BULLETPROOF
YOUR FINANCIAL FUTURE

With bulletproofing—the unique, proven investment strategy developed by noted financial planner Bruce A. Lefavi—you can have a portfolio that will protect you from the shocks of inflation, recession, or depression, as well as from personal disasters such as long-term disability.

No other financial planning book is as practical as *Bulletproof Your Financial Future*. *Specific* mutual funds, annuities, and other investments are recommended. In his easy-to-understand style, Lefavi shows you how to judge which investment vehicles best match *your* goals, and how to use them according to his bulletproofing strategy. The book includes sample portfolios that show you how—with specific investments and specific amounts of money—to structure your own investment portfolio. You'll end up with a personalized plan that's easy to set up and monitor, so you won't have to spend more than a few hours *per year* thinking about your investments.

―――――

"In straightforward language, Lefavi tells readers how to save on insurance, what to look for in a mutual fund, how to save for retirement and college costs. . . ."

—*New Orleans Times-Picayune*

"Interesting reading, particularly for someone who is relatively new to the idea of financial planning."

—*Arizona Republic*

BULLETPROOF
YOUR
FINANCIAL
FUTURE

BRUCE A. LEFAVI

POCKET BOOKS

New York   London   Toronto   Sydney   Tokyo   Singapore

POCKET BOOKS, a division of Simon & Schuster Inc.
1230 Avenue of the Americas, New York, NY 10020

Copyright © 1993 by Bruce Lefavi
Cover design by James Wang

Lefavi, Bruce A.
    Bulletproof your financial future / Bruce A. Lefavi
      p. cm.
    Includes bibliographical references and index.
    ISBN 0-671-76980-4
    1. Investments.   2. Finance, Personal.   3. Financial security.
4. Portfolio management.   I. Title.
HG4521.L337   1993
332.024 — dc20   92-34295
                                                 CIP

First Pocket Books trade paperback printing February 1994

10 9 8 7 6 5 4 3 2 1

Printed in the U.S.A.

To the two most important people in my life,
Cathy and my mother

ACKNOWLEDGMENTS

Writing a book like this requires help from a lot of people, and I especially want to thank those who work with me: Daniel A. Smith, Ann Marie Moss, and Myra K. Christensen. It took a lot of time for them to read the book, help me with research, and cover for me when I was busy. They did a great job.

Also, special thanks to what we laughingly call the Chicago Five, a group of the finest financial planners in the country who read my book and gave me comments on how to improve it. They are George Bates, Louise Googins, John M. Herr, Craig A. Smith, Dean Burchett, and Roy Alexander.

A number of experts helped check the technical content of the book. With so many facts, it was impossible to catch all the errors myself. I would like to acknowledge Richard Austin, Ann Maragaret, Rick Samson, Dexter Williams, Alden B. Tueller, John Piz, Michael Culp, Elliot Eisenberg, Gary Langer, David Schoenthal, James Bartel, Tom Holton, Bubba Power, Jahan Saleh, and Barry Rubin.

For their editing comments, I'd like to thank Caryne Brown, Sharon Cohen, Barbara Katzman, Ruth Silverman, Laurie Sutton, and especially Larry Weist, who was invaluable.

Without the help of all those named here, this book would not exist.

CONTENTS

BULLETPROOF
YOUR
FINANCIAL
FUTURE

FINANCIAL PROTECTION SO BULLETS CAN'T HURT YOU

In a world where everything is black and white, there's a 50 percent chance of choosing the wrong color. With economics, where the shades of gray are numberless, being wrong is almost a certainty.

That's why those predicting the economy's future are so often mistaken. A front-page *Wall Street Journal* article in 1991 about a stock market rally that had begun several months earlier noted: "Rarely have so many market professionals been so wrong." It ended with a quote from a major brokerage firm's chief investment strategist, who said: "To what level the market is going, we have no idea."

I agree. I don't know what will happen next year, let alone 10 years out, and I'm absolutely certain no one else does either.

Yet many financial planners and stockbrokers routinely create client portfolios and make recommendations assuming they know the future. Sometimes they don't even realize they've done this.

By the time you've finished reading this book, you will know with great precision how to bulletproof your portfolio against economic uncertainty, how to cut waste (as in avoiding unnecessary insurance), how to maximize your return with safe, proven investments, and how to create a risk-free financial future for you and your family. You can have such a future without devoting much time to your finances and without spending a fortune. Although the approach is sophisticated, the techniques are surprisingly easy to follow.

Bulletproofing is creating a mix of investments carefully calculated so that your finances can withstand any economic catastrophe while remaining highly profitable and productive. Think of it as "insurance" that removes major financial risks from your life and frees you from worries about depressions, severe recessions, or inflation. Of course, conventional risks like the failure of a company you own stock in will always exist, but I will show you ways to limit them to the short term.

My bulletproofing approach to personal financial planning has, at its core, the belief that everyone must plan their financial future as though the future is as predictable as a teenager behind the wheel of a car for the first time. In other words, you must prepare for all possibilities—and that includes the worst. Likely, the worst won't happen, but I've still taken it into account by recommending investments and strategies having the best long-term potential, whatever direction the economy takes.

I believe in the adage that "the best offense is a good defense." Basketball is a passion of mine. Every student of the game knows a good defense creates opportunities for the offense, and financial planning is no different. Protecting your assets naturally drives you toward superior investment opportunities. What's hot today is ignored because short-term popularity isn't part of a good defense. Instead, solid opportunities become your financial tools, producing the offense—excellent rates of return coupled with low risk—you want and need for a secure financial future.

Bulletproof Your Financial Future shows you, in detail, how to create a plan that financially protects you and your family against *all* plausible monetary disasters, such as recession and inflation. At no cost, you enjoy a risk-free financial future with your finances under your control, your fears and anxieties put to rest, and your life's financial goals within your grasp.

Mary's story illustrates the need we all have to protect against every potential financial catastrophe.

"Oh, what a horrible time for everyone," lamented my 75-year-old client as we sat in my office. Just thinking of the Great Depression a half century before made Mary shift in her seat uncomfortably. With a shaky voice and teary eyes, she told me of her father losing his business during the Depression and the deaths of both her parents shortly after.

I'm a baby boomer and don't know about the Depression, except from stories I've heard and articles I've read. For Mary, the Depression had been so traumatic that when she came to me for help with her financial planning, her top priority was protection against another one.

Was she crazy? Definitely not. Who foresaw the Communist bloc crumbling in a near instant in 1989? Who expected that during the first two years or so of the 1990s, commercial real estate values in many American cities would fall as much as 50 percent—the biggest drop in modern history? Is a depression any less likely? We probably won't have a depression, but one thing I am sure of: I could be wrong. With people like Mary in mind, I created a financial strategy to protect all my clients against the worst catastrophic economic situations we could face: depression or severe recession and sky-high inflation. With such protection, *every person gains control of their financial future, no matter what their income.* For the first time, by using the strategy in this book, you now have the power to reach the financial goals of your dreams. So read on, and then go out and bulletproof your financial future!

Long experience as a financial planner has taught me that we all have psychological "buttons"—fears that, when touched on, cause us to react because of our past experiences and present beliefs. Mary's button is the Great Depression. Mine is inflation, because that's the most difficult economic situation I've lived through.

My goal is to address those fears—and banish the buttons— so we all can enjoy life without financial worries. You can do this through a comprehensive strategy I call *bulletproof your portfolio.*

The Insurance Model

Financial planners refer to insurance as risk management because that's what insurance does: It helps you manage your risks. Mary and my other clients wanted me to do the same for them. They wanted insurance against the risk of catastrophe.

Thinking about Mary one day, I decided to analyze her situation as if it were a question of insurance. I began with a commonly used insurance model that begins by asking when it makes sense to have insurance and when the cost outweighs the benefits. The analysis suggests you don't insure against most risks, like those that don't happen very often and are not catastrophic when they do.

Based on experience, I know my houseplants will wilt and die within a few months after they come to live with me. I don't buy life insurance for them, however, because for one thing it's not available. More to the point, this isn't a frequent loss (I don't often buy houseplants), and when the plants die, my monetary loss is minimal. Losses with low frequency (or probability) and low costs are best absorbed.

Some situations, though, have high probabilities and low costs, such as children stealing candy from a candy store. Candy store owners are better off trying to discourage shoplifters and absorbing the losses than paying for shoplifting insurance.

And then there are risks with both high probabilities of occurring and high costs. Insurance here would be nice, but it's often unavailable. When you can get it, it's typically far too costly. Insuring an off-road motorcyclist against broken bones, for example, is not economically worthwhile. The motorcyclist is better off changing his or her behavior. Parents of toddlers childproof their houses rather than trying to find an insurance company that will insure against the destructiveness of a rampaging 2-year-old.

So when should you insure? Or, to get back to Mary and finances, what possible future situations should her strategy be designed to deal with? The bottom line is: Insure when the probability of loss is small and the cost of occurrence devastating. You carry liability automobile insurance not because you think you'll hit someone when out for a ride, but because the cost of an accident, if it does occur, is so enormous. Few home and business owners suffer fire losses, yet virtually all have fire insurance. Economic disasters, like fires, have low probabilities of occurring but are devastating when they do strike. That's why *everyone* should insure against them. In the world of economics, there are two worst-case scenarios that fall into this category. The chances of either (or both) striking each of us during our lifetimes is real, albeit unlikely.

Depression/Severe Recession

The Great Depression of the 1930s is the classic example of a depression that deeply affected everyone in our society. Unemployment, only 3.2 percent in 1929 at the start of the Depression, increased to 24.9 percent four years later. The country's gross national product fell practically 50 percent from $104 billion in 1929 to $56 billion in 1933, the depth of the Depression.

A generation of Americans, including Mary, were indelibly marked with the memories of hunger, unemployment, and helplessness brought on by this harsh and pervasive economic phenomenon. Many people, in fact, believe we'll suffer through another major depression; witness the popularity of books by such doomsayers as Ravi Batra and Howard Ruff. In Chapter 3, I will show you, in detail, how to bulletproof your portfolio to insure it against a depression or severe recession and at virtually no cost.

Inflation

Inflation is a rise in the general level of prices. If your general living expenses one year are $30,000 and the next, $33,000, then inflation that year for you was 10 percent. Inflation often affects different areas of the economy differently. During the 1980s, oil and computer prices *declined* (when the price level drops, it's called *deflation*). However, during the same period, real estate prices, college tuition, and health care costs rose. When we speak of inflation, it is the *average* price level we're referring to, which takes into account those goods and services whose prices rose a lot, a little, not at all, or dropped.

The double-digit inflation of the late 1970s and early 1980s was bad, but nothing like the inflation of 2,000 percent a year seen in recent years in such countries as Brazil and Argentina. The hyperinflation that struck Germany in the early 1920s is another classic case.

Remember the inflation we had in the late 1970s, exceeding 12 percent in 1979? The economy was drifting, unemployment was high, and the most popular topic of conversation was the increase in prices compared to the last time we were in the supermarket. Those on fixed incomes suffered most. Well, imagine 12 percent *a week* inflation! Sounds impossible, but it has happened. Runaway inflation is not likely to hit the United States anytime soon, but it could, and severe inflation is a real possibility. Chapter 4 describes strategies you can use to bulletproof your portfolio against the effects of severe inflation.

Risk-Free Financial Security

Why even worry about situations of dubious probability? They're not inevitable, after all; but they can happen. If they do, they will devastate you financially *and emotionally*. Those unprepared, like Mary, suffer the rest of their lives. Although you can't avoid depression or inflation, you can protect yourself against them. Depending upon your financial situation, your goals, and your aversion to risk, earmarking as little as 20 percent of your investment portfolio to such "disaster insurance" protects you against economic upheaval.

Plus, *this protection is free!* It's free because the types of investments that provide the protection are solid financial instruments with strong, reliable yields, such as the long-term Treasury bonds, mutual funds, and real estate that you want in your portfolio anyway.

Think of bulletproofing as the player assigned on each basketball team to watch the rear and cut off fast breaks by the opposition. Fast breaks can devastate because they get the other team pumped up and put your team off its rhythm. Bulletproofing is like having a man who's there to protect your rear. It makes sure a national economic disaster won't sneak up and become your personal disaster.

Of course, bulletproofing your portfolio against economic catastrophe does not cover all your financial needs and concerns. That's why *Bulletproof Your Financial Future* is uncommonly comprehensive. It shows how you can effectively handle lawyers, stockbrokers, insurance salespeople, and others who make demands on you and on whom you depend. You'll learn how to plan your taxes so your heirs, not Uncle Sam, get your money and how to create a retirement nest egg that will be there throughout your retirement years. You will learn ways to choose the best mutual funds and come to understand why annuities are frequently better than mutual funds. There will be tips on how to avoid wasting your money, including the kinds of insurance to avoid and those you must have. Finally, sample portfolios designed for your income level and your desired risk level will help you see how to put all of this into practice quickly and confidently.

Complete bulletproofing addresses three critical financial issues universal to all Americans:

1. Bulletproofing your portfolio to protect your assets from every reasonably foreseeable catastrophe.
2. Avoiding the waste of money so you can accumulate assets and generate income.
3. Maximizing your return to increase your assets and to provide for a desirable income.

Remember Mary, the client who was so worried about losing everything in another depression? First, I made her feel secure in the face of the recession in the early 1990s by having her invest in long-term Treasury bonds. Then I addressed her fear of a devastating depression by structuring her portfolio so her wealth would actually increase if such a calamity occurred. I accomplished this by using the three steps above. The ghosts of the Great Depression have moved on.

What I did for Mary, you'll be able to do for yourself after you've read *Bulletproof Your Financial Future*. The advice is specific and thorough, easy to understand, and nearly effortless to implement. In addition, I've illustrated what I recommend with five sample families, based on my actual clients, each of which has its own financial goal, such as creating a retirement nest egg, financing a college education, or saving for a down payment on a house. You'll find these families cropping up through much of the book. Their stories show how to create a basket of investments that protect against the unexpected, while providing the power to reach the financial goals of your dreams.

2

FINANCIAL PLANNING:
What Do You Want?

If you're like my typical client, you have a good income—not enormous wealth, but an ample living. Yet, you need more money. It's not a question of greed, it's just that no matter how much you earn, you still come up short.

"I used to think if I made $60,000 a year, I'd be rich," one client said to me. "I'm making $120,000 and it's not enough. What's going on here?"

It was as if he put his hard-earned paycheck in his pocket and walked home only to find the pocket empty. It had a hole. Do you ever wonder where your money goes? Do you ever wonder if your pocket has a hole? Many of us have found making money is easier than keeping it.

A factory owner doesn't throw people and machines together in a room and hope something good comes out of it. He has a plan. Machines, carefully chosen for specific tasks, are placed on the factory floor in a logical way, with the workers trained in the production process, and the whole coordinated with a carefully designed production schedule.

Money spent in a hit-and-miss way isn't any more productive

than people and machines thrown together haphazardly. Just as factories need a plan, so do finances. We saw in the last chapter that complete bulletproofing has three steps: bulletproofing your portfolio against catastrophe, cutting waste, and maximizing your returns. You can't maximize your returns without a plan, for planning is essential to the entire bulletproofing strategy.

Forget everything you ever read about planning. I have a plan that's simple, quick, easy, and wonderfully effective. In no time, despite your distaste for financial planning, you'll be using a plan and hardly know it. And you'll stay with it because it will be so productive.

My approach even allows you to stray from the set path without guilt or fear. With a decent plan, you need a little discipline, not a lot.

To make a success of your finances, this is all you need:

1. A plan. Any plan. Even a poorly designed plan is far superior to no plan at all. And I'll soon show you how to create a good one that'll benefit you for years to come.
2. Discipline—just a little. You don't need to be obsessive about following your plan. If you ignore the plan completely, obviously it won't do you any good. But there's no need to stick to it as though one weak moment will ruin you financially for good. In financial planning, a little bit of discipline goes a long way.

Budgeting for Those Who Refuse to Budget

Planning requires money. And this brings me to one of the most disliked words in the English language: budget. Fear not. I never put my clients on a budget. They're human beings and, as such, are as likely to stick to a budget as a kid is likely to want to hang around in a classroom on the first warm, sunny day of spring. It's the nature of things—most people don't budget. If you do, that's good. Keep doing it, since disciplined budgeting pays substantial rewards.

If you don't budget, don't despair. Here's a budget for those who absolutely, positively, unequivocally, indubitably won't budget:

THE 10–10 BUDGET

I call this the 10–10 budget because it takes 10 seconds to understand and sets aside 10 percent of your income. Unless you have a special situation where you need to budget more than 10 percent (you want to retire within five years, for instance) or your last name is Rockefeller and you have more money than you know what to do with, *save 10 percent of your gross (pretax) income*. I'm talking about total family income from investments and both spouses. Of course, you don't take out the 10 percent and then run up your credit card accounts to make up the shortfall. You want to save 10 percent without additional debt. Ten percent is a small enough percentage for most people to handle and large enough to provide the financial means to meet your goals. You won't save it if you get your hands on it, so have your employer use an automatic payroll deduction plan to remove 10 percent of your income before you ever see it. Or take 10 percent out of each paycheck yourself and *immediately* place it safely out of reach in a certificate of deposit (CD) or money market account. This is all my advice to you on budgeting.

While 10 percent of your paycheck is something whose absence you'll notice, in surprisingly short order you'll get used to your new level of income and feel good about yourself. Knowing that you're now saving for a secure financial future does wonders for your self-esteem and sense of security.

To make the transition to this new income level effortless, you can ease into it by:

1. Taking 3 percent of your gross income automatically out now.
2. Raising this to 6 percent in six months.
3. Increasing the percentage to 10 percent starting a year from today.

Everyone budgets whether they want to or not. Some are just smarter about it than others. If you spend when you don't have money—by using credit cards or home equity loans—that's *forced budgeting*. You're forced because you've put yourself in a position where you have no choice but to budget (even though most people fail to see that using credit is a form of budgeting). Each month, instead of saving for your goals, you give to your creditors and pay interest for the privilege. That's a budgetary expense that's fundamentally like mortgage payments, automobile insurance premiums, and food. Never view credit cards as a second source of income—they're not!

My recommendation is save now and pay cash later. Except for a house, an expense that is too large to save for and provides tax benefits as well, I recommend you pay cash whenever possible. By this I mean for everything from buying a car to clothes, that new CD player, and the family vacation. You're going to have to pay for the stuff eventually. The banking and credit industries don't like to call this by the hated *B* word, but it's budgeting, pure and simple. Be smart, earn from your hard work, and don't pay others to use their money.

Besides forcing you to save, the 10–10 budget has another advantage: What you do with the rest of your money is up to you. You can blow your money on anything you want—without guilt. You're doing the hard work, namely, saving 10 percent. Enjoy the rest in ways that make you happy.

Family Models Used Throughout the Book

To illustrate how goals are achieved as well as other techniques discussed throughout this book, I've created five "model" families. These represent clients of mine—their situations, their goals, their needs, their willingness to risk. It's unlikely your situation will exactly match any of these, but you'll probably find a lot of similarities. I'll introduce these families now and call them back at various times throughout the book to illustrate the things we're discussing at that time. Here, I'll give just brief biographies of these folks. Later, I'll discuss in detail how each uses our bulletproofing strategy to achieve their goals.

FAMILY 1: A COUPLE SAVING FOR THEIR RETIREMENT
Meet Jackie and Bob, who are both 40 years old and have no children. He's a government employee and she works for a high-tech company. Together their incomes total $120,000 a year, with Jackie earning more than Bob. To date, they have a total savings of $25,000, $8,500 in a retirement account and $16,500 in cash.

RISK: Medium (we will discuss risk in detail in Chapter 5).
GOAL: Both want to retire in 20 years at age 60 with a total retirement nest egg of $725,000.

WHAT THEY NEED: We assume they need 75 percent of their current income when they retire, which is $90,000 in today's dollars. To reach this income, they will need $725,000 when they retire, which, with Social Security, will enable them to reach their goal. To achieve this, their investments over the next 20 years must earn 12 percent a year on average. They are willing to take the risks to get 12 percent, so they will use the medium-risk portfolio (discussed in detail in Chapter 15), which has an expected rate of return of 13 percent.

FAMILY 2: A SINGLE MOTHER SAVING FOR HER CHILDREN'S COLLEGE TUITION

Marilyn is a 35-year-old sixth-grade teacher who is a single mother with two girls, aged 2 and 4. She assumes her retirement is covered by the money she received from her divorce, her savings, and her pension. What worries her is how she will pay for her daughters' educations. She desperately wants them to have the same educational opportunities she had and to be able to choose any profession or career they want. Her ex-husband does not pay child support, and she is not counting on him to provide any assistance with the girls' college expenses. She currently has $10,000 to put toward her goal.

RISK: Medium.

GOAL: To have $42,000 at the time her children enter college so she can pay at least half of their college educations, assuming that scholarships, loans, and other financial aid will make up the rest.

WHAT SHE NEEDS: She needs to earn a 10 percent or more return on her investments, which makes her a medium-risk investor. In truth, she's not entirely comfortable with this, but she knows she has to take some risk in order to have a return that outpaces the annual increase in college costs.

FAMILY 3: A COUPLE SAVING FOR THEIR FIRST HOME

The Santangelos are both aged 25, and want to live the American Dream, namely, own their own home. Right now they rent. These health care professionals have a total income of $42,000 a year and do not have any savings.

RISK: High.

GOAL: To accumulate $20,000 within five years for a down payment on a home.

WHAT THEY NEED: Because they are young and their income is likely to increase substantially over time, it makes sense for them to want to be aggressive, fairly high-risk investors. After all, they have plenty of time to make up for investments that go sour. What they need are investments that will allow them to reach their goal.

FAMILY 4: A COUPLE WANTING TO MINIMIZE THEIR TAXES

The more you have, the more you lose to taxes, so it's no surprise that the middle-aged Jordans' top priority is keeping Uncle Sam away from their money. Mr. Jordan owns a service business worth about $2.5 million, and Mrs. Jordan is a homemaker. Their net worth, not including the business, is $1.2 million, and their annual income is $350,000. Their children are grown and on their own, and they have the resources for a comfortable retirement. It is the tax bill each April that is driving them bananas because, though he is an excellent business manager, he's neglected to manage his personal assets. He desperately needs help in structuring his investment portfolio using tax-advantaged strategies.

RISK: Medium.

GOAL: To minimize taxes now with a goal of bringing them down to zero, or as close to zero as possible.

WHAT THEY NEED: They need to place their investments and income into tax-sheltered vehicles.

FAMILY 5: A RETIRED COUPLE

The Moriartys, each aged 60, just retired. They plan to start collecting Social Security in two years when they reach 62. Their savings total $500,000, their house is paid for, and they have no dependents. They are not big spenders, so they don't need a hefty income. Because of their age and temperament, they have a low tolerance for risk. That's okay because they need to earn only 7 percent a year on their investments, yet our low-risk portfolio (discussed in detail in Chapter 15) enjoys a 9½ percent return.

RISK: Low.

GOAL: Not to outlive their income while earning a 7 percent return on their investments.

WHAT THEY NEED: They need $45,000 in income a year to be generated by their savings and Social Security. They are not risk takers, so they need an investment strategy that will protect their principal so it doesn't run out before they die.

These are the five models we'll come back to at various times throughout the book. Each has their own specific goal, and these goals are fairly commonplace, probably closely matching yours.

It is not enough to have goals—you need a plan that assures your goals are realistic, since it outlines what you need to do to reach them. Let's assume you are 35 years old and want $1 million in income-producing assets by age 50. If you expect to earn 8 percent a year after taxes on your investments and have no money saved now, you'll need to sock away about $37,000 a year to have $1 million in 15 years. If you earn only $40,000 annually, this is not a feasible goal. Obviously, you'll want to adjust the goal so that it is possible. By completing a plan, you'll know how realistic your goals are.

The Plan

For some, drawing up a plan is almost as painful as creating and sticking to a budget. Forget your fears. Like the 10–10 budget, we can make planning simple, too.

In fact, as with budgeting, *we all plan* to some degree. We plan our day, for example, setting aside time for a morning shower, a daily commute, lunch, movies, a child's ball game, a workout at the aerobic studio. Though we all plan, some do it better than others. Many think even a half hour a week spent on financial planning is too time-consuming. This is odd when you consider that we think nothing of spending a half hour choosing a movie or a restaurant. Given how little time people spend planning what they will do with their money, you'd almost think money is unimportant.

The plan I've devised takes a little time to set up and almost no time thereafter.

The planning process has five steps:

1. Establish where you are now.
2. Set goals.
3. Create a plan.
4. Carry out the plan.
5. Periodically review the plan.

Your Financial Situation Today and Tomorrow

To plan properly, you need to know where your finances are today. This includes, in accountants' lingo, establishing your net worth. Net worth is simply your assets (what you own that has value, such as cash and property) less your liabilities (what you owe). If you have $200,000 in assets (savings, equity in your house, mutual funds, collectibles, etc.) and you owe $125,000 (credit cards, bank loans, mortgages, etc.), your net worth is $75,000. That's what you would have left if you sold all your assets and paid all your debts.

What good is knowing your net worth? Your ability to buy a home, take a vacation, finance a college education, generate retirement income, create an estate for your heirs, and other financial goals are dependent on two factors: what you've got now (your net worth) and what you're going to add to this in the future. With the 10–10 budget we discussed, you'll save 10 percent of your gross income. This will vary only as much as your income will vary in the coming years. But right this minute, you need to know where you are.

Here's a simple form to use to figure your net worth. Do it now. It will only take a few minutes.

FAST FACT: How much are you spending? Ask yourself how much income you had during the past 12 months, including wages, interest, and dividends. Subtract how much you've saved, including money in pension plans and savings accounts. The difference is how much you spent.

For some this fast fact is obvious. Yet my experience says many never think about their spending in such a simple, revealing way.

Many of my new clients frequently have little idea about how much they spend. At our first meeting I might ask a client with an annual income of $100,000, "What are your expenses?" "Oh, very little," he or she replies, "Maybe $50,000." I counter this by saying, "That means you're saving $50,000 a year." They look dumbfounded. "No," they say a little sheepishly, "I'm only saving $2,000." I reply, "That means you're spending $98,000." You can

NET WORTH

ASSETS

Savings account _____

Checking account _____

Money market account _____

Stock mutual funds _____

Bond mutual funds _____

Stocks _____

Bonds _____

Investment real estate _____

Art/collectibles _____

Pension plans _____

Market value of house _____

Market value of autos _____

Other assets _____

TOTAL ASSETS _____

LIABILITIES

Credit card debt _____

Personal loans _____

Amount due on
mortgage _____

Amount due on auto
loans _____

Taxes due _____

Medical bills due _____

Other liabilities _____

TOTAL LIABILITIES _____

almost see the light bulb light up over their head. "I never thought I was spending so much," they say.

If you've earned tens of thousands of dollars and maybe saved a couple of thousand, you probably need to save more. That's why I suggest setting aside 10 percent of your income before you ever see it.

Set Your Goals

The second step of the planning process is to set goals. A plan without goals is like a game without a scoreboard. You never know where you are. It's why first-time visitors to diet clinics immediately set a weight goal. It's why sales managers have their sales people set goals. It's why runners set time goals. It's also why goal setting is essential to the entire financial planning process.

FAST FACT: There's no guilt with goal setting. Goals are not good or bad, right or wrong. No one can tell you what the best goals are for you. It's entirely up to you. Think of goals as a means for you to get what you want out of life.

There's one hard-and-fast rule to goal setting: The goal must be specific. "I want to retire well" is not a goal, it's a hope. You have to define what "retire well" means. Is it retiring with the same amount of disposable income you have now? Is this in inflation-adjusted dollars (these are dollars after you've taken into account that the purchasing power of money drops as inflation goes up)? Can you be happy with less income but not having to work? Or do you want to retire but still work a little? When do you want to retire? Age 55 or 65 or 70? Where do you want to live? How much will you need to live there? What do you want *exactly*?

An advisor to a major celebrity once devised a simple test for all those who came to him with deals for his client. He used it to cut through the hype and reveal the substance. His test consisted of just two questions: How much money will I get and when will I get it?

That was one shrewd guy. He boiled down the process to its

essentials: Financial goals need to be specific, and they must have both money *and* time elements. When movie stars sign contracts, they make sure the document stipulates how much they'll receive and when. Take out a bank loan, and the bank, being no dummy, tells you how much it wants and when. The same must hold for your goal setting. You have to know how much you want and when you want it.

People's goals are as varied as people themselves. One client wanted $100,000 when he retired to build a three-car garage with a lot of equipment so he could work on his passion, rebuilding old automobiles.

To start, you will want to list several goals, being as specific as possible both about the goal itself and about the *how much* and *when* questions we saw earlier.

With your goals clarified, list them by order of priority. Focus on no more than three; any more will spread your energies too thin. Yes, I know Ben Franklin in his autobiography told us that he had 10 self-improvement goals going all the time, but he was Ben. I can't keep track of 10 goals, let alone accomplish them. Keep it simple and reachable. Because you'll be successful, you'll be encouraged to make more goals. This process is a confidence builder as well as a financial tactic.

When I tell you later how to construct your investment portfolio, I'll automatically bulletproof it. So don't make that a goal. Here we need your other goals.

Make an emergency fund (three to six months' worth of expenses depending on your need for security) your first goal. This is money kept in a savings account, money market fund, or other quickly accessible, safe place; this is not money you want to take risks with. After that, it's up to you what's more and what's less important.

Consider including among your goals ways to eliminate waste. To create wealth, it is not enough to generate a large income and save a lot of it—you must not waste the money you earn. Your waste-cutting goals could include

- Minimize the cost of insurance (Chapter 7).
- Cut your consumer debt. It's too expensive, given the interest rates on credit cards and consumer loans.
- Reduce taxes.

Create Your Financial Plan

You are now ready to embark on the third step of the planning process: Creating the plan. You've done most of the work already. You know where you are (net worth) and the amount your income allows you to save (at least 10 percent of whatever you and your spouse earn). With your goals established and listed in order of priority, you just need a plan to follow.

Here's an easy-to-use chart that tells you how much you need to save each month to reach your goals:

1 Time (years)	2 Current Investments	3 Growth Factor	4 Assets Would Grow to This Amount	5 Amount Needed to Reach Goals	6 Difference	7 Monthly Investment Factor	8 Amount to Invest Monthly
5	$_____	× 1.5 =	$_____	$_____	$_____	÷ 74	$_____
10	$_____	× 2.6 =	$_____	$_____	$_____	÷ 184	$_____
15	$_____	× 4.2 =	$_____	$_____	$_____	÷ 287	$_____
20	$_____	× 9.6 =	$_____	$_____	$_____	÷ 593	$_____
25	$_____	×17.0 =	$_____	$_____	$_____	÷ 2,000	$_____

As an example, we'll use the Santangelos, who want to save $20,000 within five years for a down payment on a house:

Column 1: Time: 5 years.
Column 2: Current investments: $0 (they have nothing saved toward their down payment).
Column 3: Growth factor: 1.5.
Column 4: Assets would grow to $0 (they don't have any assets at the moment).
Column 5: Amount needed to reach goals: $20,000 (they need to save the entire $20,000 during the next five years if they are to reach their goal).
Column 6: Difference [Column 5 minus Column 4]: $20,000 (this is the amount they need to save).
Columns 7 and 8: $20,000 ÷ 74 = $270.

This couple needs to save $270 a month. If they do, they'll have their $20,000 down payment in five years. Saving $270 a month is certainly feasible since they have a combined income of $42,000. They need to save about 8 percent of their income to reach their goal.

Here's a detailed explanation of each column.

COLUMN 1: TIME

This is simply how far in the future your goal is. If you are now 45 years old and want to retire at age 65, the time period is 20 years.

COLUMN 2: CURRENT INVESTMENTS

This is how much you have saved that can be used toward your goal. If you want to have $75,000 at the time your children enter college to pay for their education, and you now have $15,000 available to set aside toward this goal, then your current investments total $15,000. If your total savings are now $15,000 but you have two goals, say, saving for a house down payment and saving for a college education, you might devote $5,000 toward the house and $10,000 for college. In this case, if you are doing the calculations for the college goal, your current investments would be $10,000. You put in this column only those assets you can devote exclusively to the goal in question.

COLUMN 3: GROWTH FACTOR

The growth factors use certain assumptions. The first, 1.5, is for five years and assumes you'll earn 8 percent on your investments, compounded monthly, after taxes. Where does the growth factor number come from? If you have $1 today, invest it at 8 percent a year for five years, at the end of the five-year period, you'll have almost $1.50, 1.5 times what you started with.

The growth factors for 10 and 15 years, 2.6 and 4.2, assume a 10 percent return on your investments. You'll have 2.6 times the initial investment at the end of 10 years and 4.2 times after 15 years. The 20- and 25-year calculations, which work the same way, assume a 12 percent return on investment.

The growth factors increase with longer time periods for several reasons. First, the longer your time period you're willing to hold your investment, the more money you earn. If you start with $1 and earn 8 percent, you'll have $1.50 in five years and $2.20 after 10 years. I increase the rate of return (from 8 to 10 to 12 percent) the longer the period, because the longer you intend to hold an asset, the more longer-term, higher-yielding opportunities are available to you.

COLUMN 4: ASSETS WOULD GROW TO THIS AMOUNT

Because of the interest your assets earn, at the end of the time period they are worth more than at the beginning. Five thousand dollars now grows to over $7,300 in five years if it earns 8 percent a year. This is calculated by simply multiplying Column 2 by Column 3.

COLUMN 5: AMOUNT NEEDED TO REACH GOALS

This is your goal. If you want $20,000 for a down payment, this is where you put this amount.

COLUMN 6: DIFFERENCE

Let's say you want $20,000 in five years for a down payment and you have $5,000 in assets today that you can earmark for this goal. Using the 1.5 growth factor, this $5,000 will grow to $7,500 in five years. But you want $20,000. The $12,500 shortfall—$20,000 − $7,500—is the difference that goes into Column 6. It is simply Column 5 minus Column 4.

COLUMN 7: MONTHLY INVESTMENT FACTOR

The *monthly investment factor* is the amount you would have to pay each month to get the difference between what you have now versus what you want (your goal). If you want $1 five years (60 months) from now and you earn 8 percent on your money, then you have a monthly payment of 1.36 cents. If you divide 1 by $0.0136 (that's 1.36 cents), you get 74. You don't need to do this calculation, since I've done it for you in the table.

If your difference is $12,500, as we just mentioned, you divide $12,500 by 74. The answer goes in Column 8.

COLUMN 8: AMOUNT TO INVEST MONTHLY

When you divide Column 6 by Column 7, you find out how much you must save and invest each month. In the example just mentioned, it works out to $169. To summarize this example, someone who wants to have $20,000 in five years for a down payment and now has $5,000 to devote toward that goal must save and invest $169 each month for the next five years.

Let's take another example, namely, Jackie and Bob saving for their retirement. They have $25,000 now and want to retire in 20 years, when they'll need a total of $725,000. Their calculation would look like this:

Column 1: Time: 20 years. Their goal is 20 years in the future, the actual time they'll retire.

Column 2: Current investments: $25,000. They now have $25,000 that is set aside to reach their goal.

Column 3: Growth factor: 9.6. Since this is a goal 20 years off, the growth factor is 9.6, as listed in the table.

Column 4: Assets would grow to $240,000. Here you multiply $25,000 by 9.6 and get $240,000. This is the future value of their current investments.

Column 5: Amount needed to reach their goal: $725,000. They want $725,000 in 20 years.

Column 6: Difference: $485,000. This can be calculated by subtracting Column 4 from Column 5: $725,000 − $240,000 = $485,000. They'll be short $485,000 in 20 years unless they save more. The remainder of the calculations tell how much more they must save and invest.

Column 7: Monthly investment factor: 593. The table specifies that for a 20-year goal, the monthly investment factor is 593.

Column 8: Amount to invest monthly: $817.88. You would divide Column 6 by Column 7 to get this answer: $485,000 ÷ 593 = $817.88. This is how much they need to save each month so that they make up the $485,000 shortfall. While saving $817.88 each month, their initial $25,000 is growing. By the time they reach age 60 in 20 years, they'll have enough to retire.

Succeeding chapters will cover the investments you'll use in your own financial planning in detail. These few calculations provide your plan's structure. The framework of a house is like your plan; how you cover the framework and what you put in the house are the investments I talk about throughout this book.

You'll find sample investment portfolios in the last chapter. You can use one of them or pick and choose among the investments and strategies discussed in the following chapters.

It sounds easy, and it is. For many, the hardest part of a financial plan is getting started. How do you stop procrastinating? Simple. You already have. After all, you've bought this book and have read this far. Half your battle of getting started has been won already.

Keeping Score

The time-consuming part is now finished. As you'll see, the financial plans recommended later are easy to administer. In fact, once your plan is in place, you typically won't spend more than a handful of hours a *year* dealing with it. Keep a running score, but don't worry about tracking your investments daily. You're holding your investments for the long run, after all. What's happening now isn't important. By taking the long-term view, you don't need to worry about your investments continually and you won't panic when the market turns against you (which it will invariably at some point).

If your plan is simple, with fewer than 10 investments, a once- or twice-a-year review is sufficient. If your plan is more complex, check it every three months to see if it's performing as you want.

─────────────── H I G H L I G H T S ───────────────

For financial success, you need a plan (any plan is better than no plan) and discipline.

➡

The planning process requires that you:

- Know where you are now.
- Have specific goals.
- Have a plan.
- Carry out your plan.
- Review the plan periodically.

➡

Goals must be specific: What do you want, and when do you want it?

3

DEPRESSION BULLETPROOFING:
A Shadow from the Past

Rare is the person who goes through life without experiencing major turning points—moments that produce dramatic, permanent change.

Such moments can be economic. No single economic event demonstrated this more powerfully than the Great Depression of the 1930s, a time few Americans survived emotionally or financially unscarred. To this day, my friend's grandmother keeps no more than $20,000 in any one bank, even if that means she must have 5 or 10 bank accounts. She remembers the 1930s when collapsing banks were as common as falling leaves in autumn. Having each of her accounts insured by the U.S. government for $100,000 means nothing. She needs to know that even if a string of banks fail she won't be wiped out.

I'll bet that you carry vivid images of that dreadful decade even if you were born years later: soup lines; children selling apples on street corners; dust blowing over once-fertile plains; people lugging their belongings on their backs or in their cars, traveling west seeking work and better lives.

The power of the Great Depression lay in its ability to alter the course of history. Just as the swollen, flooding Mississippi carves new channels in the earth, the Depression forced economic history into unforeseen paths. Our entire economic system was seriously questioned, not just in the United States, but worldwide. Socialism and communism enjoyed popularity unknown before or since because the capitalist system was in such disarray. The Great Depression was the economic equivalent of a world war—pervasive, unstoppable, devastating, profound, and with enduring consequences.

Many government institutions and policies established during that pivotal decade—Social Security, the Securities and Exchange Commission, the Federal Deposit Insurance Corporation, federal deficit spending—got their start as responses to the devastating effects of the Great Depression.

No wonder, then, that of every possible economic catastrophe that can strike us, the one so many of my clients fear more than all others is a depression. True, a depression concerns older people more than younger ones. But as Elvis and the Beatles are popular with kids not even alive when these pop artists were at the height of their fame, the Great Depression lives on in the consciousness of those too young to have suffered its effects.

As I've stated before (and it's worth repeating), I don't believe you or I will experience a Great Depression during our lifetimes; but I'm not absolutely certain about that. Another depression, however unlikely, is decidedly possible. Rampaging inflation, an oil shortage, a collapse of the international monetary system due to loan defaults by third-world countries, antagonisms brought on by trade policies, widespread failures of commercial banks on a scale recently seen with savings and loans, even mistakes by the Federal Reserve that make matters worse rather than relieve a future severe recession—any of these could trigger a depression.

Yet, if I were a betting man, I'd wager that if we do have a depression, its cause will be something none of us has even thought of. Did you think you would live to see the savings and loan industry practically collapse, costing taxpayers upward of $500 billion in bailouts? I know I didn't. Before October 19, 1987, who would have thought the stock market could fall over 500 points in one day and nearly suffer a "meltdown" the next, as one New York Stock Exchange official put it? I didn't.

All my clients carry depression protection. That's a rule I enforce because the protection is free and effective and provides valuable economic and psychological benefits. And because I'm not absolutely certain we won't have a depression.

Why Worry About Something That Won't Happen?

We talked in the first chapter about the one and only situation when one must insure: when the probability of an event occurring is small but its consequences catastrophic. Suppose you had to cross an open field where one land mine was planted. Though the possibility of stepping on the mine is minimal, would you take the walk unaided if someone offered you an armored car capable of withstanding a mine blast?

The armor I offer you is carefully chosen investments that ensure against a depression. For that reason alone, having depression protection in your portfolio is a must.

Peace of mind is another great reason. Your teenager comes home late at night from a date. Even if you are sound asleep, you naturally drift into a deeper, more relaxing sleep when you hear the front door close, because you know he or she is home safe. In the same way, you may not be thinking every day about a depression, but you certainly worry about your financial future. The worry might be subtle, but it's there. The depression protection described here is a means of forever removing this financial worry from your concerns. It's a way of having everyone home safe.

The Look of a Depression

If a depression comes, what will it look like? No one knows. We have only the past to go by.

The Great Depression was probably worse than anyone who didn't live through it can imagine. The production of durable goods, such as machinery and appliances, dropped 80 percent between 1929 and the Depression's low point in March 1933. To put it another way, for every five durable goods produced in 1929, only one was made four years later. Some examples of the sales declines that occurred between 1929 and 1933 include autos, 65 percent; railroad passenger cars, 100 percent; domestic ranges, 77 percent; and electric generators, 73 percent. The output of bicycles actually increased by 3 percent, which is perhaps not surprising considering people couldn't afford autos and gasoline.

Unemployment went from 1.5 million in 1929 to at least 13 million during the Depression's depths. Official statistics said one-quarter of the work force was out of work, but with part-timers and the underemployed, the real unemployment rate probably approached one-third. This means the average American either lived in a family without a breadwinner or had a next-door neighbor in that position.

This was at a time when Social Security, unemployment benefits, and food stamps were unknown. The "safety net" created over the past half century for the poor and unfortunate did not exist in the early 1930s.

The Great Depression was the worst depression of all, though not the only one, a fact often forgotten. Between 1920 and 1921 another depression sent the durable-goods output tumbling 43 percent. There was a depression in 1907. Before that, a depression occurred between 1893 and 1896, another in 1873, and there were others.

In fact, the Federal Reserve Bank, or the Fed, has contingency plans for various types of economic collapse, including a depression. Clearly it thinks such an event is possible. The Fed activated a prearranged plan on October 19, 1987, when the stock market crashed. The media reported the next day that the market almost disintegrated entirely and was saved with the help of the Fed's actions. That may be reassuring, but I really don't rest easier knowing the Fed has rehearsed its role if we have a depression. I'd rather make my own preparations.

In his best-seller, The Great Depression of 1990, Ravi Batra argues that immutable cycles cause periodic depressions, no matter what the government does, and that the concentration of wealth is a root cause of these cycles and, therefore, depressions.[1]

Though you can argue with Batra about the causes of depressions, no one seriously disputes the existence of economic cycles. Since the start of the Industrial Revolution and the widespread use of money, economies around the world have endured busts and booms.

Cycles don't always affect entire economies; they can be selective. In the mid-1970s, the northeastern United States was in a major recession, but by the mid-1980s, it was enjoying a raging boom. In the early 1990s, it was again back in a recession.

Real estate goes through cycles on a geographic basis. The real estate boom in Texas and Arizona from the late 1970s to the mid-1980s was immediately followed by a devastating bust. A sharp downturn in California real estate in the early 1990s followed a boom during the 1980s. Some call this phenomenon a rolling recession, where economic doldrums strike one region before moving on. Although no widely accepted definition of a depression exists, it is pictured as an uncommonly severe, devastating economic period, going beyond the dislocations and difficulties found in a recession.

There have been economic cycles for at least 150 years. These include downturns that cause widespread hardships, such as the one we're going through as I write this. Before I die, I'm sure I'll see a few more. Whether any of these will lead to a depression is anyone's guess, but every downturn has the potential to snowball out of control into a severe recession or depression.

Our Model

The ambiguous nature of a future depression means that we have to make assumptions about what it would be like in order to plan effectively. Anyone can argue with assumptions, but I base mine on experiences our nation endured during the Great Depression and what I see as potential problems if another depression strikes.

What are some problems? First, poor sales and profits could close the doors of many major corporations. And the heavy debt burden so many companies assumed during the easy-money, junk-bond days of the 1980s could destroy many others. Servicing debt—paying the monthly interest—will be impossible for many companies, because debt is fixed; even though profits may decline, the company still has a set amount of interest to pay.

These big-business failures, if they occur, will have widespread economic implications. The pension plans millions of Americans are counting on for retirement could be wiped out. Government regulations, like the Employee Retirement Income Security Act (ERISA), try to protect pension plans by insuring that pension money is wisely and securely invested, but in a period of great economic uncertainty even these plans won't emerge unscathed. ERISA, for instance, considers investments in stocks and bonds to be secure, yet these are the very financial instruments likely to get into trouble in a depression. The corporate bonds many rely on for income will become virtually worthless. After all, it is this debt, in addition to market conditions, that will cause businesses to fail in the first place. Even insured bank accounts will be in trouble because the Federal Insurance

Deposit Corporation won't be able to cover the obligations of all the failed banks. (There are serious questions now, during a period of relative economic health, of whether the FDIC can cover its obligations; in a depression, the FDIC could be nearly worthless.)

The stock market will head south as surely as birds do each winter. Standard & Poor's 500 Stock Composite Index's (S&P) high in 1929 was 31.92. It got as low as 4.40 in 1932. That's a drop in value of more than 86 percent. Had you invested $10,000 in a representative sample of the S&P stocks at the 1929 high, three years later your investment would have hit a low of $1,378.45. Between 1931 and 1939, the S&P never went higher than 18.68 (in 1937) and most of the time was in the range of 8 to 13. In fact, the S&P took 25 years to recover from the Depression. Not until 1954 did it top its 1929 high.

In a typical depression, hard assets, especially real estate, get clobbered. Farm property dropped 37 percent in value between 1929 and 1933, at the same time commercial property values fell by about a third.

Based on all this, my model of the depression consists of the following assumptions:

1. Prices will decline 35 percent (probably more).
2. Interest rates will drop to 1 percent (they dropped *below* 1 percent during the 1930s).
3. Social Security and private pension plans will provide minimal income, so minimal it probably won't be worth talking about.
4. The value of stocks, bonds, and hard assets will fall precipitously by 75 percent or more.

This is scary stuff, but I think I'm being conservative.

Depression Protection: Treasury Bonds

With this picture, what's left that's worth investing in? Quite simply, U.S. Treasury bonds, commonly called *Treasuries*—the money the U.S. government borrows every day and for which it pays reasonable interest. Treasury bonds are basically like other bonds, only they are issued and backed by the federal government, and the interest they pay is not taxable. Bonds are simply a way for a government agency or company to borrow money. A bond is issued and the issuer agrees to pay back the money. The investor is merely lending the money to the issuer for a certain period and at a set interest rate. The power of Treasury bonds comes from the fact that bond prices increase as interest rates fall, all other things being equal. The reason for the inverse relationship between bond prices and interest rates will be explained in Chapter 8.

In a world of declining prices, bond prices should theoretically go through the roof, "all other things being equal," as economists love to say. But in the real world, all other things are rarely equal, and they certainly aren't for bonds during an economic calamity, hence, the second reason I recommend Treasury bonds: Of all bonds issued during a depression, the *only* ones certain to pay their interest are those issued by the U.S. government. Today's high-grade corporate bonds may not be worth much more than the stock of these companies—nearly nothing—because even major corporations will have enormous difficulties paying their debts, which includes paying you, the bondholder, interest for borrowing your money and paying you back the principal or face value of the bond when it falls due. So even if interest rates fall, no one will pay more as economic theory predicts because the likelihood of collecting the interest is slight. In fact, bond prices will probably fall, rather than rise, even while interest rates plummet.

Treasury bonds will pay for one reason—the government controls the printing presses, making it impossible for the government ever to run out of money. Sending you, the bondholder, money is easy—the printing presses run a little longer. True, the government can do the same to meet Social Security and unemployment obligations, but these are defined by legislation that Congress can change quickly. Congress will cut Social Security and other benefits rather than risk the sustained inflation that printing more and more money brings on.

Congress enjoys no such power over bonds. If the government borrows $1,000 via a 30-year bond and promises to pay 9 percent per annum, that obligation cannot be changed without the government going into default. U.S. government debt obligations are considered the safest investments *in the world* precisely because everyone believes the government's promise to pay. And here we touch on one of the paradoxes of the economic world: As much as we'd like to believe that economies rise and fall on the cold, immutable laws of mathematics, in truth the messy world of human emotion intrudes here, too. Why people believe the U.S. government will always pay its debts, even if it means printing money to do so, is like asking why the sun rises in the east. So far, it always has, and tomorrow and every day thereafter, there's no reason to think it will do otherwise. For Treasury bonds, then, it's really a question of confidence. People have more confidence in the ability of the U.S. government to repay its debts and so are willing to buy these bonds, especially in uncertain times. Partly because of this on-going cash infusion based on confidence, the government is, in fact, always able to pay its debts, living on to borrow another day. To you, the investor, the bottom line is that the government will run its printing presses into the ground before reneging on its obligations.

Now, what happens if you have a 30-year Treasury bond yielding 9 percent? Let's say you bought the bond five years before the depression when things looked good (remember that before October 29, 1929, few people saw a major depression coming, so don't expect a lot of warning signs). The bond has 25 years left to maturity. When the depression hits, interest rates fall to 1 percent. Most bonds are traded freely across their term, meaning that you don't have to hold your $1,000 30-year bond for 30 years; you can sell it, even for a loss (at less than $1,000), at any time if you have a buyer. The bond's market value changes over time, too. Initially, the biggest factor affecting the bond's value are interest rates. When a bond is almost mature, however, its value reverts to the redemption value since the period of time it has left to pay interest to the holder is so short. Interest rates are important during the life of the bond because every bond has a fixed interest rate over its life.

When interest rates across the market fall (say to 1 percent, 8 percent less than your bond pays), the market value of the bond goes up and vice versa. This is because someone wanting to buy a bond that would have an equivalent value at maturity would, of course, have to pay more initially to make up for the 8 percent fall in interest rates. In this case, a $1,000 30-year bond paying 9 percent interest has the same value as a $2,765.71 bond paying 1 percent interest, which means that suddenly your $1,000 bond paying 9 percent is worth (given a buyer) $2,765.71. (This calculation, by the way, is called a *future value* calculation.)

Now let's look at depression-proofing your whole portfolio, which we'll say is worth $100,000 before the depression. What's important is to have enough assets during a depression so that no purchasing power is lost compared with what you have today.

My model assumes that prices decline 35 percent, based on what occurred in the 1930s. This means a bond worth $2,765.71 during the depression will buy $4,254.94 worth of goods and services in today's dollars since what once cost $1 now costs 65 cents. (This is done with simple arithmetic: $1 - 0.35$ divided into $2,765.71.) Why does the value go up as prices decline? Because the more prices drop, the more you can buy with each dollar you have.

Let's say when you bought the bond, movie tickets cost $5 for adults and $3 for children. Taking your family to the movies— you, your spouse, and your two children—cost $16. When the depression hit, movie theaters lowered their prices 35 percent: $5 movie tickets now cost $3.25; $3 movie tickets now cost $1.95. The total cost for you and your family at the movies: $10.40. That's $5.60 less than what you used to pay for the same outing. Assume now you buy popcorn for $2.90 and drinks for $2.50. The evening still costs $16, but now you're getting popcorn and drinks for the same money that before only bought tickets. In the same way, the value of bonds increase (you can buy more) as prices decline.

The bond cost you $1,000, so for every $1 you paid, you've now got about $4.25 worth of buying power. This provides us with a multiplier of 4.25. Every dollar invested today in a Treasury bond, if a depression hits, will buy $4.25 worth of goods and services.

If about $23,500 of your $100,000 in assets are in long-term Treasury bonds and a depression comes, the purchasing power of those bonds becomes $100,000 ($4.25 × $23,500). You are completely covered in that your ability to buy $100,000 of goods and services has not declined, the difference is made up by the enhanced value of your bond.

In the real world, though, you wouldn't need to put so much into Treasuries because your other assets, although less valuable, will almost certainly be worth something. Let's say that you put $80,000 of your assets in non–depression-protection assets (stocks or real estate), and during a depression, the value of those assets fall 75 percent. What was worth $80,000 is now worth only $20,000. Because we're assuming prices fall 35 percent, these assets can now buy, in today's dollars, $30,769.31 worth of goods and services. With this $30,000, you need additional assets worth about $70,000 in purchasing power to make you whole. Since our multiplier is 4.25, you need $16,470.59 in depression-protection assets. The assets you buy with this $16,000+ are Treasury bonds.

Looked at from another angle, with a little over 16 percent of your portfolio invested in 30-year Treasury bonds, your net worth is *completely protected against a depression*. And this protection is free. Why? Because Treasury bonds are damn good investments even if we never have a depression. However, recognize that during periods of high inflation, such as we had in the late 1970s and early 1980s, Treasury bonds, like all fixed-income investments, lose value as prices increase. As prices rise, the value of the interest paid by the bonds declines. To counter inflation, we use investments that increase in value with rising prices, which are discussed in the next chapter. No matter what you think of the likelihood of a depression occurring, you need Treasuries in your portfolio because of their safety and their yield. Their depression protection is a welcomed bonus.

Another caveat: Don't make the mistake of thinking you are protected by investing in a government-bond mutual fund (or annuity), which is a mutual fund that invests exclusively (or nearly so) in government bonds. The longer the length of maturity of a bond, the more protection it affords. Fund managers sometimes have short- to medium-term investment horizons, such as 5 or 10 years. That's a lot shorter than the 30-year bonds I recommend you buy.

Another major shortcoming of mutual funds is that when the bond market fluctuates (which it certainly will in a depression), fund managers will likely sell off their bonds. Managers will act this way because the prices of the bonds will rise and the managers, to make their track records look good, will want to lock in profits—to have the money in hand so to speak. It's an approach exactly opposite from what I recommend, which is buy and *hold*. The only time you sell in the depths of a depression is if you absolutely need the money. By the time we get into the deepest trough of a depression, I predict most fund managers will have largely sold out and will be holding cash. Though the value of those dollars will increase as prices decline, it won't compare to the increase in values we'll see with Treasuries.

As with most things, there is an exception to the rule that you shouldn't buy Treasuries through mutual funds or annuities. Franklin Valuemark II Zero Coupon Fund Maturing 2010 is the only annuity (or mutual fund) I know of that invests in one type of security—Treasuries that mature in the year 2010—and never varies its portfolio. In other words, it buys this one type of security and holds it. That's why it can be used instead of the actual Treasuries.

Except for this one fund, I recommend you buy Treasuries—the Treasury bonds themselves.

Depression Protection: Strips

A second type of financial instrument also provides superb depression protection, namely, strips. A *strip* is a long-term, say, 30-year, Treasury bond that an investment banking firm has stripped of its interest. They sell at prices heavily discounted from their face value.

Before everything was electronic, bonds were printed pieces of paper. Along the bond's edge were small coupons, each of which represented an interest payment. Each six months or whenever the interest fell due, the bondholder would clip the coupon, bring it to a bank, and redeem the coupon for the interest due. (This is all done electronically today.) When you think of strips, picture the investment banking firm stripping, or clipping, off all the interest coupons and keeping them for itself and selling you just the bond (without interest).

Why would anyone want to buy a bond that pays no interest? First, the bond itself has value because when it matures, it can be redeemed for its face value. Second, because the bond doesn't pay interest, the investment banking firm sells the bond at a steep discount from the face value. The difference between the bond's face value and what you pay is calculated so that it represents (surprise!) the market's prevailing rate of interest. There's nothing unusual about this arrangement. After all, U.S. EE savings bonds are strips; they don't pay interest periodically but sell at a steep discount from their face value. Strips and EE savings bonds are also *zero-coupon bonds*, which means they do not have coupons.

Assume you buy a $1,000 30-year strip for $75.37. The imputed rate of interest of this bond is 9 percent, the prevailing interest rate. Five years later, a depression is raging. Based on interest rates having fallen to 1 percent and with accrued interest, the bond is now worth $779.77 (calculated as we saw earlier by using future values).

Assuming prices have dropped 35 percent, the purchasing power of that $779.77 bond based on the present value of a dollar is $1,199.65. (To calculate this number, take 1 − the percentage drop in value, or 0.35, which is 0.65, and divide this into the present value, which is $779.77.) The bottom line is, you invest $75.37 and get $1,199.65 in depression protection. That's a multiple of 15.92; for every dollar you invest, you receive $15.92 worth of depression protection.

With about 6 percent of your portfolio invested in strips, your net worth is fully protected. This supposes the unlikely event that the value of the remainder of your portfolio drops to zero. Assuming the rest of your portfolio drops 75 percent, you can fully protect yourself against a depression by devoting less than 5 percent of your portfolio to strips.

However, there are disadvantages to strips compared to conventional Treasury bonds. Because strips don't provide a stream of income (Treasuries pay their interest every six months), you don't get any cash from your investment until the strip matures. Also, even though you get zero cash until the bond's maturity, you have to pay taxes on the accumulated interest every year. So, not only do strips not provide any cash flow, they actually create negative cash flow. Placing the strips in a tax-deferred account, such as an individual retirement account (IRA), postpones the tax liability.

Strips are also more volatile than Treasury bonds, which makes some investors nervous. The volatility is not because investors are concerned about their quality (these are, after all, government securities), but because strips reflect changes in interest rates only through their prices. Conventional bonds are not quite as volatile because, no matter what their prices, bondholders know they will get a stream of guaranteed income; their only volatility comes in the market price of the bond should they want to sell any time before maturity. The situation is similar to stocks. Growth stocks, which rarely pay dividends but have considerable growth potential (their price increases), are more volatile than utility stocks, which typically pay sizable dividends but change slowly in value, if at all.

Volatility is good. The more volatile the bond, the more depression protection it provides. If the economy goes into a tailspin and the investment hardly responds, then it provides little protection. Only when the investment responds strongly, such as with a strip, do you get significant protection. Strips provide lots of bang for the buck—much protection for little investment—precisely because they are so volatile. The volatility is not an issue of risk because you won't even consider selling the strips unless there's a depression. You sell only when the condition for which the investment was bought occurs, such as a depression. In the long run, volatility will have zero effect on your strips' value, and you'll get the guaranteed return at maturity. When it comes to that part of your investment portfolio providing depression and inflation protection, volatility is your friend. The remainder of your portfolio will provide steady, secure growth in assets.

The type of security best for you—Treasury bonds or strips—depends on your need for cash and the risk you're prepared to take over a certain span of time. (Risk is discussed in detail in Chapter 5.) Conservative investors usually go with Treasuries. They like the cash flow and the low volatility, and the secure, conservative nature of Treasuries is appealing, even discounting their protection characteristics.

More adventurous investors go for strips, which allow them to devote a greater percentage of their portfolio to other investments. Other investments are, by definition, more aggressive because every investment is riskier than U.S. government obligations. Many investors take part of their portfolio and devote it to growth stocks and other higher-potential/higher-risk investments. They don't want to have too much of their money tied up in government securities.

Sometimes, investors have their money tied up in illiquid assets (the harder it is to turn an asset into cash, the more "illiquid" it is), such as real estate or annuities, and it is hard for them to come up with the cash to buy Treasuries equal to 15 percent or so of their portfolio's value. But few people have so many illiquid investments that they can't get 5 percent of their holdings in cash. Using strips, this 5 percent provides very adequate depression protection.

An Example

One day a client walked in. Like most people, he came to me with virtually no depression protection. He had recently gotten a 65-page financial plan from one of the largest and oldest national financial planning firms in the country. Its cost: $800. Its value: $0. The plan was so complex that it was practically beyond comprehension. Further, its recommendations were so difficult to implement that it wasn't worth the time and expense required. The ongoing costs of tracking a complex portfolio was an additional factor, too. In desperation he came to me.

In this analysis, like all others, I include only investment assets, not assets for personal use, such as the house one lives in. I assume that use of personal assets will continue in the same way whether or not there is an economic catastrophe.

Briefly, he had about $19,000 in cash and CDs, money he could get his hands on quickly. There was another $16,000 or so in corporate bonds and about $24,000 in stocks and stock mutual funds. A piece of undeveloped land was worth $20,000, and he had another $50,000 tied up in a limited partnership. All this added up to $129,000. But the bulk of his estate was in a fixed-income annuity (an annuity that guarantees repayment of the principal) worth $139,000 (oh, the persuasiveness of insurance salespeople who sell these annuities that are such poor investments). Because fixed-income annuities are debt instruments issued by the insurance company, they are equivalent only to low-grade corporate bonds: The value of both depends on the ability of private organizations to repay their debt during times of financial upheaval (annuities are discussed in detail in Chapter 9).

What was his problem? He had virtually no depression protection. The annuity, though secure in normal times, would drop dramatically in value during a depression because the insurance company wouldn't be able to pay it. Insurance companies can pay interest on their annuities—the "income"—because of the returns they earn on other investments. Those other investments, however, are real estate and corporate stocks and bonds, which may plummet in value in a depression. It's a safe bet that insurance companies will be in deep trouble during a depression (as in 1929) and policyholders will be left holding the bag. My advice to him—and to you: Don't count much on your insurance policies if we get into a depression.

He had another common problem. Most of his investments were illiquid; it was hard for him to turn these investments into ready cash. He could get cash from the annuity, for instance, only on a slow piecemeal basis of 10 percent a year. Turning the limited partnership and real estate into cash was also difficult and would be proportionally more so in a severe downturn.

As a result, I advised him to place 5 percent of his assets in Treasury strips this year and 5 percent in Treasury bonds next year. His entire estate was worth about $258,000, so 5 percent meant coming up with about $13,000 in cash. With his savings account and CD, that was not a problem the first year. And with only $13,000 in strips, he handled his small tax liability easily. The following year would be soon enough to start liquidating some of his illiquid assets, such as the annuity and limited partnership, so he wouldn't have to tap into his cash reserves to raise this second $13,000. And because he was putting the money into Treasury bonds, there was a positive cash flow, which helped pay the taxes on the strips.

Most important, he was protected against a depression. I used a conservative 15 multiple for the strips and a 4 multiple for the Treasury bonds. Every dollar he invested in a strip would be worth $15 in the event of a depression. The strips would have a value of $195,000 and the bonds, $52,000, for a total of $247,000. Since his current portfolio was worth $258,000, this left his protection $11,000 short, which the value of his remaining portfolio would easily cover.

Here was a man who had virtually no depression protection and few liquid assets. Yet, with a couple of simple easy-to-implement investments, I could protect him from a depression while putting him into investments that provided excellent returns with absolute safety. He's since thrown away his useless 65-page financial plan and now sleeps soundly.

Depression-Protection Portfolio Basics

We'll learn in detail all about risk and how it relates to you in Chapter 5, but here are some simple guidelines:

Low-risk. If you are a low-risk investor, the investments of choice are 30-year Treasuries or plain cash. These are low risk because they don't involve leverage (borrowed money or debt), are sure to pay interest, and are less volatile than long-term Treasuries. About 35 percent of your portfolio should be in Treasury bills (one year or less) or 17 percent in 30-year Treasury bonds.

Medium-risk. Medium-risk investors should put 4 percent of their portfolio in Treasury bills and 10 percent in Treasury bonds.

High-risk. Aggressive, high-risk investors can put 7 percent in strips (in fact, 6 percent is adequate but the asset allocation model uses 7 percent). Strips have a low risk of default, but they are volatile, which usually makes low- and medium-risk investors nervous. That's why these are recommended only for high-risk investors. Strips can provide all the depression protection you need.

Our Five Model Families

FAMILY 1: A COUPLE SAVING FOR THEIR RETIREMENT.

Jackie and Bob have $25,000 in savings. We'll put 14 percent of that ($3,500) into depression protection and maintain this percentage as their portfolio grows. Of this, $2,500 (10 percent) will be put in 30-year Treasury bonds and $1,000 (4 percent) will be kept in cash and cash equivalents, such as money market accounts and CDs. Cash and cash equivalents offer good depression protection because as prices fall, their value increases.

PORTFOLIO
30-year Treasury bond	$2,500
Cash and cash equivalents	1,000

FAMILY 2: A SINGLE MOTHER SAVING FOR HER CHILDREN'S COLLEGE TUITION

Marilyn has $10,000 saved, which needs to be protected. Being a medium-risk investor like the previous couple, her portfolio will be structured in a similar way, namely, having 10 percent in 30-year Treasury bonds ($1,000) and 4 percent in cash and cash equivalents.

PORTFOLIO
30-year Treasury bonds	$1,000
Cash and cash equivalents	400

FAMILY 3: A COUPLE SAVING FOR THEIR FIRST HOME

Because these are aggressive, high-risk investors, unlike the previous two families, the Santangelos' portfolio is structured differently. They have no assets now. But as they accumulate assets, they will first put their money into a savings account at their credit union or savings and loan. The money will stay in this account until they have enough to buy the minimum for Treasury strips, which is usually set at $1,000 by the brokerage firm that sells the strips. Their goal is to put 7 percent of their assets into strips, which will provide complete depression protection.

PORTFOLIO
Treasury strips $1,400

FAMILY 4: A COUPLE WANTING TO MINIMIZE THEIR TAXES

The Jordans are a medium-risk couple, so their portfolio essentially looks like those of Families 1 and 2, though the numbers are larger. We want to protect their $1.2 million net worth, which does not include the business. We'll put $120,000 (10 percent) in a Franklin Valuemark II Zero Coupon Fund Maturing 2010 and $48,000 (4 percent) in American Funds' U.S. Treasury Money Fund of America. The Franklin annuity provides tax-deferral advantages, which, given this couple's goal of minimizing taxes, is important.

PORTFOLIO
Franklin Valuemark II Zero Coupon Fund
   maturing 2010 $120,000
American Funds U.S. Treasury Money
   Fund of America   84,000

FAMILY 5: A RETIRED COUPLE

Because the Moriartys don't like much risk, their portfolio is different than any of the others. They have $500,000 that needs protection. We'll put $260,000 into this protection, specifically in cash and cash equivalents and 30-year Treasury bonds. This is much more protection than they need (they need about 16 percent of their portfolio and this is 51 percent). The model for low-risk investors calls for 35 percent of the portfolio to be in cash and cash equivalents and 17 percent in Treasury bonds.

These are precisely the assets used in depression protection.
Rather than complicating things by listing some of their investments in these vehicles in this chapter and the others in later
chapters (the end result, namely, 35 percent in cash and 17 percent in Treasury bonds is identical), I've listed all these assets
here.

PORTFOLIO
Cash and cash equivalents	$175,000
30-year Treasury bonds	85,000

—————————— H I G H L I G H T S ——————————

In a depression:

- Hard assets, like real estate and gold, will lose much of their value.
- Stocks will lose much of their value.
- Prices will decline.
- Interest rates will decline.

In a depression, the only investments that are sure to increase in value are U.S. government securities.

The losses incurred in one's investments during a depression can be offset by the gains of long-term U.S. government securities.

4

INFLATION BULLETPROOFING:
Winning the Race Against Prices

"The sins of the fathers are to be laid upon the children," Shakespeare wrote. He wasn't referring to *inflation* (a rise in the general level of prices), but he could have been. Children today are finding their parents have committed the "sin" of lacking enough retirement money. Inflation is the culprit. Singlehandedly, it erodes retired parents' incomes, leaving their children to pick up the slack.

Professionals Joan and Mark have three children. Their incomes are good, but they came to me to gain better control of their finances. As we discussed their financial situation, I innocently asked if they had any dependents besides their children. That's when I heard the harrowing story of Joan's parents. Her father, employed by the same firm all his working life, retired with what seemed to be an adequate pension. Adding Social Security, their financial future was secure. They thought.

Joan's father retired in the late 1970s when inflation was building steam. Within five years, Joan's parents saw their expenses increase nearly 70 percent. At the same time, their income increased a mere 20 percent, which came entirely from Social Security cost-of-living adjustments since the pension payout was fixed. Today, these two elderly people are dependent on

Joan and Mark just to keep a roof over their heads and food on the table.

Were Joan's parents profligate? Unwise with their investments? Unconcerned with their future? No. Their spending was responsible; they invested conservatively and planned thoroughly for their future. In a sense they suffered from something they never dreamed about: bad luck.

They were unlucky because they began their retirement when inflation was dramatically increasing. And inflation—at *any* level—can be devastating. At a modest 6 percent annual inflation rate, prices *double* in 12 years and *triple* in 19. At 12 percent inflation, prices double in 7 short years and triple in 10.

Let's say you have a retirement nest egg of $250,000 that's in a long-term bond yielding 8 percent a year or $20,000.

A couple of years later, inflation is running at 10 percent and stays there, say, five years. (This is not impossible; we averaged better than 10 percent a year inflation during the four years of 1978 to 1981.) At the end of five years, you are still earning 8 percent and getting $20,000, but you're paying $20,000 for the goods and services that $12,418 could buy in the first year. You've lost 38 percent of your purchasing power in five short years. And in another five years at the same inflation rate, the purchasing power of your $20,000 would drop to $7,711, or 61 percent. You can see how devastating inflation can be in Table 1.

▶ **TABLE 1** _____

Effects of 10% Inflation on Purchasing Power

Year	Investment	Yield (%)	Income	Amount of Income Needed to Keep Pace with Inflation	Purchasing Power of Income
1	$250,000	8%	$20,000	$20,000	$20,000
2	250,000	8	20,000	22,000	18,182
3	250,000	8	20,000	24,200	16,529
4	250,000	8	20,000	26,620	15,026
5	250,000	8	20,000	29,282	13,660
6	250,000	8	20,000	32,210	12,418
7	250,000	8	20,000	35,431	11,289
8	250,000	8	20,000	38,974	10,263
9	250,000	8	20,000	42,872	9,330
10	250,000	8	20,000	47,159	8,482
11	250,000	8	20,000	51,875	7,711

At the beginning of Year 1, you receive $20,000 annually. One year later, you are still getting $20,000, but because inflation is 10 percent a year, that money can buy only $18,182 worth of goods and services compared with what it bought the first year. (To calculate, take your beginning income and divide by 1 plus the inflation rate. The equation looks like this:

$$\frac{\$20,000}{(1+0.1)} = \frac{20,000}{1.1} = \$18,182.$$

Two years out, your purchasing power is down to $16,529. You're still getting $20,000, but its value has dropped as prices have risen.

You're stuck with the 8 percent return because the bond pays a fixed interest rate and its price declines dramatically if interest rates rise (which they will very likely do during inflation). It doesn't take much inflation to decimate a retirement nest egg.

Think of inflation as radiation. A little X-ray radiation now and then causes no harm. But, over a lifetime, radiation damage builds up in the body. It never goes away. Too many doses, even if each is small, cause serious problems, even death.

Inflation has the same insidious effect. A few percentage points of inflation won't greatly erode anyone's buying power and financial health. Yet, over time, it destroys. Even the nest eggs of the truly wealthy are not immune. With inflation bullet-proofing, however, you cannot be caught unawares. Your financial health will blossom, and you can retire knowing inflation won't decimate your savings. Your bulletproofing keeps you unharmed.

Our Number 1 Economic Fear

In the last chapter, we talked about depression and its devastation on an entire generation of Americans. Today, most of us of a later generation have another fear, and that fear is inflation. Its immediacy to us is simple: We experienced it recently. I know of depression only through stories, books, paintings, photographs, movies, but I know of inflation because it made my life a roller coaster ride of highs and lows for years. For me, inflation is Economic Enemy Number 1. Nothing else comes close, not unemployment, not disability, not taxation, not economic downturns. If financial devastation comes my way, I am convinced inflation will do it.

Judging from my clients and radio listeners, I am not alone in fearing inflation. Over and over they tell me: "By the time I retire, I think my pension and Social Security won't be enough." If they are saving for their children's college education, they expect the ravages of inflation to make it impossible to finance anything but four years at the cheapest state university. If it's a house they want, they don't think they can save for a down payment fast enough to match rising prices.

My clients and listeners represent most Americans. Every month, without fail, the government releases such statistics as the consumer price index (CPI), the wholesale price level and the prices of various goods and services, like real estate, gasoline, and food. The news media dutifully reports these. Inevitably, the news stories conclude with a discussion about that beast inflation. Is it about to awake from hibernation, or for the moment at least, is it asleep and content? Everyone wants to know because inflation worries them. If the government's budget deficit starts to feed it, if imports increase in price, if the dollar's value goes down, if demand outstrips supply, if the public begins to think inflation has arrived and will be around for sometime, if inflation resurfaces—watch out. Prices can quickly go crazy.

Stopping inflation on the run is like trying to change a supertanker's direction on the high seas. It takes many miles and much time just to bring the ship to a halt. And even longer to turn it around. If inflation lets loose, it can take years to get it under control, during which time it will exact a considerable economic price.

The diverse, insidious nature of inflation makes protecting against it all the more difficult. If a flak jacket is enough to bulletproof your portfolio against depression, you need a suit of armor to get you as much protection against inflation.

Postwar Inflation

Through the 1950s and early 1960s, inflation was generally less than 3 percent. Observers set the beginnings of postwar inflation in the United States at about 1965. That's when the Vietnam War buildup started without higher taxes to fund the expanded defense expenditures. By 1970, inflation was 5.6 percent. Then-President Nixon imposed wage and price controls, which had little long-term effect. Once lifted, prices hit levels they likely would have if the controls had never been imposed in the first place.

The CPI rose 3.5 and 3.4 percent in 1971 and 1972, respectively. It jumped to 8.3 percent in 1973. By then, the controls were being phased out (they were gone entirely by 1974). Poor harvests and a strong demand for food at home and abroad helped push up food prices, too. Then the Organization of Petroleum Exporting Countries (OPEC) quadrupled the price of oil in 1973.

The end of the decade saw an even stronger inflation surge. In 1978, the CPI rose 9.0 percent. During each of the next three years, it reached 12.8, 12.5 and 9.6 percent before settling down to 4.5 percent in 1982.

But what real effects and consequences do these numbers imply? Is 4.5 percent really inflation? Well, at this rate, prices double in 16 years. Many Americans live 20 years or more in retirement. In 20 years, price increases of 4.5 percent mean that what cost $1 in Year 1 cost $2.50 by Year 20. Yet, most of us think of 4.5 percent price increases as not even being inflation. This is a sort of a "natural" increase, something to expect over time. Yet, such innocuous price increases devastate a person's retirement income during their lifetime. And during any 20-year period, the chances are good that prices will shoot ahead far faster than this rate for at least a few years.

When I think of the late 1960s, the Beatles, the Vietnam War, Richard Nixon, the promise of peace, and an idyllic future come to mind. It was a mixed bag. When I reflect on the late 1970s, inflation is all I picture. I recall restaurants whose menu prices increased with practically every visit. Union workers demanded huge wage increases and claimed, with justification, that all they wanted was to maintain their buying power in the face of rapidly rising prices.

It was a time out of control. My economic destiny was largely beyond my influence, and the government appeared equally powerless. Ronald Reagan kicked Jimmy Carter out of the White House in part because Carter was blamed for the country's economic morass.

Although that was a trying time for most Americans, we've been lucky in never having experienced hyperinflation, as occurred in Germany in the early 1920s, and in other countries much more recently. Between 1970 and 1978, Argentina had an average annual inflation rate of 120 percent. In March 1990—in just this one month—inflation reached 95.5 percent in Argentina. Supermarkets were ransacked, food trucks were hijacked, and 15 deaths resulted from the rioting in this one month, all because of the runaway inflation. Such inflation is not ancient history but is happening in the world today.

Inflation: A More Detailed Definition

Exactly what is inflation? George W. Wilson, in his book, *Inflation: Causes, Consequences and Cures*, states that inflation is "the *persistent* rise in the *general* level of prices" [his emphasis].[2] Researchers claim to have found evidence of inflation as far back as ancient Greece and Rome, so there is nothing new about it.

What really constitutes inflation and at what level rising prices begin to be seen as "high" inflation is open to interpretation. Personal values and experience color our perceptions of it. Recent U.S. history proves the point. Inflation throughout much of the 1980s hovered in the 4 percent to 5 percent range, yet President Ronald Reagan boasted loud and long about the expanding economy and "moderate" inflation. Appealing to the fear I and so many others had in the late 1970s, he claimed he had brought the economy under *control*.

Yet, the 1950s and 1960s saw the economy grow rapidly while price increases stayed below 2 percent annually. In fact, it was the 5 + percent inflation in the early 1970s that motivated Washington to impose wage and price controls for the first and only time in this country's history. Barely 10 years later, similar price increases would have hardly raised an eyebrow to most economists, politicians, and Americans.

Will the United States go through inflationary periods similar to those of Germany in the 1920s or even our own in 1978–1981? No one knows. I don't think we're headed for a German-type hyperinflation. It would surprise me though if during the 1990s we didn't struggle through at least one period of sustained, pronounced inflation, something in the two-digit range.

What's important is not whether we run into a stretch of foul economic weather, but that we wear the protective clothing needed if we do.

It is more difficult to create a model for inflation, unlike recession. We've never had hyper- or even sustained severe inflation, so we have no history to go by. Inflation-protection investments are also more varied than those for depression. In addition, the price fluctuations of such investments over time are more difficult to calculate. Bond prices, for instance, move in fairly predictable ways when interest rates move. That's not true of real estate prices during inflation. However, certain parameters can be constructed that help us create inflation-protection portfolios.

The Inflation Scenario

If we have severe inflation, I see certain investments increasing *faster* than the inflation rate. If inflation turns into real hyperinflation, say 100 percent or more a year, the investments I recommend will work remarkably well. In fact, the more inflation there is, the better protection these investments provide. You actually need fewer of these investments if inflation goes bananas because these recommendations skyrocket in value with price increases.

The reason for this is that the values of certain investments (like commercial real estate) go up at an *increasing* rate as inflation builds up steam. I estimate certain inflation-protection investments, which I'll discuss shortly, will increase at the following annual rates:

Inflation rate of 10 percent: Inflation-protection investments increase 13 percent.
Inflation rate of 20 percent: Inflation-protection investments increase 30 percent.
Inflation rate of 100 percent: Inflation-protection investments increase 200 percent.

Here's an example. You buy a piece of commercial real estate for $250,000. For the five years after your purchase, inflation runs at 10 percent a year. When inflation is at this rate, we expect inflation-protection investments, like commercial real estate, to increase 13 percent annually. By the end of Year 5, your property is worth a bit over $460,000, but in real buying terms (the original worth of money in Year 1 dollars), it is worth $286,000 or about 14 percent more than you originally paid for it.

At 14 percent for the five years, or about 2.7 percent (again, in *real* terms), you haven't made much money. You have, however, more than kept up with inflation, which is quite an accomplishment in itself.

The arithmetic looks like this:

First year: $250,000 × (1.13) = $282,500
Second year: $282,500 × (1.13) = $319,225
Third year: $319,225 × (1.13) = $360,724
Fourth year: $360,724 × (1.13) = $407,618
Fifth year: $407,618 × (1.13) = $460,609

Since prices have gone up 10 percent a year, $460,609 just doesn't buy what it used to. $460,609 at the end of Year 5 can buy what $286,002 could buy at the beginning of Year 1 (this is calculated by discounting the 10 percent a year that prices increased). This discounted figure of $286,002 is $36,002 more than you started with.

If inflation jumps to 20 percent a year, we expect commercial real estate to appreciate *30 percent annually*. By the end of Year 5, it has a nominal value of $928,000. What is this $928,000 worth in real terms? Since prices increased 20 percent a year, it buys what $373,000 could at the beginning of Year 1. That's an increase in *real value* of about 50 percent over your initial $250,000 investment (this is calculated by discounting the 20 percent a year that prices increased). You could now buy commercial real estate worth $373,000 (in present dollars) without any additional strain on your finances.

And if inflation moves into a white-hot phase, say 100 percent a year, you make out like a pirate on an unarmed Spanish galleon. With 100 percent annual inflation, I predict your real estate will appreciate 200 percent a year. At the end of five years, that $250,000 property would be worth a joyous $60,750,000. Unbelievable? As we saw, this degree of inflation happened in Argentina in a single month.

In real buying power, of course, your $60,750,000 property isn't worth this much. What it is worth is about $1,900,000. While not the same as 60 million bucks, it is close to *eight times in real terms* what you initially invested. This is enough to make Scrooge happy.

What accounts for the power of certain investments to increase in value? Is this smoke and shadows created by economists *cum* magicians? The most important reason hard assets increase faster than inflation is the famed economic law of supply and demand.

As inflation surges, those with money in other places—bonds, stocks, money market accounts, CDs, mutual funds—find their rates of return fixed or at best unable to keep up with inflation. So they bail out. They beeline to the dollar signs with a heedlessness that could make Michael Milken blush. The supply of hard assets remains the same while the demand for them dramatically increases. Real estate, gold, and other hard assets attract the attention of the cash-rich, and they almost throw money at these investments.

The greater the inflation rate, the more investors will want to jump on the hard-asset bandwagon. Their actions amplify the increase in prices of these investments, pushing them up faster than inflation, which just attracts even more investors and more money. The United States has always been a safe haven for money, a place where money flows to when times are bad in other countries. It is conceivable that there might be a flight of capital from the United States to other nations in such high inflation times, but I think it unlikely. Americans have never acted this way (though, admittedly, there's always a first time), and more importantly, if the United States is experiencing runaway inflation, much of the rest of the world probably is, too.

These investors aren't being stupid. Money market accounts, bonds, stocks, and the like just can't keep up with full-speed-ahead inflation. Pension plans frequently lack inflation-adjustments clauses, leaving those dependent on such pension plans financially ravaged.

Social Security is also problematical. At best, its price adjustments always lag by one year, since they are calculated on what the CPI did the *previous* 12 months. If inflation runs at 20 percent a year, this lag time seriously affects the buying power of Social Security payments. A severe period of inflation may even force Congress to curtail the Social Security cost-of-living adjustment for fear of bankrupting the whole system. Even in the late 1980s, there was talk about limiting Social Security payments. And this was when inflation was moderate.

The last word is that tangible assets with inherent value, like real estate, will always have value, so the flight of capital to them makes a lot of sense. And this is what I see happening if we get a bout of serious inflation.

The downside is, if inflation doesn't happen, the recommended investments will produce solid, though unspectacular, returns. There's no question that inflation-protection investments are not sterling performers in a recession. But they'll do okay, and the rest of your portfolio, which we discuss in the remainder of this book, will do quite well. Since we're in for the long term, a year or two or three of recession isn't significant. As I write this book, we're in a recession. Chances are good that when we climb out of it, a strong bout of inflation will appear, and these investments will take off. On the other hand, a depression will devastate inflation-protection investments. That's why you balance inflation protection with depression protection. Also, inflation-protection investments do well when the economy does well. During times when we're not in a severe recession/depression or strong inflation, these investments should be highly productive.

Bulletproof Your Portfolio Against Inflation

Bulletproofing your portfolio against inflation involves a basket of investments to look at now. In later chapters, I'll discuss these in more detail.

Real Estate

For most people, real estate, in the form of one's home, is their largest one-time *expense*. Many mistakenly view their home as their largest *investment*; a home is not an investment because it is for personal use, not for generating income or capital gains. You have to live somewhere, so even if you sell your home, you'll have to pay rent rather than use the money for nonhousing purchases. The assets you accumulate for retirement will likely be your largest investment.

Real estate does well during inflationary periods. The annualized rate of return on commercial real estate, as calculated by T. Rowe Price, Baltimore, for the decade of the eighties was 12.1 percent, while inflation averaged 5.1 per year. That's pretty good considering that, although some real estate markets, such as California and the Northeast, did very well for most of the decade, others stagnated or even collapsed. Arizona, Texas, and the

Rocky Mountain states were among the weakest real estate markets then. As I write this, the Northeast now has a terrible market and California's is weak.

Because we take a long-term view of investing, these periodic ups and downs are not significant. Over the long run, real estate does quite well. In fact, Peter S. Spiro, in his book, *Real Interest Rates and Investment and Borrowing Strategy*, claims "there is . . . no perfect hedge against inflation, but real estate . . . appears to be the best of the alternatives."[3]

Lack of liquidity is real estate's most important shortcoming, for it cannot be quickly converted into cash. Stocks and bonds are far more liquid: Call up your broker, he or she sells them, and you have cash within days. That's liquidity, which we'll discuss more in Chapter 6.

For some people, though, illiquidity is an important advantage. If the market disintegrates and they panic and want to sell, they're stuck. They have to hold onto their property until the market turns up. By then, they have weathered the worst of the market and can earn a decent return on their investment. This makes the real estate market a nearly perfect investment regulator—it lets you sell when the market's high and prevents you from selling when it's low.

Real estate is available in a variety of forms. Real estate investment trusts (REITs) and real estate limited partnerships (RELPs) are more liquid than real estate in the form of land or buildings. When you buy into an REIT or an RELP, you're buying shares of a company that, in turn, invests the money in a whole range of real estate investments. Because REITs and RELPs typically invest in many properties, they also limit the investor's risk by spreading it across a diversified portfolio of real estate investments of which, hopefully, the majority perform well and more than cover the losses of those that don't, generating an overall profit. Those who buy mutual funds will appreciate the similarity between these investment vehicles and REITs and RELPs. They all give the investor an easy way of creating a diversified portfolio.

Real estate's leverage potential is a bonus to the investor. This refers to your ability to multiply the amount of property that can be bought by using credit; if you have $100,000 for a 20 percent down payment, you can borrow the rest to purchase $500,000 worth of property. As little as 10 percent or 20 percent down can get you a piece of property. This way you can control real estate worth 5 to 10 times the amount of money you have on hand. During times of inflation, this advantage becomes even greater because you are paying off your mortgages with "cheaper" dollars (dollars that are less valuable because of inflation).

It also offers tax advantages, such as writing off the interest paid on real estate purchased for investment purposes, and deducting depreciation if your income is below $100,000. This is one of the few tax shelters left to the moderate income earner. One never knows what Congress will do with tax laws, but at the time of this writing, real estate offers some decided tax advantages.

Real estate's advantages during inflation are that

1. Its value increases faster than the general price level.
2. It can be bought in a variety of ways.
3. Leveraging is easy.
4. It has tax benefits no matter what inflation is doing.

My experience with real estate illustrates these points: In 1974, as a full-time sales engineer for Westinghouse, I bought two condos in Park City, Utah, a ski resort 35 minutes from downtown Salt Lake City. The condos had reverted to the bank, and I bought them with $5,000 down. I lived in one and rented the other.

The whole condo complex was in trouble, and shortly thereafter, I bought eight more condos, putting down only $1,000 apiece. I rented these out, their rents more than covering my mortgage, taxes, and upkeep costs. In the late 1970s, with inflation heating up, so did Park City's real estate market. It peaked in 1980–1981. By then I had bought and sold many properties, commercial as well as residential. At the market's peak my initial investment of $5,000 for the first two condos and $8,000 for the next eight had turned into about $2.5 million. Westinghouse was a distant memory as I was able to work full time on my investments.

By the early 1980s I had sold all but a few of the properties. Starting in about 1983, the market began really dropping. Skydivers fall more slowly than Park City's real estate market did then. Between the early 1980s and the market's nadir in about

1988, the market lost about 60 percent of its value, and I took a bath on a number of properties.

What happened? Inflation fizzled and real estate, perhaps the ultimate inflation hedge, floundered. Between 1988 and 1990, however, though inflation was no higher than it had been in the mid-1980s, the market recovered most of its losses. By 1990, it was probably down only about 25 percent from its peak. By 1993, I predict the market will be at least equal to where it was in 1981, and probably higher. The boom came because Utah's economy, which struggled through the mid-1980s, turned up in 1988, spurring demand for Park City real estate. At the same time, excess inventory had been sold off (virtually nothing was built for several years), which also helped boost prices.

The lesson: During inflationary periods, real estate is a wonderful inflation hedge. And, over the long term, it is a solid investment, one destined to return a good profit, even though it may suffer significant short- to medium-term downturns.

In a later chapter on hard assets, I'll discuss in detail the pros and cons of various types of real estate investments and ways to choose the best ones.

Gold

Another classic inflation-protection investment is gold. When the economy does well and inflation is moderate, as during the 1980s, gold tends not to perform well. For most of the 1980s, it was in the $350 to $450 per ounce range. However, it can be a strong hedge when the economy falters because of high inflation.

Gold is perhaps history's oldest and most enduring investment vehicle. For thousands of years, people have bought, hoarded, traded, hidden, and coveted gold. The Spanish conquistadors came to the New World to find gold. The alchemists of the Middle Ages tried turning lead into gold. The glittering metal has long held a fascination for people around the world exceeded only by their passion for religion, politics, and possibly sex.

Mary, my client who grew up during the Great Depression, learned to appreciate gold at an early age. Her father always kept gold bullion coins for a rainy day. Over time, as his wealth increased, he increased his holdings. He had a hoard when Nixon, in 1971, set the price of gold free. Overnight, gold jumped from $35 an ounce to about $60 and Mary's father's coins jumped in value, too.

When I suggested to Mary she use gold bullion coins for part of her inflation protection, she loved the idea. She knew from her father just how solid a hedge gold can be. In this regard, Mary is a bit different from many folks. Most people believe bank accounts and stocks and bonds are the investments of quality. Gold, to them, seems slightly offbeat.

It isn't, and history proves it. Unique among investments, it has minimal practical uses yet is universally valued.

Like real estate, gold is available in a variety of ways. Bullion—as gold bars or ingots—is one. The problem here is twofold: Bullion is both relatively illiquid and a pain to store.

Gold bullion coins are another investment vehicle. South African Kruggerands, Canadian Maple Leafs, American Eagles, and Chinese Pandas have ready markets and an easily calculated value, explaining why many investors find they are an excellent vehicle for inflation protection.

Consider gold stocks. These are the stocks of companies exclusively or principally in the gold-mining business. Gold stocks are particularly worthwhile because they provide exceptional leverage potential (I will discuss this in detail in Chapter 10).

Another way to invest in gold is to buy a mutual fund that invests only in gold stocks. Like REITs and LPs in the real estate world, mutual funds enjoy both liquidity and lower risk because the fund spreads its investments among a number of gold companies.

In sum, as an inflation hedge, gold is a good performer that deserves serious consideration. I'll talk more about this precious metal in Chapter 10, which is on hard assets. Of course, inflation protection comes with other investments, too. Various collectibles, such as numismatic coins, are examples. Chapter 10 covers these as well.

The Downside

Every investment with an upside (profit potential) has a downside (loss potential). Investments used for inflation protection will likely do poorly in a depression and give a mediocre return in a period of relative price stability. I've already discussed my experience with real estate during periods of inflation and stability. Gold, too, has had its ups and downs, having rocketed to $850 an ounce during the height of the late 1970s inflation, then dropping to the $350 to $450 level and languishing there to the present day.

That's all right because if the remainder of your portfolio is properly constructed, you do well overall. We don't expect inflation-protection investments to sparkle during periods of very moderate inflation—and they don't. If the 1980s had been a period of high inflation, these investments would likely have done extremely well, and overall, your portfolio would have done well. Remember that the task at hand is to design your portfolio so that if a particular economic situation develops, you'll have investments that take advantage of it, while others will do adequately or poorly. It doesn't matter what happens economically, as long as the portfolio can handle all possibilities. This is what bulletproofing your portfolio is all about.

An Example

When Sarah came to me after the death of her husband, this was her situation. Together, they had amassed net assets worth about $1.8 million. Of this, about $5,000 was in gold coins, $100,000 was in stocks, $40,000 in a condo, and the rest was essentially in cash and cash equivalents, such as Treasury bills (these are short-term investments) and money market accounts. Her inflation protection: $45,000 out of $1.8 million, or about 2.5 percent.

The level of risk Sarah was comfortable with was low to medium, so she should have had between 20 percent and 33 percent of her portfolio in inflation-protection investments. (The rest of her portfolio was put in other low- and medium-risk investments discussed throughout the book; for specifics, see the portfolios in Chapter 15.) We put $410,000, or 22 percent, in inflation protection. These were her inflation-protection investments:

Gold	Coins: $80,000
	Van Eck Gold/Resources Fund (a gold-stock mutual fund discussed in Chapter 8): $40,000
	Total in gold: $120,000, or 29 percent of inflation-protection portfolio
Real estate	Conservative real estate limited partnership: $250,000
	Condo: $40,000

Total in real estate: $290,000, or 71 percent
of inflation-protection portfolio

We expect Sarah's inflation-protection portfolio to at least double in value in severe inflation. This should more than offset any decline in real value in her total portfolio due to inflation.

Inflation-Protection Portfolio Guide

Low-Risk Portfolio

For those not wanting to take on much risk, devote about 30 percent of your total assets to inflation protection. If you have $250,000 in investment assets (remember, this does not include your home), then $75,000 should be in inflation-protection investments. Two investments are for you:

1. *Real estate.* Twenty percent of your total assets should be in real estate—fully paid real estate, not leveraged real estate bought with something down and the rest borrowed. If you don't have enough money to buy actual land or buildings, buy into an REIT or LP (limited partnership). In our example, roughly $56,000 should be in nonleveraged real estate.
2. *Gold bullion coins.* Ten percent of your total assets should be in gold bullion coins. Kruggerands, Eagles, Maple Leafs, and Pandas are all good. Each contains one ounce of gold. Don't pay more than 5 to 15 percent above the current price for an ounce of bullion. If gold is selling for $400 per ounce, your price for gold coins should be between $420 and $460.

Moderate-Risk Portfolio

As a middle-of-the-road risk taker, put 25 percent of your total portfolio in inflation protection. You need less than the low-risk investor because you are willing to take on a bit more risk and be a bit more aggressive with your investments. Two investments are for you:

1. *Gold-stock mutual fund.* I recommend you make this 12 percent of your total portfolio.
2. *Real estate.* Unlike the low-risk investor, you can use leverage with your real estate—up to 50 percent—to buy real estate worth the remaining 13 percent of the inflation-protection portion of your total portfolio.

High-Risk Portfolio

For those really willing to take a flier, only 20 percent of your total portfolio needs to be in inflation protection. Here are your primary investments:

1. *Real estate.* In keeping with your risk taking, use highly leveraged real estate, meaning you borrow 80 percent or more of the purchase price. Highly leveraged real estate gets all of your inflation-protection portfolio.

Now you have the tools needed to create a portfolio that will protect you against moderate to severe inflation. Chapter 15 contains sample complete portfolios that include depression and inflation bulletproofing, plus excellent investment returns. This chapter will tell you exactly what your entire portfolio should look like.

Our Five Model Families

FAMILY 1: A COUPLE SAVING FOR THEIR RETIREMENT

These moderate-risk investors will use real estate and gold for their inflation protection. As our model calls for (see Chapter 15), 13 percent of their portfolio is put into a real estate annuity (which provides tax-deferral benefits) and 12 percent in gold.

PORTFOLIO	
30-year Treasury bonds	$2,500
Cash and cash equivalents	1,000
Franklin Valuemark II Real Estate Securities Fund	**3,250**
Franklin Valuemark II Precious Metals Fund	**3,000**

FAMILY 2: A SINGLE MOTHER SAVING FOR HER CHILDREN'S COLLEGE TUITION

Like the previous couple, Marilyn is a moderate-risk investor and therefore puts the same percentage of her portfolio into real estate (13 percent) and gold (12 percent). However, since she wants to withdraw the money before retirement, we have her use a real estate mutual fund for inflation protection rather than an annuity. This way she avoids early withdrawal penalties.

PORTFOLIO

30-year Treasury bonds	$1,000
Cash and cash equivalents	400
Templeton Real Estate Securities Fund	**1,300**
Franklin Gold Fund	**1,200**

FAMILY 3: A COUPLE SAVING FOR THEIR FIRST HOME

Because these folks don't have much money and investments usually require a minimum amount of money, the Santangelo's first goal was to put depression protection in place. Once they have the $1,400 saved for that, they can move onto the next step in their portfolio building, namely, inflation protection. Being high-risk investors, their portfolio should have 20 percent of its assets in real estate. So, the next $4,000 (that's 20 percent of the $20,000 they want to save) should be invested in real estate. This couple has a short-term goal, so their real estate investment is a mutual fund rather than a tax-deferred annuity.

PORTFOLIO

Treasury strips	$1,400
Templeton Real Estate Securities Fund	**4,000**

FAMILY 4: A COUPLE WANTING TO MINIMIZE THEIR TAXES

Medium-risk investors, the Jordans should put 13 percent of their portfolio into real estate and 12 percent into gold. Because they want to minimize taxes and will not withdraw any money before the age (59½) at which they need to worry about IRS penalties, we'll have them put their money in annuities.

PORTFOLIO

Franklin Valuemark II Zero Coupon Fund Maturing 2010	$120,000
American Funds U.S. Treasury Money Fund of America	84,000
Franklin Valuemark II Real Estate Securities Fund	**156,000**
Franklin Valuemark II Precious Metals Fund	**144,000**

FAMILY 5: A RETIRED COUPLE

These are low-risk investors, which means they put 20 percent of their portfolio in real estate and 10 percent in gold.

PORTFOLIO

Cash and cash equivalents	$175,000
30-year Treasury bonds	85,000
Franklin Valuemark II Real Estate Securities Fund	**100,000**
Gold bullion coins	**50,000**

H I G H L I G H T S

Runaway inflation quickly devastates the value of all money-based assets, such as CDs, bonds, and money market funds.

To protect against inflation use hard assets:
- Real estate properties.
- Real estate investment trusts.
- Real estate limited partnerships.
- Gold.
- Collectibles.

5

RISK DOESN'T HAVE TO BE RISKY

You're now saving, planning, and ready to move into a new world of financial security. Only one problem: What do you do with your money?

There's plenty of choices, and in fact, that's what the rest of this book is about. First, though, you'll need to know something about the risks you face and the strategies to use. In this chapter we'll learn all about the issues involved with risk before introducing easy-to-use strategies in the next chapter.

I ask every client, "How much risk are you willing to take?" "Very little," is the typical reply. I don't know whether being a risk taker conveys a shoot-from-the-hip wild image people want to avoid, or risk just frightens folks, but few seem comfortable thinking about taking much risk. "Americans are investment wimps," says the *Wall Street Journal* about Americans' aversion to risk.[4]

My bulletproofing strategy cuts most risk over the long term, but no strategy can completely eliminate risk, especially in the short to medium terms. Even if a strategy could, you wouldn't want it. That's because risk and reward are related: The more carefully chosen risks you take, the greater your rewards.

Risk

One important aspect of risk that is paramount, but often unacknowledged in making investment decisions, is its effect on your behavior. If you don't like risk, yet put money into commodities futures contracts (the riskiest of risky investments), you'll probably react quickly to market fluctuations and endanger your investment, giving in to panic at the first wide swing in price and getting out when you should stay in. Or you freeze and do nothing. People don't think rationally or effectively when panicked and afraid, and that's not a good frame of mind in which to make crucial decisions affecting your financial future. If you can't put your head on your pillow and fall asleep free of worry each night because your investments scare the hell out of you, you're making the wrong investments.

A woman of 80 once came to my office and before I could introduce myself asked, "What's the market doing today?" She was in trouble and scared silly about her financial situation, and this made her chronically nervous.

Going broke wasn't her concern, for she had plenty of money. Instead, she fretted unhealthily about losing money. In short, her investments were too risky for her personality. She owned aggressive growth stocks that do well in the long term but, day by day, are as explosive as a 2-year-old's temper. Together, we changed her investments to match her personality, dumping the high-risk stocks in favor of income-oriented mutual funds and secure and calming bonds. As her portfolio stopped its manic swings, she mellowed and eventually lost her nervous edge entirely.

Moderate risk takers are just as susceptible to investments with inappropriate risks. If they buy boring CDs, disappointment will follow. They like the excitement of bigger returns, and the gambling aspect of taking such risks is obviously exciting. So they do something stupid, like buying the penny stock of a firm that's never sold a thing and is unlikely ever to do so. Or they go into commodities they know nothing about. Soon they're having more excitement than they ever wanted. I call this a recipe for trouble. Successful investing requires a match between risk and your personality.

Where There's Reward, There's Risk

The more risk, the greater the potential reward or profit; the less risk, the smaller the likely reward. This trade-off is basic to all investing, with risk having an essential role in every investment decision you make.

Risk affects you directly through price fluctuations. The prices of everything you buy have moments that are, by their nature, short to medium term. That's how long they affect you. Yet you should hold for the long term so that your earnings reflect the long-term growth trends of your investments, leaving temporary worries about short-term fluctuations behind you.

One of my clients learned this the hard way. During the two years she held a gold mutual fund, its price dropped about 20 percent, and she wanted to sell. I advised her not to, but she sold it anyway. Within three months, the fund's price doubled. This is price fluctuation, pure and simple. A fundamentally sound investment should be held because it will eventually perform. No investment goes up all the time. You wait because most good investments create profits for their investors eventually. Over the past 60 + years, the stock market has risen at a double-digit average per year. It's that kind of long-term power you want to harness for yourself. If you hold for the long term, you don't need to be Ross Perot to make money.

A Risk-Reward Example

Most major issuers of debt in the form of bonds—corporations, states, cities, and even towns—are rated in terms of their financial state (and therefore their ability to make good on interest and principal payments to bondholders) by several internationally reputed rating firms, most commonly, Moody's and Standard & Poor's. (Appendix A at the back of the book lists and explains the ratings of these ratings services.) As the rating declines, the interest the issuer must offer to attract buyers increases. Very low or unrated bonds are "junk" bonds, which offer the highest available returns for bond buyers—and the most risk. They are most often issued by companies with lots of debt already, those that have fallen on hard times, or just small companies whose bonds lack ratings by the major rating services. Every unrated bond fits into the junk category. Companies that must cover crushing interest and principal payments on their bonds or appear risky because their debt is unrated have to offer high rates of interest.

Those who buy junk bonds are less likely to get paid than investors who buy triple-A-rated bonds. Don't get me wrong. I'm not saying junk bonds are likely to default. Yet, if you bought two bonds, one junk and the other investment grade, the bond more likely to turn into a black hole is the junk.

Investors know this, but they're willing to buy junk bonds because they demand—and get—greater rates of return and are willing to take the risk. Otherwise, investors would put their money into low-risk and less-enriching government bonds and be done with it. Why take a chance with a junk bond if you can get the same return with a government security? Junk bonds have at times been excellent investments, especially when the market has made them pariahs. That's when they've produced superior "devastation dividends," which I will discuss in Chapter 6.

Your tolerance for risk must be matched with the rewards you expect. If your financial plan requires a rate of return of 25 percent a year for 20 years, you better be on friendly terms with Lady Luck and expect to see her dark side once in a while. Anticipate losing money with such a plan, because to get such a high rate of return you'll have to take on a high degree of risk. If that's not acceptable, then create a plan that does not require a high rate of return and this high level of risk. A more easily attained 12 percent a year, for instance, allows for a financial plan carrying much less risk.

The Modern Portfolio Theory

What does someone with a job on Wall Street, a loft in the trendy Soho area of Manhattan, and a portfolio of bank and brokerage firm stocks have in common with someone who owns an employment agency in Silicon Valley, has a house nearby, and invests in high-tech mutual funds?

The answer: Neither are diversified. The New Yorker's job is dependent on the financial industry, as are the values of the loft and her stock investments. The Californian lacks diversity because the employment agency is dependent on the high-tech industry, as are the values of his house and mutual funds.

There's a direct relationship between risk and diversification. Diversification by using asset allocation (putting your eggs in many carefully chosen baskets), which will be discussed in Chapter 6, appears to offer the proverbial free lunch—higher returns with lower risk. This actually happens and it's not due to alchemy. Diversification works because it helps eliminate unnecessary risk, which is any risk you can reduce without diminishing your return. By reducing this risk, you lower your overall risk and enjoy greater rewards. Asset allocation does this by combining investments that move in different directions in similar circumstances. If interest rates go up because of inflation, bond prices fall. The losses on the bonds are made up with gains elsewhere, such as in real estate, which increases when inflation heats up.

So powerful is this theory that those who helped develop and quantify it—Harry Markowitz, William Sharpe, and Merton Miller—shared the 1990 Nobel Prize in economics for their work in this area. The theory is often called the *modern portfolio theory*, or *asset allocation*, because it focuses on how to allocate assets to maximize the return for a given risk level.

In the realm of investing, we face three choices:

1. Which individual investments to buy.
2. When to buy and sell them—this is timing.
3. The overall mix of investments, namely, diversification or asset allocation.

If asked to rank these three in order of importance—which will have the greatest effect on how well our investments do—most people will usually say individual investments are most important. Second, they'd probably pick when to buy and sell (the famous "buy low, sell high"). I'm sure the overall mix would come last. It should come first.

Lower risk, better returns—that's what diversification promises. And the research proves it works. In a study published in the *Financial Analysts Journal* analyzing the performances of 91 large pension plans between 1974 and 1983, on average, 93.6 percent of the differences in performance among the pension plans were explained by diversification (asset allocation) alone.[5] Add market timing, and you have 95.3 percent of the differences explained. Diversification plus security selection explained 97.8 percent of the differences.

In referring to this study, Roger C. Gibson wrote: "The study dramatically supports the notion that asset allocation policy is the primary determinant of investment performance, with market timing and security selection both playing a minor role."[6]

Diversification is more difficult to do than it appears, which is why I provide the sample portfolios in Chapter 15. I provide the balance; you just need to implement it.

Though such strategies as diversification help you avoid risk in investing, you still need to understand the various kinds of risks and how each affects your financial well-being. Following are the more important kinds.

Liquidity Risk

Liquidity is the ease with which an investment or financial instrument can be turned into cash. A checking account is more liquid than a car, which is more liquid than a house, which is more liquid than a major office building. The more illiquid the investment, the harder it is to turn it into cash.

A house is a classic example. Because of the difficulty of finding buyers and the trouble buyers have getting mortgages, rarely can you quickly turn a house into cash. It usually takes at least a couple of months and often much longer. That's a lack of liquidity. How much money you get for the house is also a factor, and that relates to marketability.

Illiquid investments aren't necessarily poor investments. In fact, there's evidence that investors pay a price for liquidity. After all, it's valuable, so there's no reason to think the desirability of having ready access to cash comes free.

Buying liquid investments may mean you're paying for something (liquidity) and not using it. Even stocks can be fairly illiquid when they lack buyers. This is particularly true with smaller, obscure stocks on the over-the-counter market. But even on the New York Stock Exchange (NYSE), some stocks are more liquid than others. There're about 1,900 companies on the NYSE, many of which you've never heard of and which don't attract much trading. With such stocks, it can be difficult to get a buyer, and if you do, the price might be low because of the lack of buyers. One academic study calculated that between 1961 and 1980 the least liquid stocks on the NYSE averaged an 8.5 percent a year higher return than the most liquid stocks.[7] An extension of the study for the 1980–1985 period found the least liquid stocks outperformed the most liquid by almost 6 percentage points a year.[8] Those willing to buy and hold the least liquid stocks came out significantly ahead in the long term.

What to do about liquidity risk: Use the buy-and-hold strategy; that is, plan for the long term. It minimizes liquidity risk.

FAST FACT: If illiquidity is a significant factor in the value of an investment, plan to hold it. With real estate and thinly traded stocks, five years is the minimum recommended holding period.

Examples of illiquid investments or those it's difficult to get your money out of:

- Real estate.
- Thinly traded stocks.
- Art and collectibles.
- Precious metals.

Examples of highly liquid/easy-to-sell investments:

- Stocks of major corporations.
- CDs.
- Savings and checking accounts.
- All Treasuries.

Interest Rate Risk

Interest rates change, sometimes daily. The prices of bonds, mortgages, and other financial products rise and fall directly in response to interest rate changes and thus expose the investor to interest rate risk.

Investing in an asset subject to interest rate risk is a little like committing to a family picnic in uncertain weather. You can check the weather report and get a forecast for the evening of your outdoor extravaganza. Likewise, you can read about the Federal Reserve and talk to pundits about what interest rates will do. But once the commitment is made—going to the park and setting up the picnic table or buying a bond—events are out of your control. You have to sit back and hang on for the ride. All you can do is hope it doesn't rain on your head or pocketbook. If it does, getting out at a good price won't be easy.

What to do about interest-rate risk: Hold the asset for the long term.

Inflation Risk

"The dollar just doesn't buy what it used to," people say. They're right, and we can blame inflation. As prices rise, each dollar buys less. Inflation risk is so important that it is a major part of our bulletproofing protection. The evil of inflation is discussed throughout this book, especially Chapter 4 on inflation protection and Chapter 12 on retirement.

What to do about inflation risk: Bulletproof.

Financial Risk

The risk that debt won't be repaid is a financial risk because companies can and do veer suddenly toward default (just like individuals). The credit ratings of Moody's and Standard & Poor's place a lot of emphasis on this risk.

What to do about financial risk: Invest in mutual funds and variable annuities whose diversity significantly reduces this risk.

Reinvestment Risk

You're 45 years old and buy a 20-year bond that pays 10 percent. You dream about what you'll do with that steady income "guaranteed" until you retire. Think again. Many bonds have "call" features, which means the issuing company can call (redeem) the bond any time during the call period. This usually starts two years or later from the date of issue and continues until the date of maturity. Of course, the company recalls (repays) your principal plus accumulated interest. When CDs mature, it's a similar problem.

An investment you **must** liquidate, leaving you with the need to find a new place to park your money, places you at reinvestment risk, the risk that you can't get the same return you were getting.

What to do about reinvestment risk: Invest in bonds that lack call features and invest in stocks.

Company-Specific Risk

The market can gyrate, interest rates can bounce off the walls, inflation can simmer or go ballistic, all of which affect the price of a stock. But the company behind the stock counts, too. If it's a star performer, the stock usually responds. If the company stumbles, well, boulders have fallen off cliffs slower than some stocks have dropped on bad news. Call this company-specific risk. It's the risk directly attached to the performance of the individual company you invest in.

What to do about company-specific risk: Invest in mutual funds or variable annuities so you have a diversified portfolio of stocks.

Leverage Risk

Borrowing money to pay for an investment is *leveraging*. The more you borrow, the greater your leverage risk. Buying on *margin*, you can borrow up to 50 percent of the cost of a stock. Usually 80 or 90 percent of a real estate property's value can be borrowed, whereas commodities may require as little as 3 to 5 percent of the value to be paid with cash. Leveraged stocks are often less risky in turn than highly leveraged real estate, which is less risky than very highly leveraged commodities. With commodities, you can quite easily lose more than you invested, which is why they are the riskiest of investments (see Figure 1).

What to do about leverage risk: Match your risk level to your leverage. Don't borrow to pay for your investments if you're a low-risk taker. Borrow a lot if you share the same feelings about risk that rock climbers, Formula One racers, and sky divers do. Simply limit your borrowing to amounts you are comfortable with and can still service from other sources if your investments don't work out.

Catastrophic Risk

Catastrophic risk is a label I coined for the risk that you'll lose everything. This was the risk that prompted me to create the bulletproofing strategy.

Everyone is subject to catastrophic risk. Though less likely to happen than other risks, its importance lies in its consequences. You may lose money if you invest in an illiquid asset, live through moderate inflation, or buy the wrong type of interest-paying instrument. But you can lose *everything* in an economic catastrophe.

What do do about catastrophic risk: Bulletproof. Period.

Market Risk

Many a money manager and stock market observer has read Charles Mackay's 1841 classic treatise *Extraordinary Popular Delusions and the Madness of Crowds.*[9] Why? Because it discusses mass psychology and mass psychology moves markets.

Market risk is also called *systematic risk.* It's the part of price movements that come from the whole market, the psychology underlying the entire market. If the market thinks we're heading out of a recession, stocks will go up, including stocks of companies not doing particularly well. A slide into a recession causes the market to tumble, including the stocks of very sound companies. This is market risk. The rest of the price movement relates to risks associated with the specific asset, called *specific, nonsystematic,* or *diversifiable risk.*

How influential is market risk? Very, particularly when you diversify your portfolio, as I suggest. One study says that an investment portfolio of 30 or more common stocks eliminates so much specific risk (that's the risk associated with the specific company you're investing in), that 85 to 95 percent of all the risk left in the portfolio is market risk.[10] Put another way, with proper diversification, 5 to 15 percent of the risk you face is with the specific investments you make, and the remaining risk is with the overall market (if the market gains, you gain, and vice versa). My approach to investing reduces much of the concern over market risk because I recommend you hold for the long term and diversify between markets. The stock and real estate markets, for instance, expose you to considerable market risk in the short to medium term. Over decades, though, their values will increase. If you hold for years, then you don't worry about market risk.

What to do about market risk: Use the asset allocation model discussed in Chapter 6 and hold for the long term.

Risk and You

All these risks are important in a couple of ways. They highlight subtle risks we often overlook. They stimulate thinking about how you, personally, relate to risk.

Most of us are bigger risk takers at 17 than at 47 or 77. The younger we are, the less we know and the more time we have to make up for our mistakes. It's too bad because this results in very few of us starting to save at an early age.

The best time to start saving is early, preferably before age 30. Frequently, though, this is when we have little money and even less concern about our own mortality. What money we do have, though, should go into high-growth, risk-oriented investments. The power of compound interest is never stronger than now because we never have more time to put our money to use. So any money made during these years can create a huge nest egg later. Chapter 6 illustrates how powerful early saving can be through the magic (sometimes also the tyranny) of compound interest.

A few years ago the *Federal Reserve Bulletin* reported that 43 percent of all American families took no financial risks. Of the nation's wealthiest families, though, the Fed found only 5 percent took no financial risks.[11] These wealthy people know something important: It's almost impossible to build a sizable net worth without taking reasonable chances.

It's nice to talk about taking risk, but the energy is wasted unless you can handle taking the risk represented by your investment. *Take the level of risk you can live with so you don't panic and sell before you should.* As with goals, there is no right or wrong amount of risk for everyone. What's right is what you can and want to live with.

Being conservative can also prove quite risky. Conservative investors think securities such as Treasuries are safe havens. In a very real sense, they're not. Figures compiled by Ibbotson Association, Chicago, as reported in the *Wall Street Journal*, reveal that between 1926 and the end of 1991, long-term government bonds provided returns (bond-price changes plus interest) of 4.8 percent a year. Shorter-term Treasury bills gained 3.7 percent annually. The problem: Inflation rose 3.1 percent a year during the same period. What was a less risky investment? Stocks. They provided a pretax total return, including reinvested dividends, of 10.4 percent a year on average, for the entire 65-year period. Playing it safe with an investment that barely keeps up with inflation is playing a high-risk game. The way you deal with the risk (namely, price fluctuations) of stocks is by diversifying and holding for the long term. If history is a guide, that's actually less risky than government bonds.

The reason I recommended Treasuries earlier is that they are great for bulletproofing. It is worth taking a part of your portfolio and putting it into Treasuries because of the protection against severe recession and depression that they provide. It is not worth putting *most* of your portfolio in these bonds because they generally don't provide an adequate return.

How Much Risk Can You Handle?

It's often hard to picture how much risk we're willing to take, so I've drawn up a risk pyramid that graphically shows how much risk different investments have in relation to one another, which is shown in Figure 1. The higher the investment is on the pyramid, the more risk—and the greater potential reward. Investments on the same horizontal line have about the same degree of risk.

How to use this pyramid:

1. What types of investments appeal to you? If you're like most people, the desirable investments will cluster in one area toward the top, middle, or bottom of the pyramid. If you like futures, speculatives, and collectibles, you like risk. Someone more attuned to collectibles, growth mutual funds, and high-grade preferred stocks is a middle-of-the-road investor (most of my clients fall into this category). If you feel most comfortable with high-grade preferred stocks, money market accounts, and Treasuries, then you like little risk.
2. Structure your portfolio to match your feelings about risk. Place most of your money in the investments with the amount of risk that allows you to be comfortable. Near the end of this book I will give you sample portfolios. They are rated high, medium, and low risk. Use this pyramid to find the category you fit into.
3. This pyramid is a guideline. Just because you like no-leveraged real estate, for instance, doesn't mean you can't take

▶ **FIGURE 1**

Investment Risk Pyramid.

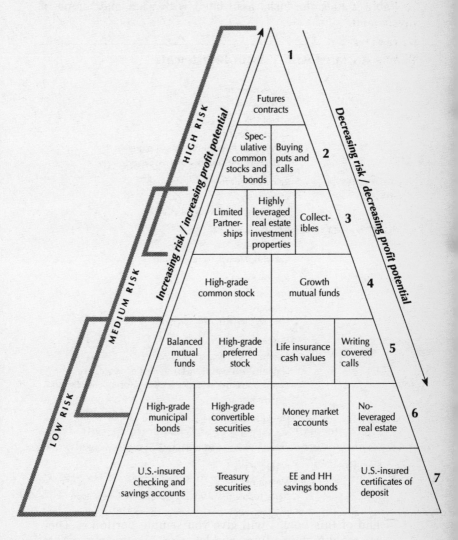

a flier with a speculative stock or limited partnership. Focus on the investments that match your needs, and use the corresponding sample portfolio that is in Chapter 15.

Table 2 lists the risks associated with each major type of investment.

▶ TABLE 2 _____

Risks Associated with Various Investments

BONDS	Interest rate risk
	Inflation risk
	Credit risk
	Catastrophic risk
	Inflation: Price of bonds will plummet
	Depression: Bonds won't be repaid
CERTIFICATES OF DEPOSIT	Reinvestment risk
	Inflation risk
	Catastrophic risk with inflation
MONEY MARKET FUND	Reinvestment risk
	Inflation risk
	Catastrophic risk with inflation
TREASURIES	Reinvestment risk
	Interest note risk
	Inflation risk
	Catastrophic risk with inflation
STOCKS	Market risk
	Company-specific risk
	Liquidity risk especially for thinly traded stocks
	Catastrophic risk with depression/severe recession and inflation
REAL ESTATE	Liquidity risk
	Market risk
	Catastrophic risk with depression/severe recession
COMMODITIES	Leverage risk
	Market risk
	Catastrophic risk with depression/severe recession
COLLECTIBLES	Liquidity risk
	Market risk
	Catastrophic risk with depression/severe recession
PRECIOUS METALS	Liquidity risk
	Market risk
	Catastrophic risk with depression/severe recession

———————— H I G H L I G H T S ————————

Risk affects your behavior, which, in turn, influences how successful you'll be as an investor.

Risk and reward work together: Typically, the greater the risk, the greater the reward, with the reverse holding true.

The modern portfolio theory proves that diversification provides higher rewards at lower risk.

Types of risk: liquidity, interest rate, inflation, financial, reinvestment, company specific, leverage, catastrophic, and market.

Use the risk pyramid to clarify how much risk is right for you.

6

INVESTMENT STRATEGIES:
What Smart Money Knows

Think of financial planning as a basketball game. You're the coach, and your money is your team—the means to get you to your goals. In basketball, the coach has one goal—winning. In the game of life's finances, you have the same goal. The difference is how you keep score.

Basketball gives you 2 or 3 points for a bucket, 1 for a foul shot. In finance, however, you make points (dollars) every time a goal is scored (an investment pays off), but you lose points every time you miss (an investment's price falls below what you paid). With an investment strategy, you're the coach and a strategy is simply your game plan. Every basketball coach has a plan that matches his players against the opponent's. He'd never go into a game hoping chance would produce the best matchups, and smart investors don't go into the game of finance hoping chance smiles on them.

Your investment strategies are like your financial plan—an essential part of bulletproofing. Without effective strategies, maximum returns are impossible to reach.

Some popular strategies work, others don't. In the next few pages, you'll learn a couple of strategies to use and a popular one not to. The recommended ones are easy to understand, easy to put into practice, and require little money.

Up to this point, we've covered budgeting, goal setting, and risk, as well as depression and inflation protection, and you're probably beginning to get a good picture of some of the basic elements that go in to creating an effective portfolio. You know you will need to dedicate small portions of your portfolio for bulletproofing, such as Treasuries for depression protection and real estate for inflation protection.

You're beginning to understand how to start choosing *the right investments for you* because now you've got an idea of how risk and reward relate and how much risk makes sense for you. If you think about it, in just a few chapters, you've learned what it takes to create a firm foundation for your financial future, including how to control your spending, how to choose investments, and how to protect yourself from whatever the economic future holds.

But there's still the remainder of your portfolio to consider— the parts not directly designed to bulletproof your assets. And you have goals to reach, such as retirement, buying a home, and financing a child's college education. Now we get to take a look at the nuts-and-bolts strategies of how to get there from here. To reach your dreams, you need effective strategies, and that's what we'll discuss now.

The Sequence of Investing

Complete bulletproofing involves the following.

1. Protection of your portfolio from devastation.
2. Cutting waste.
3. Maximizing returns.

I've mentioned these before and will return to them throughout the book. Essential to putting these into practice is a tax strategy I call the *sequence of investing*, which lists by order of priority the sequence used to pick investments based on their tax implications. This is an important place to start because it gives you a framework that minimizes your tax liabilities. The less you pay Uncle Sam, the more you have to invest for yourself, your family, and your future. The strategy is simple and obvious. And infrequently followed; though it can be as important as what you invest in. It is the following:

- First, place your money in investments that offer *tax deductions and tax deferrals*. Examples: Charitable remainder unitrusts and pension options, such as IRAs, Keoghs, and 401(k) and 403(b) plans (discussed in Chapter 12).
- Second, place your money in investments that offer *tax deferral only*. Examples include variable annuities (discussed in Chapter 9) and non-income-producing hard assets, such as gold bullion coins and real estate (discussed in Chapter 10)
- Third, and last, place your money in *taxable* investments. These are everything else, such as mutual funds (discussed in Chapter 8), dividend-paying stocks, and the like.

This approach reduces waste (money spent on taxes that needn't be) and maximizes returns, which addresses two of the three goals that make up bulletproofing. Table 3 illustrates the power of using this sequence of investing to maximize returns based on minimizing your tax liability. It assumes you start with $100,000, earn 10 percent a year, and have a 35 percent tax liability. If you are using a tax-deferred/tax-deductible investment, you start with the full $100,000 and it earns the full 10 percent a year. If it is just tax deferred, you start with only $65,000 ($100,000 less 35 percent) but earn the full 10 percent a year. A taxable investment means you start with $65,000 and earn 6.5 percent (that's deducting the 35 percent tax rate from the 10 percent you earn).

By using tax-deferred/tax-deductible investments, after 30 years, you have $1,744,940. Tax-deferred investment doesn't do quite as well, but it's still a strong performer, yielding $1,134,211. Taxable investments are the Chicago Cubs of the investment world: long-term losers with virtually no hope of ever being champs.

Holding down your tax liability substantially increases your ability to make money, as Table 3 vividly illustrates. If you can get both a tax deduction and tax deferral, you'll have 57 percent more money at the end of 30 years than if you just got a tax deferral ($1,744,940 versus $1,134,211) and *three times* more than if you have no tax benefits at all ($1,744,940 versus $429,934). However, taxable investments tend to be more accessible than tax-deferred and tax-deductible ones. Those that provide tax benefits, such as pension plans, often have penalties that

▶ **TABLE 3**

The Power of Compounding When Taxes Are Minimized

Initial Investment: $100,000

		Tax Deductible/ Tax Deferred	*Tax Deferred*	*Taxable*
Initial year		$100,000	$65,000	$65,000
Year	1	110,000	71,500	69,225
Year	2	121,000	78,650	73,725
Year	3	133,100	86,515	78,517
Year	4	146,410	95,167	83,620
Year	5	161,051	104,683	89,056
Year	6	177,156	115,151	94,844
Year	7	194,872	126,667	101,009
Year	8	214,359	139,333	107,575
Year	9	235,795	153,267	114,567
Year	10	259,374	168,593	122,014
Year	11	285,312	185,453	129,945
Year	12	313,843	203,998	138,391
Year	13	345,227	224,398	147,387
Year	14	379,750	246,837	156,967
Year	15	417,725	271,521	167,170
Year	16	459,497	298,673	178,036
Year	17	505,447	328,541	189,608
Year	18	555,992	361,395	201,993
Year	19	611,591	397,534	215,058
Year	20	672,750	437,287	229,037
Year	21	740,025	481,016	243,924
Year	22	814,027	529,118	259,779
Year	23	895,430	582,030	276,665
Year	24	984,973	640,233	294,648
Year	25	1,083,471	704,256	313,800
Year	26	1,191,818	774,681	334,197
Year	27	1,310,999	852,150	355,920
Year	28	1,442,099	937,365	379,055
Year	29	1,586,309	1,031,101	403,694
Year	30	1,744,940	1,134,211	429,934

the taxable investments do not. That's why you should always keep a part of your portfolio in highly accessible accounts, such as cash, Treasury bills, and money market accounts. But as long as you don't need to take money out, generally tax-beneficial investments are far more profitable than taxable ones, as Table 3 shows.

Dollar-Cost Averaging

To reduce fear, there's probably no strategy better than dollar-cost averaging. This is a periodic-investment approach in which you invest a regular amount of money according to a set timetable at time intervals you choose. The most popular intervals are monthly, quarterly (every three months), and every paycheck.

The strategy is simple. You buy the same stocks, bonds, group of investments, or mutual funds without variation. Purchases are made regardless of what's going on in the market in general or with your investments in particular. That's it. What could be easier?

In fact, I use dollar-cost averaging with clients unfamiliar or uncomfortable with investing because it is so easy and safe. It's an introduction to the investment world one step at a time. Like the perfect spouse, it's easy to live with. Eventually these clients move up to the more sophisticated asset-allocation strategy discussed later.

Dollar-cost averaging works because it lets you ride the long-term increase in the stock market. Over the past 65 years, the market has provided average annual returns of better than 10 percent; during the past 50 years or so, which excludes the Depression, the market's annual gains are about 12 percent. Many investors wish they did this well with their money. At this rate, if you had put $50,000 in the stock market 20 years ago, today that money would be worth nearly a half million dollars.

Why do so many stock market investors not do this well? Because they try to guess when the market is low (that's when they buy) and high (which is when they sell). No one can consistently time the market in this way, which is why so many individual investors lose money in stocks or never get good returns, even though the market keeps going up. *Dollar-cost averaging averages the prices you buy at so you get the full effect of the market's long-term rise.* It gives you the power to maximize the profits you earn from the market's tendency to increase. It takes the guessing out of investing. It's an automatic, effective, and economical way to ride the market's coattails. And if you invest in a good mutual fund (I recommend some in the next chapter), you can earn even more; 15 percent a year is very reasonable. Dollar-cost averaging plus the upward trend of the stock market together make for a very potent investment strategy.

The benefits of dollar-cost averaging are many. These include the following:

- *It is simple.* This is a no-brainer strategy that works! You don't need fancy record keeping or advanced math. In fact, you may be using dollar-cost averaging without realizing it. If you have a set amount of money withdrawn from your paycheck and put into a 401(k) or 403(b) retirement plan, profit-sharing plan, or U.S. savings bonds, you are dollar-cost averaging.
- *It complements your bulletproofing strategy.* Dollar-cost averaging works no matter what's happening with the economy. That's why it's a perfect complement to bulletproofing your portfolio. Early on, I said the ideal is a situation where you don't need to guess what the economy will do because the economy can't be predicted. Dollar-cost averaging makes no assumption about what the economy or the markets will do (except that over the long term, they'll go up more than down). That's exactly what you want. This strategy lets you sleep at night.
- *It is economical.* Because you buy more shares when prices are down (you invest the same amount each time so lower prices get you more shares) and less when prices rise (the opposite of when prices decline), dollar-cost averaging lets you buy for less than if you bought at an investment's average price. And the more choppy and uncertain the market, the better it works.
- *It fits perfectly with our buy-and-hold strategy.* As I mentioned, dollar-cost averaging assumes the price of your investment will increase over time. (In fact, it's possible, in certain circumstances, that when the market is flat, you will make money because dollar-cost averaging gets you to buy more when the price is down and less when the price is up.) The stock market has always increased over the long

term. Of course, major drops have occurred. But, overall, there's been an upward trend. Dollar-cost averaging takes full advantage of this trend, making it ideal for our buy-and-hold strategy.

There's nothing magical about dollar-cost averaging, which is why it can't *guarantee* you a profit. If your investment keeps falling in price and you cash out, you will lose money. No amount of averaging can change this outcome.

In a steadily rising market, you'll sometimes lag the market using dollar-cost averaging. On the other hand, if the price falls over the short term, you'll lose money, but not as much as you would if you had fully invested at the beginning of the period and stayed put.

Dollar-cost averaging requires some *discipline*. You have to invest regularly. You can't skip one period and try to make it up the next. Prices will probably differ from period to period, making it impossible to "catch up." Nor do you want to guess about when is a good time to buy. If you do, then you're in the realm of using a market timing strategy and that's among the worst strategies. Ironically, asset allocation, a more sophisticated approach to investing than dollar-cost averaging and a strategy we'll discuss shortly, does not require this degree of discipline.

Investing regularly does not mean you have to invest a lot. Some mutual funds have minimum investments as low as $25, so you can use this strategy very effectively on as little as $25 a month. At the end of this chapter is an appendix, giving a numerical example of how dollar-cost averaging works.

Let the power of dollar-cost averaging work for you.

The Power of Early Saving

It's never too early to start saving because the longer you can compound your earnings, the more money you will make. Compounding is so powerful because you earn money not just on the money you initially invest, but on all the money, including interest and profits, you earn over time. A snowball starts small, but the bigger it gets, the larger is its surface area and the more snow is able to stick to it. The more snow that sticks to it, the larger its surface area, and the effect keeps feeding on itself so the snowball continually grows.

With compounding, the more you have, the more money you make. And the more you make, the more money you have to work for you. Your stake just keeps increasing in size like a snowball. If still in your twenties or thirties, I strongly encourage you to set up a savings/investment program. You are in the enviable position of being able to maximize the power of time to your great advantage. But if you're middle-aged or older, there's nothing you can do to take advantage of the power of compounding over decades. You have to use other techniques we discuss throughout this book.

Here's an example. Suppose you're 25 years old this month, you save $100 per month for the next five years and make your last payment during the month before your 30th birthday. On your 30th birthday you will have $7,396, assuming you earned 8 percent on your money annually and never took any money out of this account. Now, at the ripe age of 30, you decide you are through saving. You never add any money but leave your $7,000 + nest egg to grow until you retire on your 65th birthday. During the intervening 35 years, providing you continue to earn 8 percent annually, your nest egg will grow to $351,428.

Now let's suppose at your 30th birthday party you tell your best friend, who's your age, that you've been saving for the past five years and now you are through. He or she sees the light and decides the time to start their own savings program is now. Following your example, they sock away $100 a month. They want a real cushy retirement so they save *each month*, without fail, for 35 years until they too reach the age of 65. Assume he or she also earns interest of 8 percent a year, just like you. After 35 years of saving, they'll only have $350,971. Not only is that $457 less than you, but you saved each month for only five years versus your friend's 35 years. How can this be? The reason is simple. When you both were 30, you had more money ($7,396 versus $0) to benefit from compound interest. Your friend never quite caught up. Do you need any more proof of why starting a savings/investment program *today* is so important?

Timing

Before I even tell you what it is, let me say that timing doesn't work. Period. Charles D. Ellis wrote: "The evidence on invest-ment managers' success with market timing is impressive—and

overwhelmingly negative."[12] Whatever you do with your investments, don't try to time buying and selling decisions to take
advantage of market swings.

Timing is simply the attempt to buy investments at the "best"
time (when prices are lowest) and sell them at the "best" time
(when prices are highest). This approach is directly contrary to
the bulletproofing philosophy, which posits that no one knows
what's going to happen. If you don't know what will happen in
the economy six months or a year from now (let alone in 5 or 10
years), what makes you think you can consistently pick a stock
or real estate markets' lows and highs? You can't, I can't, no one
can.

One thing you can be certain of: The market will move. It
will go up, it will go down. You just don't know when or by how
much or in what direction. That's why I recommend a buy-and-
hold strategy. Certain investments, such as stocks and real estate,
have upward trends lasting for decades. I could be wrong, but
I'll bet they will continue to go up over the long run. It's the
short and medium term that scares me. In these dips and troughs,
fortunes have been lost. With stocks, "investors have historically
suffered negative annual returns approximately 30 percent of the
time."[13] These are the dreaded troughs.

You can't avoid this 30 percent, but stay in long enough and
you'll be there for the 70 percent when money is made. Even if
something happens (your child goes to college) and you have to
get out during a down market, you still come out ahead because
you've benefitted fully by the previous up markets. The up markets last longer and are more pronounced than the down ones,
which is why the market over time has gone up. If you're in there
for the upturns, the downturns can never be devastating.

Timing is popular because if it could work, fantasy-size fortunes would be within the reach of many. Roger C. Gibson, in
his excellent (if somewhat technical) book *Asset Allocation* gives
a revealing example of this.[14] Imagine meeting with a person with
perfect market timing ability on December 31, 1925. This seer
makes forecasts of 1926 security returns for Treasury bills, long-
term government bonds, long-term corporate bonds, common
stocks, and small stocks. He correctly predicts common stocks
will produce the best returns from these five investments. Big
spenders that we are, we bet $1.00 on his advice and at the end
of 1926 have $1.12.

Impressed, we do the same the next year and the year after. We are timing. This mythical seer precisely predicts when the market is at its absolute low (that's when we buy) and at its absolute high (a signal to sell). By the end of 1988, our $1.00 is $2,650,000. Sounds too good to be true? It is. It's true that if you perfectly timed a $1.00 investment year after year and let it compound, between 1925 and 1988, you would have $2,650,000. Nobody can do it, especially over time. Imagine if the initial investment was $1 million. By 1988, we would have $2.65 trillion, more than the market value of all outstanding shares of all publicly traded common stocks in the United States at that time. You wouldn't be merely rich, you'd own corporate America. This is the seductiveness of market timing and why so many desperately want to believe in its reality. In theory it's great, in practice it's impossible. Betting on market timing is a sure road to ruin.

Don't confuse this with dollar-cost averaging. Timing is investing no set amount of money at a time you think the market is at its low. Rather than being an automatic approach, timing is by definition irregular. It uses whatever research or intuition you have about the market.

A study done on the stock market by Trinity Investment Corporation that Gibson cites looked at nine peak-to-peak cycles that occurred between May 29, 1946, and August 25, 1987.[15] It found the following:

- Up months outnumber down months 309 to 187, or 1.7 up months for every down month.
- The average bull market is up 104.8 percent. The average bear market drops 28 percent.
- Up markets last 41 months versus 14 for down markets, or nearly three times as long.
- Even within down markets, about 3 to 4 months out of 10 are up months on average.
- During bull markets (lasting 41 months on average), eight months account for more than 60 percent of the total gain.

The bottom line to this study is that the market has many ups and downs but overall goes up more than down. If you don't worry about when the market is up or down at any one moment but just get in and stay in, you'll be glad you did.

An unpublished study of 100 large pension funds cited by Charles D. Ellis found that "not one of the funds had improved its rate of return as a result of its effort at timing. In fact, 89 of the 100 lost as a result of 'timing'—and their losses averaged a daunting 4.5 percent over the five-year period."[16]

Need I say more? "Buy low, sell high" assumes you can time your trades. A buy-and-hold strategy assumes you can't time your trades, but that you can benefit from such long-term trends as the increasing value of stocks and real estate over many years.

Gibson studied investment returns for four types of investments over various time horizons. His analysis yielded two important conclusions. One is that common stocks, when compared with corporate bonds, long-term government bonds, and Treasury bills, are the best performers.

The second is that your investment time horizon directly affects your risk exposure. The shorter the time you hold, the greater your risk. Conversely, the longer you hold, the less your risk. That's why I recommend the buy-and-hold approach.

No one can time the market over many years, yet we all must invest over much of our lifetimes. We can't choose one year or a few years to invest and then say we'll never invest again. Even if we put our money in our mattress, we are making an investment choice. Since we live for decades and must therefore invest for decades, the only smart and prudent investment strategy is to invest for the long term.

Devastation Dividends

There's a time to do things automatically, such as dollar-cost averaging, and as with most things in life, a time for exceptions: When you can capitalize on what I call a devastated market, go for the gusto. Investing in battered markets provides higher-than-usual rates of return—a devastation dividend. There are risks with this approach, but because you're buying when prices are very low, the risks are limited.

Just about every investment has a rough period when its small world falls apart. Park City real estate, one of my first big investments, fell more than 50 percent in value from its high in the early 1980s to its low in the late 1980s. I stayed in too long and took some hits, but overall my profits were in seven figures. As the real estate portion of my portfolio grew, had I kept the entire portfolio in balance by selling some real estate and reinvesting elsewhere, I wouldn't have suffered the losses I did. That's because I would have less in real estate and more in other investments. A balanced portfolio maximizes returns and limits risk.

The stock market crash of 1987 is another example. Within a couple of days, the market fell more than 20 percent. Yet, as I write this in 1992, less than five years later, the market is at a record high. When Drexel Burnham Lambert disintegrated, so did the market for junk bonds and, with it, bond prices. Lots of money has been made by those who realized that most junk bonds wouldn't default (not pay) and that when the market was down, it presented a wonderful buying opportunity.

Mazda was on the ropes in the mid-1970s when its rotary engine gained a reputation for being a gas guzzler. Now it's a star among the Japanese carmakers. In fact, I view Japan and Germany after World War II as investments that were disasters that later became major winners.

Many, many examples exist of a devastated investment that eventually rose from the ashes. Such investments offer the savvy, risk-taking investor devastation dividends. A world war doesn't have to break out or a major corporation go bankrupt to offer these dividends. They happen with surprising frequency. Just look at what's struggling because of the economy or getting blasted in the press today. Chances are these will provide devastation dividends later.

Of course, you can't buy just any stock, mutual fund, piece of real estate, or other investment without sometimes getting clobbered. Some years ago, according to one article, a major management firm with a solid long-term record bought a big block of Braniff Airlines stock at just about its historic low. Sounded like a good bet for a while. A very short while, it turns out. Within *hours*, the airline declared bankruptcy.[17] Since the early 1980s, pundits have been proclaiming that gold, which fell in price by half after its big run-up in 1980, would make another run for the $800 + per ounce stratosphere. We're still waiting.

Not every investment runs contrary to the law of gravity. Not all that goes down comes back up. But many do. Why? The market overreacts. What it likes becomes overpriced. Eventually, the light is seen, the emperor's clothes (or lack of) are noted, and the selling begins. Wham-o. The pendulum doesn't just swing, it races headlong to the other side.

Devastation is at hand. Now the investment is underpriced. And devastation dividends are possible. Recent example: junk bonds. With the arrest of Michael Milken and the end of the junk bond empire he created at Drexel Burnham Lambert, the market for junk bonds collapsed.

What didn't collapse were all the companies that issued these bonds. Some were in trouble because of their debt, but most could service their debt. This meant that investors sharp enough to pick the viable companies (not that hard since most of these firms were okay) did well with junk bonds. As early as 1989 I recommended junk bonds to my clients and the listeners of my radio show.

FAST FACTS: When looking for investments that have declined but are likely to soar upward again, concentrate on those whose value now is no more than half their highs during the past three years. Real estate that falls 50 percent or more in three years is worth buying, for example.

Devastation dividends work so well because investors who go contrary to a trend are rare. Mass psychology dominates the market. The courageous who battle the prevailing wisdom are a decided minority. That's good, because by definition it's impossible to make above-average gains if you act averagely.

Be on the lookout for devastation dividend opportunities. They could be close to home, such as in local real estate. Or, they could be as far away as a foreign country floundering economically but that, over time, may become a winner. Some Eastern European countries, for example, Hungary and maybe Poland, could have solid economies by the turn of the century. Portugal might be another. Buying stocks in their corporations may be one of the best investments of the 1990s.

FAST FACTS: *When to sell.* I recommend a buy-and-hold strategy with all investments. Sometimes, especially with devastation dividends, it pays to cash out sooner than later. The promise of big profits can tempt you to be greedy—a bad attitude with investments. When should you sell? When your portfolio gets out of balance. If you want 30 percent of your assets in real estate to bulletproof, and a surge in the real estate market makes real estate 40 percent of your total portfolio, sell the excess real estate and buy more of the other investments in your portfolio to keep everything in balance and to benefit from diversification.

Asset Allocation/Diversification

If you put all your money into one investment whose price reaches the heavens, you will not only become rich, but people you have known for a lifetime will suddenly consider you a financial genius. Your opinions will be sought, your words listened to enthusiastically, your newly hired chauffeur will be proud to work for you.

Sound like a dream? It usually is. The original John D. Rockefeller made millions by focusing just on oil, Sam Walton of Wal-Mart stores was worth billions when he died because he put all his assets into discount retailing. Bill Gates, still in his 30s, is a billionaire because his assets are all in one company and that company, Microsoft, is the largest computer software firm. In addition, each of these men ran his own business rather than investing in someone else's.

Most of us, though, don't have an aim-for-the-heavens business in which to place all our eggs. We have to shop around for investments, whether they're stocks, bonds, real estate, collectibles, money market funds, or Treasuries. To put all our eggs in one investment is practically a sure way to financial disaster.

We need a different strategy, and that strategy is diversification, which I discussed in Chapter 5. Diversification is merely the idea of putting our money in a variety of investments to reduce the risks inherent in any single investment. By taking this view of our overall portfolio of investments and not just looking at investments individually, we not only cut our risk but improve the total performance of our portfolio.

Suppose you owned stocks in airlines, auto parts manufacturers, fertilizer companies, petrochemical companies, and long-distance trucking firms. Five different industries, right? True. Yet not true in terms of asset allocation/diversification. Price changes in oil affect the profits of all these firms in the same way. A price in black gold increases the operating costs of the airlines, fertilizer, petrochemical, and long-distance trucking firms and lessens the demand for cars, thus lowering demand for the products of auto parts manufacturers. The bottom line of each gets hurt. A price decline has the opposite effect.

When the stocks of companies in different industries tend to move in the same direction, they are said to have a *positive coefficient* by statisticians. Stocks of firms that move in opposite directions (oil companies versus airlines, steel- and carmakers—price increases in steel hurt carmakers) have *negative coefficients*. Our sample portfolios in the last chapter, based on the well-known asset allocation model, use these coefficients as a guide to choosing investments.

For example, if the expected rate of return on a car maker's stock is 8 percent and an oil company's is 12 percent, by buying each, you average the rates of return while decreasing your risk. The risk is less because the stocks move in opposite directions (have negative coefficients) in reaction to the same event, such as an oil price rise. This, in turn, lessens the price fluctuations of the combined two investments to less than the price fluctuation of either by itself. The amount of price fluctuation of an investment is how we measure risk—the lower an investment's price fluctuations, the lower the risk.

To create a portfolio with maximum profit potential and minimum risk, you need to factor in how various investments move in relation to one another, which requires a complex computer program. The portfolios recommended in Chapter 15, however, have been carefully chosen to create true diversification. Use them and you will enjoy the benefits of asset allocation.

For people like you and me, diversification isn't just theory. It is something we all can use because it's easy and doesn't require a lot of money. We use it by focusing on the "big picture" rather than individual investments. As we have seen, research proves that the *areas* you invest in and *how much* you invest in each area are far more important than the individual investments in each area or when you buy and sell.

Investments such as stocks and real estate—solid, reliable performers over many decades—are the big picture. Which individual stocks or real estate you buy is not that significant. If you don't have enough money to diversify within major areas such as stocks, buy stock mutual funds (mutual funds that invest in a variety of stocks rather than, say, in bonds) with strong long-term track records. And hold them. For a long time. Many mutual funds will let you invest as little as $25 at a time, so this strategy, just like dollar-cost averaging, doesn't need much money.

Fine-Tuning Asset Allocation

Sometimes, one area of the portfolio takes up more or less of the total than is intended. It needs to be fine-tuned. Here's how.

I'll assume you started with the following $200,000 portfolio, with the percentage of the total portfolio represented by each investment in parentheses. This is our standard medium-risk portfolio discussed in Chapter 15, along with each investment's role in the overall makeup of the portfolio.

$8,000 in Treasury bills (4 percent)	Depression protection
$14,000 in U.S. small-company stocks (7 percent)	Growth of capital
$20,000 in Treasury bonds (10 percent)	Depression protection
$20,000 in domestic stocks (10 percent)	Growth of capital
$48,000 in international stocks (24 percent)	Growth of capital
$40,000 in international bonds (20 percent)	Income
$24,000 in gold (12 percent)	Inflation protection
$26,000 in real estate (13 percent)	Inflation protection
Total: $200,000	

Assume within a year of creating this portfolio, the overseas stock market skyrockets and the international stock mutual fund you've invested in has doubled to $96,000. To make things simple, we'll assume all your other investments have stayed the same. The total portfolio is now worth $248,000, of which 39 percent is in international stocks.

That's too much, since we only want it to represent 24 percent. So we sell $36,500 of the international stock. This leaves us with $60,000 in foreign stocks or 24 percent of the total portfolio—just what we wanted.

We add $1,900 to our holdings of Treasury bills, so they now make up 4 percent of the total, which is right on target. U.S.

small-company stocks gain $3,400 to maintain their 7 percent share of the total portfolio. Domestic stocks get an additional $4,800, international bonds gain $9,600, gold and collectibles have $5,800 added, and real estate gets $6,200.

Our portfolio now looks like this:

$9,900 in Treasury bills (4 percent)
$17,400 in U.S. small company stocks (7 percent)
$24,800 in Treasury bonds (10 percent)
$24,800 in domestic stocks (10 percent)
$59,500 in international stocks (24 percent)
$49,600 in international bonds (20 percent)
$29,800 in gold and collectibles (12 percent)
$32,200 in real estate (13 percent)
Total: $248,000

You don't have to be exact when rearranging your portfolio, only approximate. If you're contributing to the portfolio on a regular basis, you might not have to sell anything. Just take the new monies and put them into the areas of the portfolio that need further investment to create balance.

When first creating a portfolio, your goal is to pick the best portfolio you can. The fine-tuning comes later. With the right choices, you can sit back and ride the inevitable ups and downs of the markets. You rest easy knowing that, over the long run, you'll come out okay because of your portfolio's design and because the investments in it will perform well over the long run. This gives you the stamina to hold through the tough times.

Two attitudes hinder most investors: fear and greed. If you take the asset allocation approach, you'll never suffer the consequences of fear or greed because they will never motivate your actions.

Our Five Model Families

The strategy of choice is asset allocation. Eventually, all my clients use it. Those who are nervous about investing should use dollar-cost averaging, until they are comfortable with having their money in stocks, bonds, and other investments. Of our five model families, Family 1, Jackie and Bob saving for their retirement; Family 4, the Jordans wanting to minimize their taxes; and

LEFAVI'S LAWS OF INVESTING

Here are some simple rules to live by when investing:

- Keep a rainy-day fund, at least enough for three months' worth of expenses. An emergency, by definition, strikes unexpectedly, which means you had better plan for it now.
- Don't develop a timing mentality. Buy and hold.
- Don't look over the shoulder of the next guy for investment ideas. He's no more likely to be right than you.
- Plan. Otherwise, your financial future is dependent on Lady Luck. She's usually hard to find.
- Diversify your investments. If you put all your eggs in one basket, it's easier for some—or all—to break.
- Commit yourself to your plan and follow it. If you won't commit, don't expect the plan to work for you.
- Have realistic goals. If your income is good, don't expect extraordinary wealth. Be content with considerable wealth.
- Follow the sequence of investing. If you don't, Uncle Sam will become more than an annoyance; he'll become your full-fledged partner.
- Listen to the investment advice of a good independent financial planner. Rarely listen to the investment advice of your accountant. Never listen to the investment advice of a lawyer, insurance agent, or stockbroker.
- If sleep eludes you and you count stock prices rather than sheep, get out of your investments and into something less risky.
- If you find a good idea, have the courage to make it your own. Use it before it becomes popular. Originality is not necessary for success.
- Don't panic. If you have done your homework, the inevitable downturns in your portfolio will prove temporary.
- Don't be greedy. There's a saying on Wall Street: The bulls make money, the bears make money, and the pigs get slaughtered.

Family 5, the retired Moriartys, have all had experience investing. They are untroubled by having their money at some risk, and so all will use asset allocation. Family 3, the Santangelos saving for their first home, is a young couple chomping at the bit to make some money, so they are eager to use asset allocation. When they've saved enough money, they'll immediately use it. Of our four families, only Family 2, Marilyn, the single mother saving for her children's college tuition, is anxious. As a result, I have her using dollar-cost averaging until she is secure enough to want to use asset allocation.

Appendix: An Illustration of Dollar-Cost Averaging

Here's an illustration of dollar-cost averaging at work. Say you invest $200 per month for six months, and to compare it, we'll say you could have put that money in a single investment, a mutual fund, all at once.

	Month					
	1	2	3	4	5	6
Amount Invested	$200	$200	$200	$200	$200	$200
Price per Share	$30	$29	$28	$27	$26	$25
Number of Shares Purchased	6.67	6.90	7.14	7.41	7.69	8.00
Number of Shares Owned	6.67	13.57	20.71	28.12	35.81	43.81
Total Invested	$200	$400	$600	$800	$1,000	$1,200
Average Cost per Share	$30.00	$29.48	$28.97	$28.45	$27.93	$27.39

During the six-month period, the mutual fund's price steadily fell. In total, you invested $1,200. If you had put all of that in the fund during Month 1, your average price per share would have been $30, you would own 40 shares and their value at the end of the six-month period would be $1,000 ($25 × 40).

By dollar-cost averaging, you still invested $1,200, but you bought 43.81 shares and your average cost per share was $27.39. Note: If you just take the average of the share prices—add $30, $29, $28, $27, $26, and $25 and divide by 6—the average price per share is $27.50, more than you paid using dollar-cost averaging. The benefit is clear. You paid less per share—and got more shares—than if you had put down your money at the beginning of the period or *just bought at the average price*. The reason is, with dollar-cost averaging, you buy more shares when the market is going down because you keep investing the same amount of money each time, precisely what you want to do when prices decline. The key to dollar-cost averaging is consistency, namely, always investing the *same amount of money on a regular basis no matter what the stock market is doing*.

The converse is also true. When prices rise, you want to buy fewer shares because the shares are getting more expensive. Let's assume that in the six months following the above example prices steadily rose.

	Month					
	1	2	3	4	5	6
Amount Invested	$200	$200	$200	$200	$200	$200
Price per Share	$26	$27	$28	$29	$30	$31
Number of Shares Purchased	7.69	7.41	7.14	6.90	6.67	6.45
Number of Shares Owned	7.69	15.10	22.24	29.14	35.81	42.26
Total Invested	$200	$400	$600	$800	$1,000	$1,200
Average Cost per Share	$26	$26.49	$26.98	$27.45	$27.92	$28.40

Now the share price is steadily increasing. Of course, your average cost per share therefore rises. Because the number of shares you buy each month decreases, the average share price is less than if you had averaged the prices over the six-month period ($26 through $31 divided by 6), which would be $28.50 versus $28.40 using dollar-cost averaging. The downside is, if you had spent the entire $1,200 at the beginning of the period, your average share price would have been $26.

Let's look at these two examples as if they were one continuous 12-month period. With dollar-cost averaging, at the end of 12 months, you would have invested $2,400 and owned 86.07 shares for an average cost per share of $27.88. If you had bought a set amount of shares each month regardless of price, your average cost per share would have been $28.

In this example, the market was not volatile but had gradual price changes. The more volatile the market, the more pronounced the benefit of dollar-cost averaging. As a quick example, let's say you invested $200 per month in a mutual fund that over three months was priced at $20, $30, and $40. Your average price per share would be $27.69 versus $30 if you just bought the same number of shares each month, taking the average price of the stock over the three-month period ($20 + $30 + $40 ÷ 3 = $30). That's a big difference. The more pronounced the price swings in the market, the more dramatic the savings you get from dollar-cost averaging.

HIGHLIGHTS

◆

Sequence of investing:

- Place your money where you receive tax deductions and tax deferrals.
- Place your money where you receive tax deferrals.
- Place your money where it is taxable.

◆

Investment strategies:

Dollar-cost averaging: Make investments on a periodic basis with a set amount of money without regard to how the investments are doing.

Early saving: If you are in your early 20s into your 30s, saving *now* unleashes the power of compounding fully.

Timing: This is a classic strategy of trying to time when the market is low (time to buy) and high (time to sell). This strategy is almost sure to lose you money, because no one can consistently time the market.

Devastation dividends: Go against the prevailing wisdom and buy when the market is devastated. Used to maximize returns.

Asset allocation/diversification: Use the modern portfolio theory to diversify, which provides high returns at lower risk.

7

INSURANCE:
The Good, the Bad, and the Ugly

Insurance is a curious word: widely used, universally accepted—frequently misunderstood. We think of it primarily as "risk protection," and many of us believe that protecting us from financial ruin is its role in our lives.

Insurance can't really protect us. Auto seat belts and airbags help protect against the risk of injury in a car accident—not auto insurance. Fire alarms and sprinklers help protect against the risk of injury and damage—not fire insurance. A healthy diet and exercise help protect against the risk of disease—not medical insurance. As we all know, life insurance does nothing to prolong life.

According to the U.S. Bureau of Labor Statistics, the average household spends close to $1,700 annually on insurance. Of course, this includes people at all income levels. Many with lower incomes spend little or nothing on insurance. I estimate my clients spend on average about twice this figure, probably more.

Because insurance can't protect and is expensive, what is it good for? Risk management. It can't protect us against the risks we all face daily, but it can help manage those risks to minimize their effects if they happen. What risks do we all face? Some are death, disability, job loss, lawsuits, theft, fire, death or disability of the family breadwinner, accidents, divorce, and disease.

Consider insurance as a form of bulletproofing. It's different from pure monetary investments, but it too protects you against catastrophe. It also fits into our overall approach because it is probably the single most important source of wasted money. Most of us spend too much on insurance. And even though we do, we still leave ourselves unprotected in certain areas. We can't fully bulletproof ourselves unless we deal with these risks, and that's the job of insurance.

Insurance has been around for a while. In fact, when Joseph in the Book of Genesis warned the Pharaoh to save food against a drought, it was an early recommendation for insurance. Food storage couldn't prevent the drought, but it could let the Egyptians manage the risk of starvation.

Since then, insurance has become big business. Much of it is worthwhile, but a lot is nothing but waste. Among my clients, unnecessary insurance is the single most important source of squandered money. In a moment, I'll discuss this in more detail. Here, I'd like to return to something mentioned in the first chapter of this book, namely, when insurance is appropriate.

Figure 2 is a diagram in which the vertical axis measures the cost of a loss: the higher on the vertical, the greater the loss. The horizontal axis measures the frequency or likelihood of a loss; the further to the right, the more likely a loss will occur.

I've divided the box into quarters. Let's look at each of these boxes in turn.

Box 2. Both the cost and frequency of a loss is high in this situation. This is not the place to try to manage your risks by insuring against them. Better to reduce the risks.

Insurance where likelihood and cost are high is often unavailable or prohibitively expensive. If you live in a high-crime area, burglary insurance may be unavailable at any price. If it is available and you buy it, it could bankrupt you. So eliminate the risk as much as possible. Bars on the windows and several locks on the door are one approach. Moving to a safer neighborhood is another.

Box 4. This is a situation where the cost of loss is low but the frequency of loss is high. Here you reduce the risk as much as possible.

► FIGURE 2 ─────────────────────────────

Risk Management: When to Use Insurance.

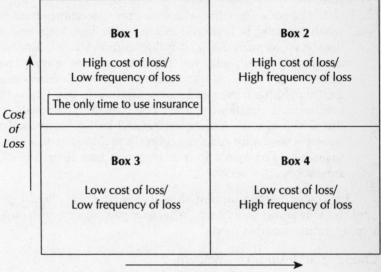

Cost
of
Loss

Box 1

High cost of loss/
Low frequency of loss

The only time to use insurance

Box 2

High cost of loss/
High frequency of loss

Box 3

Low cost of loss/
Low frequency of loss

Box 4

Low cost of loss/
High frequency of loss

Frequency of Loss

Glasses and dishes probably break everyday at restaurants, yet restaurant owners don't insure against such losses. The losses happen so frequently and cost so little that insurance is not economical. Instead, restaurant owners are better off buying less fragile glassware and training their staffs better.

Box 3. When the cost of loss is low, as is the likelihood of loss, forget about getting insurance, even when available. Just *retain* the risk yourself. Extended product warranties are an example of inappropriate insurance. These are popular with electronics, such as radios and videocassette recorders. The problem is that electronics rarely break down, and they don't cost much to fix or replace when they do. In addition, they usually come with a free warranty good for 90 days to a year. Electronic devices, if they break, usually do so shortly after being bought. Those that get past this initial period usually last a long time. Because the high-risk period is covered and the cost of repair or replacement is small, don't buy electronic-product warranties.

Avoid all extended warranties no matter what the product. Self-insure. Don't try to manage this risk by buying insurance.

Box 1. The only situation where insurance is appropriate is when the cost is high and frequency is low. Your house doesn't often burn down. If it does, however, the costs are devastating. That's why you buy fire insurance. Rare is the time you go for a ride and have an accident. When you do, though, the costs can be catastrophic, so you buy auto insurance. It's unlikely you will be disabled by an accident. But if you are, the consequences will be long and costly, which is why most of us not retired should carry disability insurance. For many, it is more important than life insurance.

This model helps pinpoint situations where you should insure and where you should not. Whenever you're faced with buying insurance, use this model.

Choosing an Insurance Company

Long, long ago, in another time and another era when financial stability and reliability characterized the insurance industry—about four or five years ago—no one worried about the financial health of their insurance company. These companies rarely failed. Of those that did, industry mechanisms prevented policyholders from losing money.

It's hard to remember, but such innocence once typified the savings and loan industry, too. We all know about that nightmare. What the S&Ls were to the 1980s, the insurance industry may be to the 1990s. Already, several important insurance companies have failed this decade, and several of the biggest are tottering on the edge of financial collapse.

When you buy a car, you don't worry if the carmaker will be there in 20 or 30 years, because you know your car won't. A house, on the other hand, has long-term use, but you don't concern yourself with who built it. When something goes wrong with a house, rarely do you go to the builder looking for repairs. In fact, few people who buy existing homes even know who built their house and are uninterested in finding out.

Insurance is another matter. We count on the decades-long survival and financial viability of the company we buy from. If you are 35 years old and buy life insurance you expect to need until you retire, you are assuming the insurance company will be around in 30 years.

That is one massive assumption. Thirty years ago, the Vietnam War hadn't happened; raging inflation hadn't happened; the missile gap with the Soviets was the big foreign threat; and companies like General Motors, Sears, Pan Am, and U.S. Steel were the pride and joy of American industry.

Pan Am is out of business, and General Motors, Sears, and U.S. Steel are largely has-beens. The Eastern Bloc countries are independent, and the Soviet Union is rapidly fading into memory. The Soviets, Vietnam, Cuba, and nuclear war are no longer the major threats to the United States. Instead, we fear the economic might of Japan, Germany, Taiwan, South Korea, and the European Economic Community. We're secure with our military superiority; it's our economic position that scares the hell out of us.

In a short 30 years, we practically have a new world. Items we use in daily life were undreamed of three decades ago. Personal computers, VCRs, microwave ovens, big-screen TVs, auto seat belts, avocados, compact discs, "gourmet" chocolate chip cookies—these are the stuff of everyday life in the 1990s. Triple-bypass heart surgery, contact lenses, and tummy tucks are no big deal. AIDS, the homeless, depletion of the rain forests, and the hole in the ozone layer are widespread concerns. What did we know of these in the early 1960s?

Today, the big corporate names are Sony, Toyota, McDonald's, Wal-Mart, Microsoft, the Gap—all of which were regional firms 30 years ago if they even existed. Falling performances of American students and the high cost of medical care are sources of national concern now. Then, we were building bomb shelters and worrying if rock and roll would spoil the minds of our young.

If our world and our outlook can change so fundamentally so quickly (and 30 years really isn't so long), what makes us think our insurance company will be as "solid as the rock" by the time we need it to pay? Obviously, we're making a bet here, and for many of us, it's a bet we're going to lose during the next several years.

How much of a bet is it? In July 1991, Mutual Benefit Life Insurance Company, the country's 18th largest insurance company, was seized by New Jersey officials because of its financial condition. This was no backwater company. "One of the most conservative and respected insurance companies in the country," is how the New York Times described Mutual Benefit in an article reporting on the company's failure with the headline "Financial Plight of a Top Insurer May Shake Faith in the Industry."[18]

You're probably thinking that even if the public didn't know of Mutual Benefit's problems, the experts did. That's what's so scary. They didn't know either. The oldest insurance rating company, A.M. Best, totally blew it. This is a quote from the New York Times from an article that came out on the day Mutual Benefit failed: "Until 10 days ago, the A.M. Best Company had assigned Mutual Benefit an A+ rating [which is classified as "superior"], meaning the rating agency considered the insurer's claim-paying ability to be unimpeachable."[19]

What happened? Something no one dreamed of. The insurance industry experienced the equivalent of a run on the bank. Publicity in the media spread the word of Mutual Benefit's troubles, which were due to poorly performing mortgages. People got understandably scared and started taking money out of the firm. This led to insolvency and the government takeover. No one seriously considered that policyholders would panic like bank depositors have so often. So new was this phenomenon that the press gave this new risk a name: run risk.

Time magazine published an article in 1991 about insurance companies whose ratings had recently been lowered by Moody's, a major ratings agency.[20] Among the faltering firms were such household names as The Travelers, John Hancock Mutual Life, Massachusetts Mutual Life, and Aetna Life. The Wall Street Journal in early 1992 reported that Moody's had downgraded the rating of the nation's largest insurer, Prudential Insurance, saying this was a "milestone for the industry," because of Prudential's size and its marketing image of being as steady as "the rock."[21]

Standard & Poor's, a major rating agency, instituted a review of nearly 2,600 insurance companies, finding more than 500 of them, mostly small ones, were vulnerable to financial trouble. These had 13 percent of the industry's assets, or about $60 billion.

In fact, some observers say one-third of today's insurance companies will fail by the end of the decade.

So how do you know if your insurance company will live longer than you? The truth is not easy to take: You don't. It is impossible to be absolutely certain whether any particular company will survive as long as you need it to.

One action to take is to bulletproof your portfolio. Insurance companies are more likely to get into trouble when the economy is as tangled as weeds than when the economic flowers smell sweet. Bulletproofing works best during tough times, which is precisely when you need it. With properly protected assets, your insurance company's disaster needn't become your disaster.

Avoiding an insurer's failure is your best and least costly route, of course. You want to reduce the chance your insurer will be one of the insurance industry's failures during the 1990s and beyond. Here are a few steps to take to improve your chances of finding a long-term winner.

- Avoid firms promising you eye-popping rates of return. If CDs are paying, say, 7 percent, and an insurance company promises you 12 percent for the life of the policy, watch out. Either the firm is overstating the rate of return you'll actually get (very common) and/or is investing in risky high-yield investments, a rocky place on which to bank your financial future. Anyone who promises you the sun, moon, and stars is likely to sell you the Brooklyn Bridge, too.
- Here's an adage as powerful as the law of gravity: If it sounds too good to be true, it probably is.
- The best and really only practical way to try to pick a winner is to use the rating services. Yes, I know I just bashed them. But there's no other way to go. Don't ask your insurance agent which is best. He or she has an interest in telling you the companies they represent are the best or at least safe. It's a risky business trusting what whole life insurance agents tell you, and this is especially true when he or she extols the virtues of their favorite insurance companies.

The ratings industry has five major players. A.M. Best is the oldest and best known. Standard & Poor's and Moody's are well known. Duff & Phelps is also big but doesn't seem to rate as many firms as the other agencies. Finally, there's Weiss Research, a relative newcomer. Of these, I like Weiss the best, because it is generally the most conservative. There are plenty of insurance companies around, so why take a chance when you don't have to? Go with the best ratings from the most conservative rater.

Best, Standard & Poor's and Moody's ratings are frequently in libraries. Your insurance agent can show you the ratings of all five agencies. You can get Weiss's ratings directly from the company. The rating for one company costs $25, three quotes cost $55. A year's worth of the ratings for all the insurance firms Weiss analyzes costs $376. Located in West Palm Beach, Florida, Weiss's telephone number is (800) 289-9222.

Ratings between the agencies can vary widely. *Stanger's Investment Advisor* did a comparative study of the five rating services.[22] We'll use Alexander Hamilton Life Insurance Company of America (Michigan) as an illustration. It had an A+ rating by Best, their highest rating. Standard & Poor's gave this firm an AA rating, its third-highest. Weiss gave it a C, its eighth-highest rating. (The other two services didn't rate it.)

Giant Equitable Life Assurance Society of the U.S. got Best's second-highest rating, a contingent A+. S&P gave it an A, its 6th-highest rating, as did Duff & Phelps. Moody's gave it its 7th-highest rating, an A3, whereas Weiss really didn't like Equitable, giving it D+, its 10th-highest rating.

In general, Best gives the highest ratings, Weiss the lowest, with the other three services somewhere in between. (For an explanation of each service's ratings, see the appendix at the end of the book.)

Why do the ratings differ so dramatically? Some ratings services apply more rigorous standards than others. In fact, when Moody's downgraded Prudential Insurance, the *Wall Street Journal* said the insurance company's chairman "attributed the downgrading to a more aggressive stance at Moody's rather than a change at Prudential."[23] Weiss is the leader in aggressive ratings. It's the newest rating service and seems to have learned from the mistakes of its older peers, while not being as hidebound.

This is my recommendation to you: Emphasize Weiss, but limit your exposure to insurance company troubles through such tactics as buying term rather than whole life (we'll learn about these next) and not buying insurance you don't need. Don't go with an insurance company that Weiss doesn't give at least a B+ (its fourth-highest rating). If possible, go with firms that the other agencies also give their fourth or higher ratings to. For Best, this is A− or above; Standard & Poor's, AA−; Moody's, Aa3; Duff & Phelps, AA−. Use an insurance company with at least these minimum ratings by three or more rating agencies, including Weiss. Of course, you want the insurance company to have maintained its high ratings over several years.

Let me say this. Although it is desirable to have an insurance company with a high rating, don't panic if the rating is a little lower than you'd like. For example, if a firm's Weiss rating is B rather than B+, but it has other positives, such as a reasonable insurance policy or lower-than-average commissions, then consider using the firm. These ratings can change with the fortunes of the insurance company, so nothing is set in stone. Use the recommendation of a B+ rating or higher as a guideline, not an absolute, but check a company's ratings *before* buying its policy.

Here's another tactic to lessen your exposure to insurance companies' financial instability. Using term life means only your premiums for the current period are at risk. If you have whole life and can't economically get out of the policy, or you need whole life because you can't get term, reduce your exposure by borrowing as much money as possible against the policy. This way you've got much of your money outside the policy if the insurance company goes belly up.

Whole Life versus Term Life: Know the Difference

Whole life works like this: You pay a premium (which usually stays constant during the life of the policy) for a period specified in the policy (often until retirement). Part of the premium goes toward life insurance: When you die, your survivors receive a specified amount. The remaining part of the premium is not insurance but, rather, an investment. It is a savings plan where the insurance company pays interest on the money invested. You can generally borrow against this money during the life of the policy. At some point, typically after retirement, this money can be taken out of the policy (called the *cash surrender value*) in a lump sum or placed in an annuity. Withdrawing money from a whole life policy usually decreases the size of the death benefit.

Term life works like this: You pay a premium and, in return, gets life insurance. It is "pure" insurance, as there is no investment, cash value, or dividend portion to it. It comes packaged in 1-, 5-, 10-, or 15-year periods. As you get older, its cost increases. That's as it should be, because the likelihood of you dying increases with age. If you die while the policy is in force, the insurance company pays the face amount of the policy to your beneficiaries.

Whole Life

In a rational world, whole life insurance wouldn't exist, and we wouldn't be talking about it here. Yet, many of you probably have whole life. Many more will be pitched whole life by insurance agents. And many will want to know what it is. That's why I'll give you a brief description of how it works and why it's a bad deal. If you already know why it's a waste, skip this section and jump directly to term life. Sometimes, whole life is called by other names, such as universal life. This is a name change to protect the guilty. Whole and universal life are, for all intents and purposes, the same.

The phrase *whole life* sounds like a single product. It isn't, and that's the problem. It's two very different financial products that have been bundled together. The two parts are life insurance and investment. Sometimes, there's a third element, dividends. Ignore dividends. The federal government actually defines insurance dividends as overpayments of premiums. You've paid in more than was needed for the insurance and so the insurance company is giving you back your overpayment. Hardly a great return on one's investment.

The biggest problem with whole life insurance is that it tries to be both insurance and an investment vehicle. And it does both poorly. The insurance portion is typically overpriced, whereas the investment part provides anemic rates of return.

Let's look at how insurance companies have structured whole life insurance policies. Usually, these policies come with a set yearly premium for the policy's duration. That sounds good. You know today what you will pay 10 years or 20 years down the road for life insurance coverage.

Logic tells you something is amiss here. If you're 30 years old, why are you paying the same insurance premium you will when you're 60? This is life insurance, and you are decidedly more likely to cost the insurance company money when you're 60 than when you're 30, because you're more likely to die the older you are. The insurance company is overcharging you early in the policy's life for the insurance. In theory, the excess goes into the investment or cash portion of your policy. Don't bet on it. Besides, why pay for something today you won't need for years?

If you really look at what your rate of return is on these policies, you wonder how insurance companies have stayed in business so long. Rarely have I seen a policy pay more than about 4 percent. Insurance companies are geniuses at creating tricks and organized confusion to obscure what's really happening. They promise a rate of return, for example, but then deduct such expenses as commissions and overhead. And if, God forbid, you want to get your hands on your own money, they'll assess penalties for good measure.

The promised returns may be real, but only for a limited time. Insurance companies love to provide large rates of return, but the small print usually reveals that these big numbers only last a year or two, and then the return gets back to normal—3 or 4 percent. A classic adage is never more true than when it comes to life insurance: Buyer beware.

In fact, within the first five years of the policy, most if not all of your so-called accumulated cash goes to commissions and other expenses. Later, the yield goes up, but it still doesn't equal what's available with other investments.

One of the country's major insurance companies likes to use a picture of its handsome Manhattan headquarters in its ads to show how stable and conservative it is. The ad's headline: "New York Life is large, conservative, and dull. Reassuring in times like these, isn't it?" It's worrisome when a major insurance company uses the public's need for reassurance for its primary marketing pitch. That alone makes me uneasy.

This firm also thinks a big building is reassuring. Well, it may be reassuring to the insurance company, but not to me. The building costs a lot to maintain and even more to fill with workers. Money that should go toward your return on investment is, instead, going toward the insurance company's overhead. No wonder whole life is such a poor investment. Few industries are as inefficient as insurance. They live in fat city, and you pay for it.

If you tell your insurance agent the yield on his policies stinks, he'll counter by saying, "Look at what you'll be earning in 20 years." Actually, a few whole life plans do provide okay (but not great) returns after 20 years. The problem: Only about 3 percent of the people hold their policies for 20 years. You can earn better in other investments without having to defy the odds.

The reason whole life pays poorly early on is the commissions—amounts of 150 percent of the first year's premium and 10 percent per year thereafter aren't unheard of. Over time, commissions decrease relative to the value of the policy, which is why the rate of return improves. Too bad you have to wait decades for a mediocre rate of return.

Of course, many people say they like whole life because it's a form of "forced savings." They have to pay the premiums anyway since they need the insurance, so the savings part is forced on them. There are other more desirable ways to "force" you to save. If you need some outside motivation, have a set amount of money taken out of each paycheck before you even see the money. Or ask your frugal spouse to handle the money. Put all your change each evening in a cookie jar. Put the money into CDs or even savings bonds. Do anything but buy whole life. Believe me, other investments can get you to save while being a lot more productive than whole life.

Insurance agents claim whole life can be a savings account of sorts. Sure, like jail is a good way to avoid getting run over crossing a street. You're better off looking both ways. You can take money out of a life insurance policy when you need it, so why not view it as a savings plan with life insurance? claim the agents. Would that it were true. Money in an insurance policy isn't nearly this accessible. Actually, you can't take money out of the policy directly. If you do, your policy ends. That's because you must take the entire cash value you have built up; you can't take a little. And remember, when you've taken it all out, there's no insurance policy left.

What you can do is borrow against the policy. In fact, the insurance policy stipulates what the interest rate will be if you decide to borrow against it. That should be a red flag. Why is the insurance company expecting, even encouraging, you to borrow against your policy? Because it makes money from it. *It charges you to borrow your own money.* Don't view whole life as a substitute for a savings account. If you want a savings account, get one. Don't get a whole life policy.

Most insurance agents extol the virtues of whole life based on its tax advantages. It's true whole life lets the cash value of the policy grow tax deferred. But this holds for various pension vehicles, such as IRAs, Keoghs, and 401(k)s, which I will discuss in Chapter 12, and it's also true of annuities, which I will cover in Chapter 9. Put another way, whole life isn't the only way to let your money grow tax deferred. And it's certainly not the best way. In most situations, annuities can be used in place of whole life.

As with most things in life, there are exceptions to the rule. With whole life insurance, there is one situation, and one situation only, in which it makes sense to buy it: If you can't get term life because you have an illness and every insurance company refuses to cover you as a result, then, and only then, buy whole life.

I'm emphasizing the problems with whole life because it is so heavily promoted and the horror stories about it abound. Once, a 25-year-old man came to me for advice. He had bought a whole life policy that would pay him $100 a month from age 65 to the time he died. The agent, of course, proclaimed this a wonderful deal. I calculated that the policy paid a miserable 2.34 percent rate of return. If he used the money paid in premiums over the life of the policy and invested them at 10 percent a year in a tax-sheltered vehicle, such as an annuity, he would have $468,000 by age 65. If, at that point, he took this money and invested it so he got 9 percent a year after taxes, his income would be over $3,500 a month. Assuming this was all spent so his principal did not increase, the income from this $468,000 would last as long as he did. And when he died, it would remain intact to pass on to his heirs. The insurance policy left nothing for heirs. Stories such as this are all too typical.

The bottom line: Don't buy whole life insurance or any life insurance with cash value.

Whole Life Insurance Agents' Favorite Lies

Let me say that while I have little respect for whole life insurance agents, agents who sell other types of insurance, such as casualty, I've found to be quite knowledgeable and honest. It's the whole lifers who are the problem. Here are some of their favorite lies. When you hear one, you know it's time to get another agent.

You need life insurance to cover medical bills. This fabrication is usually directed at couples nearing retirement. It feeds on people's fears. The agent claims there's a good chance one spouse will suffer a long, debilitating—and expensive—illness. This will bankrupt the couple, so the survivor will have nothing left to live on. Garbage, I say. If you'll be bankrupted by an illness then the life insurance will come too late. Avoid financial trouble in the first place. Life insurance doesn't address the problem, medical insurance does. If you're worried about medical expenses, get proper medical insurance, not life insurance.

You need life insurance for retirement. Watch out if the agent suggests life insurance is a good way to finance your retirement. The pitch usually includes the claim that monies in an insurance policy accumulate tax free, and you can borrow against a life insurance policy without paying taxes. This is all true, as far as it goes. But there are a couple of fundamental problems. According to this argument, one is that the whole basis for investing in a life insurance policy is to get the tax benefits. Tax bennies are nice, but don't count on them. Congress can change them at any time. The 1986 Tax Reform Act left untold numbers of limited partnerships high and dry when Congress did away with multiple tax write-offs. *Never invest in anything that's not fundamentally sound financially without its tax benefits.* Any tax benefits are just icing on the cake, not a reason for making an investment. Second, investment vehicles offering better returns and as good or better tax benefits exist. Pension plans, for example, provide both a tax deduction when the money is placed in the plan and tax deferral while the money remains in the plan. Using life insurance for retirement is like using it to cover medical bills—using a product designed for one purpose for another purpose (the proverbial round peg in a square hole). If you want retirement money, use a pension plan. Don't stake your retirement on the survival of your insurance company.

You need life insurance on children. Agents frequently say parents need life insurance policies taken out on their young children. This doesn't make sense. If, heaven forbid, a child dies, expenses go down, not up. Some agents try to bolster their argument by claiming whole life is a good investment vehicle to use for financing a college education. Why use insurance for a goal that's entirely dependent on the amount of money saved and the rate of return? Again, this is an inappropriate use of insurance. Really unscrupulous agents say parents should insure children now to be certain the children can get insurance later in life. Rarely does a healthy child need to worry about getting life insurance when they become young adults and need it. Also, the amount of guaranteed insurance is usually so small as to be unimportant. Forget life insurance for children.

Term Life

Question: How do you know term life is good for you?

Answer: Few life insurance agents will voluntarily recommend it.

They won't recommend it because it pays them lower commissions than whole life. If they get less, that means you get more. If you need life insurance, this is the only kind to get.

Term life involves premiums that increase over time. If you use one-year policies, the premiums will increase each year. Increasing premiums make many people uncomfortable. They prefer the security of stable premiums. That's why I recommend getting a 10-year term policy. The premiums will be level for that period, but you won't pay a lot extra for this fixed rate. That's because, unlike whole life, the premiums aren't set for life. Be sure the policy is renewable without your having to undergo a physical exam.

Also, as you get older, typically you need less insurance. Your children become independent, and your assets increase so your family won't be in such dire straights if the breadwinner dies. Over time, you'll probably want to decrease the amount of your coverage. Of course, less coverage means less cost. As a result, you'll probably find that while the rates of term will increase as you get older, your premiums will not.

Some term policies carry a guarantee that in the future, the insurance company will renew the policy without you having to take a physical examination or otherwise prove you're insurable. Some are renewable until age 100, others to 65 or 70. Most likely, you won't want life insurance after 65, but be sure it lasts at least this long.

Cost is term life's chief advantage. It is considerably cheaper—often 80 percent!—than whole life. Several years ago, Consumer Reports magazine did a study.[24] A 35-year-old woman buying the magazine's top-rated term policy would pay, in the first year, *one-tenth* what a top-rated whole life policy cost for the same coverage. It's true that the premiums on the term policy increase over time rather than stay the same as with the whole life. But it wouldn't be until the 21st year, when the woman was 56 years old, that the premiums on the term policy exceeded those of the whole life, according to the magazine. During the years she's paying lower premiums, she can take the "extra" money and invest it. Then, for those few years past age 56 when she still needs insurance, she would have far more than enough to cover the higher premiums. Not only that, by the time she's in her mid-50s, she probably needs less coverage anyway, and is most likely paying lower premiums than whole life.

How Much Life Insurance Do You Need?

Before you can know how much insurance you need, it's essential to know what you want the insurance for. Two situations characterize the reasons most people have for needing life insurance.

1. *To take care of those you leave behind.* If you have dependents, such as children, a spouse, or elderly parents, you may want to have life insurance if you die. I say "may" because if your assets are sufficiently large and liquid to produce a reasonable income, you don't need it, even with dependents. Taking care of loved ones is by far the most popular reason for having life insurance.
2. *To pay estate taxes.* To pay estate taxes, some heirs have to sell assets or borrow heavily. This can cause emotional difficulties. There also may be significant financial losses when the assets are largely illiquid, such as real estate or ownership of a business. Let's say a business owner's estate is worth $2 million and just about all of this is in a business. The estate taxes on it are $500,000. If the heirs don't have $500,000 in liquid assets, they must either sell the business or go into debt to pay the taxes. A life insurance policy that pays an amount sufficient to cover the taxes makes sense in this situation.

If you fit into one or both of these categories, your next question must be, How much insurance do I need?

If you need insurance to take care of those you leave behind, first calculate the amount of money they need to live on. Remember that the person whose name the policy is in will not be alive. Include dependent children, but take into consideration that the closer they are to becoming independent, the less insurance is needed. College costs count, too. As for your spouse, calculate his or her needs from the time of your death to the time he or she is likely to die. If you're both in your 60s, the surviving spouse will need money for about 15 or 20 years. If you're both now in your 30s, and the spouse isn't likely to work at least for some time (say, there are young children), then money is needed for 30 or 40 years.

FAST FACT: For a quick calculation of how much income your survivors will need if you die, work on the assumption they'll need 75 percent of the family's current income. If the annual income is now $100,000, the family needs $75,000. This can come from the spouse's income, Social Security investment income, and other sources. Use insurance to make up any shortfall.

Assume you or your heirs need $75,000 a year to live on. If your spouse works (or will be able to work if you die), deduct this salary from the $75,000. Let's assume there's a shortfall of $45,000, since the spouse earns $30,000. If you earn 9 percent on your investments after taxes, your family will need a nest egg of $500,000 to generate the needed income (9 percent of $500,000 is $45,000). Five hundred thousand dollars is how much insurance you should get.

If you need life insurance for estate purposes, estimate what your estate taxes would be if you died today. Currently, the first $600,000 of an estate's assets pass to the next generation free of federal tax, though that tax can run as high as 60 percent on the remainder. There may also be state taxes. If the total estate taxes are likely to be $200,000, then buy $200,000 worth of insurance.

Making Sure Proceeds Pass on to Beneficiaries Tax Free

Proceeds from a life insurance policy can pass on to the next generation free of estate taxes—provided the policy is initially set up correctly. I don't know why, but many life insurance agents don't always do this. The following procedure must be closely adhered to if your heirs are to avoid paying estate taxes on your policy:

1. The insured (you) must not be able in any way to benefit or control the policy. Once a beneficiary is set, it must be irrevocable.
2. The insured cannot have any control over the proceeds.
3. The proceeds cannot be made payable to the estate.
4. The insured cannot be the owner of the policy.
5. The insured or the insured estate must not benefit in any way from the proceeds of the insurance.

Disability Insurance

Fact: You are five-and-a-half times more likely to be disabled at least 90 days than you are to die before you retire.

Fact: If you're now in your early 30s, there's a one in three chance that you will be disabled for at least six months before age 65.

Fact: Over 100 million American workers lack insurance against the risk of long-term disability.

When you die, life insurance provides for your family. Become disabled, and the financial hardship is greater—your income stops while your expenses continue and likely increase. It's no wonder that disability is called "living death."

It's amazing how many of my clients lack disability insurance. Most people have too much insurance of almost all types. But with disability, rare is the person who has enough.

Disability policies are complex and costly. A recent survey found that for a person aged 45 the annual disability premiums on policies paying $5,000 per month coverage and a 90-day elimination period ranged from $1,600 to $2,900. The elimination period is like a deductible—it's the time between the start of the disability and when the insurance starts paying.

Many companies provide employees with disability coverage, but it is often inadequate. The plans pay a percentage of a worker's income but do not include in that income bonuses or profit sharing. If you change employers, you may lose your coverage.

To determine the amount of disability coverage you need, remember that you probably won't have to rely entirely on the disability insurance. You may get workmen's compensation, company policies, even auto or liability coverage.

Also, no disability policy will cover your entire salary. Insurers want you to have some incentive to return to work.

FAST FACT: Be sure your disability insurance will provide 60 to 70 percent of your current pretax income. If you now earn $6,000 per month, coverage of $4,000 per month should be adequate.

Look carefully at the policy's definition of *disability*. Some cover you as long as you cannot work in your occupation. Others may cover you only as long as you cannot work in *any* suitable occupation. A doctor or lawyer too disabled to practice their profession can perhaps teach. If so, they may not be covered, even if they never wanted to teach.

Look for policies that the company cannot cancel and that are guaranteed renewable so the insurance company can't raise your premiums or leave you out in the cold. These are features worth having. You also want a policy that will cover you to at least age 65. A cost-of-living option is desirable, since benefits increase with inflation. Find a policy that gives you the option of increasing coverage as your income rises, preferably without requiring you to take a medical examination.

One way to hold down the cost of disability insurance is to take a long elimination period—the time you have to wait for benefits to begin. This functions like a deductible on medical insurance. A higher deductible and a longer elimination period translates into lower premiums.

Determine how long your savings and other income sources can support you and your family until the first insurance check arrives. If you need $50,000 a year in take-home (after-tax) income and you have savings of $15,000 and can get another $10,000 from other sources, then you can do without receiving the disability premiums for six months. Your elimination period should be six months.

Although disability coverage is expensive, especially for the self-employed, going uncovered can prove far more costly.

Money Savers

Here are tips for saving money on insurance:

- Take out the highest deductible you can afford. Minimum deductible: $500; preferable, $1,000. This applies to auto, medical, property, and any other insurance you buy that has a deductible. The higher the deductible, the lower the insurance premium. In the long run, you're better off assuming the risk associated with the deductible.
- Never buy specialty insurances. These include automobile towing, uninsured or underinsured motorist protection (in most states, that's just medical, for which you're already insured), extended product warranties (many of these pay as little as 10 or 15 cents for every dollar they collect), cancer, funeral, nursing home, airline flight, and any other insurance product the insurance industry can conjure up. These are a waste. Period.
- When insuring your home, don't insure the land—it's not going to burn, blow down, or be stolen. Insure just your house and its contents. Have insurance that will cover the replacement costs of the house and contents. Very valuable items need coverage with a policy added to the standard coverage, called riders. I have art insured with a rider. Some property is covered only to a specified limit. For instance, silver usually has coverage up to $1,500. If you have silver worth more, get a rider. Gun collections, art collectibles, antiques, and cash (which is usually insured only to $500) need special coverage.
- Credit life. You frequently see this attached to mortgages. It pays off the mortgage if the beneficiary dies. The idea of this is fine; it's the execution that's dubious. What you're buying here is declining term insurance. Over time, you pay off more and more of the mortgage so the insurance com-

pany has less and less exposure (that's the declining part). It's term because it provides only life insurance (no investment part) for the duration of the policy. What's the problem? Being tied to mortgages, people think they have to buy it. This allows insurance companies to charge outrageous prices. By purchasing declining term, which provides identical coverage, you can save as much as 75 percent on the cost.

- As your assets increase, your need for life and disability insurance declines. The more assets you have, the more income they'll generate for you in case of disability or death. The more income you'll have, the less insurance you need. When you have enough assets to generate income sufficient for you and your heirs' needs, you no longer need any life or disability insurance. Don't believe the insurance industry's claims that everyone needs life and disability insurance.

Our Five Model Families

FAMILY 1: A COUPLE SAVING FOR THEIR RETIREMENT
Since both work and there are no dependents, Jackie and Bob do not need life insurance. Both do need disability, which they get from their employers.

FAMILY 2: A SINGLE MOTHER SAVING FOR HER CHILDREN'S COLLEGE TUITION
Concerned about the children's finances if she were to die, Marilyn took out a $100,000 term life insurance policy. This should be enough to cover the children's expenses and college education, assuming they go to live with their father or grandparents.

FAMILY 3: A COUPLE SAVING FOR THEIR FIRST HOME
Both the Santangelos work and there are no dependents, so life insurance is not needed. They should have disability. Neither has disability coverage from their employer. Such insurance is not cheap and they opted to take the risk of not being covered for disability so that they could more quickly save for their home. I don't entirely agree with this approach, but I leave to my clients which risks they want to assume.

FAMILY 4: A COUPLE WANTING TO MINIMIZE THEIR TAXES

The Jordans have plenty of money, so they don't need life insurance for the survivor to live on. However, they do own a business, so we did an analysis of the tax liability that the business would create. Since they have over $1 million in assets outside the business, the surviving spouse would have no trouble paying the tax liability. This would give him or her time to decide what to do with the business rather than having to sell under pressure. Again, life insurance was not needed. Also not needed is disability insurance since there is plenty of money if the breadwinner were to become disabled, plus the business would continue to generate income.

FAMILY 5: A RETIRED COUPLE

This couple has more than enough money to cover survivor's expenses if one were to die, so life insurance here is not needed. In fact, the Moriartys had a whole life policy when they came to me that I recommended they liquidate, which they did. (There were no tax consequences because there was no gain, which is common with whole life.) Since they don't work, there's no need for disability insurance.

─────────────── H I G H L I G H T S ───────────────

The only situation in which insurance is appropriate is when there is a high cost if there's a loss while the likelihood of a loss is low.

Choose an insurance company that gets a fourth-highest or higher ratings by Weiss and two of the other four rating services.

Do *not* buy whole/universal life.

Buy term life, but only if you need life insurance.

How much life insurance you need: An amount equal to 75 percent of your family's current income.

Almost everyone who has yet to retire needs disability insurance.

8

MUTUAL FUNDS:
Only the Best

Jonathan came to my office with a gripe. He had gotten into individual stocks and stock mutual funds (which are pooled funds that invest in stocks and are managed by professionals) early in 1985 when the Dow Jones was less than 1300. Now five years later, the market was over 2800. The Dow had more than doubled, so one would think with so much money in stocks, that he would have been as happy as a stockbroker after a record day on Wall Street. But Jonathan was angry, very angry. He hadn't made any money during the past five years. I don't mean his investments didn't keep up with the rapid rise in the market. I mean he didn't make a cent. He literally broke even at a time the market more than doubled.

Even though he had had the foresight to be in the market during one of the greatest bull markets in history, he lost out for two reasons: (1) He invested in poorly performing stocks and mutual funds, and (2) he made frequent trades rather than using a buy-and-hold strategy. Just one of these mistakes can wipe out a person's profits; together they are sure to be deadly. Jonathan's investments were dead in the water.

Lacking a game plan and relying on a stockbroker's recommendations got Jonathan stuck in a losing proposition. His plan should have been to take a long-term buy-and-hold view. Instead, he acted more like a speculator. As for his broker, he put Jonathan into stocks and funds sponsored by the broker's own firm and encouraged him to trade liberally, generating commissions.

Most major brokerage and financial planning firms sponsor mutual funds. The problem comes because these firms typically pay their brokers larger commissions to sell investors the in-house funds rather than those sponsored by other companies. It's no surprise, then, that brokers push their own firm's products first. In fact, some firms require their brokers to push the in-house stuff. Sadly for the investor, funds sponsored by major brokerage firms are typically weak. Poor performers, these funds always enrich their sponsors and salespeople, but far less frequently outperform the market.

Jonathan's situation was made worse by an especially greedy broker. Not only couldn't he pick a decent stock or fund, but he had Jonathan do a great deal of trading, generating commissions for himself for every buy and sell order while taking away Jonathan's profits.

Within weeks of coming to me, I had Jonathan into solid, consistent funds, and his portfolio increased in value over 30 percent in 18 months. Had he stayed with his broker, I'm sure he would have been lucky to break even during this time.

Over many years I have developed a highly effective approach to picking mutual funds and strategies for using them. I've simplified it so you can use it with ease and complete confidence. By the time you finish this chapter, you'll know how to invest in mutual funds and which ones to choose.

Why Mutual Funds

"There's strength in numbers," goes the adage, and that's true with mutual funds. These ever-popular financial instruments capitalize on the idea that individual investors have a hard time beating the market by themselves because of high costs, the difficulty in investing in more than a few stocks, and bad advice. If they pool their resources, however, they can hire the best money managers in the world who know how to pick winners and gain the clout of the big boys.

This is a very appealing scenario. So appealing, in fact, that of the $21 trillion in total assets in the United States, $1.2 trillion is invested in more than 3,000 mutual funds.

There are solid reasons why mutual funds are so popular. They provide an easy way to build a diversified portfolio (making them a valuable tool for bulletproofing) because they invest in dozens of stocks, which creates far more diversification than the average investor could by him- or herself. As we've learned, diversification, properly done, increases returns while limiting risks.

Fund managers typically are seasoned professionals. They've studied the market for years; have enjoyed success as investors; have information, personnel, and technology at their disposal to exploit the best investments; and provide the individual investor with access to sophisticated portfolio management only the superrich could afford on their own. Mutual funds have access to markets not readily open to individual investors, particularly with overseas investments.

Funds usually come bundled as a "family of funds" by their sponsor. Several mutual funds are offered, each with its own investment objectives and management. The American Funds Group, for example, has a number of funds, among them: the EuroPacific Growth Fund, which invests in the securities of companies based outside the United States and seeks long-term capital appreciation; Washington Mutual Investors Fund, whose goal is current income gained through investments in U.S. companies; and American Balanced Fund, which invests in both stocks and bonds and has as its objectives the conservation of capital, current income, and long-term growth of both capital and income. You can switch between them at no cost. While you don't want to switch because you think one fund is likely to be hotter than another, you do at times need to move a portion of your assets to maintain balance in your portfolio and your bulletproof protection according to our asset allocation model.

Cashing in your shares in mutual funds is easy, so there's ready access to your money. Bookkeeping for tax purposes is simple because the fund does the work. And the fund will automatically reinvest your dividends and capital gains if you want.

Funds can also be a source of income, as you can withdraw money when you wish. This will limit your profitability, of course, but a good fund, the Templeton Growth Fund, for example, will still be a star performer even when factoring regular withdrawals. If you had put $10,000 into this fund on December 31, 1977, and withdrew 6 percent of your investment a year (that's $600 or $50 per month), on December 31, 1991, you'd have $59,347 in the fund and over time would have withdrawn over $8,400. If you withdrew 9 percent ($900 per year/$75 per month), you'd still have $43,174 in your account by the end of 1991. Good funds are useful to build assets and provide income.

The principal disadvantage of mutual funds is that they're taxable—the interest and dividends you earn from them and their capital gains are taxed each year, so they offer neither tax deductions nor tax-deferral benefits. This is why we frequently use annuities, which are discussed in the next chapter, instead of mutual funds.

All in all, mutual funds work hard to make investing in them easy. Largely, they succeed.

The Downside

As with any investment, mutual funds have their shortcomings. Performance is often one. With all the money, professional management, and computers at their disposal, one would think mutual funds would be stellar performers. A few are, and I'll recommend these shortly. Most aren't. One reason is that many funds are now too big.

As more money comes into a fund, less and less of the fund's overall portfolio can be in lesser-known undervalued stocks. Essentially, there's so much money to invest that managers can't find enough of these hidden gems to absorb it all. So they start putting money into the same stocks everyone else does, which by definition means they don't outperform the market. In fact, many can't even keep up with it. The costs of running a fund dictate that a manager has to have better-than-average returns just to stay even with the market. In practice, as many as 80 percent of fund managers lag the market. This accounts for the popularity of index funds that try to mirror the stocks found in indices, such as the Standard & Poor's 500 (which tracks price movements of 500 major corporations and is used as a measurement of how the stock market overall is moving), and just put money into those stocks. The idea is, if you basically have the stocks that comprise an index, you'll do as well as the index. It makes you wonder what you need a manager for; an investment novice could manage an index fund. In fact, even these funds often underperform the index because of their costs.

In late 1991, with interest rates falling, money was flowing into mutual funds so fast it made Niagara Falls seem like a mere bath spigot. Fidelity Investments, the largest mutual fund firm, had the assets in its bond funds *double* in 1991. The firm's director of fixed income was quoted in the *Wall Street Journal* as saying: "The big issue is whether we'll be able to continue to invest this enormous cash flow at reasonable rates."[25]

A variation on this problem with size is when firms become so popular they needed to start several new funds each year. Fidelity Investments is a prime example. It's hard to manage a dozen funds; Fidelity has over 160. How many can be productive especially when there aren't that many proven managers available to manage them? Maybe one or two are adequate performers and if you happen to invest in these, you come out okay. Chances are, you'll get one of the dogs. Stay away from sponsoring firms that have many funds because the numbers are against you.

Cost is another consideration, although not as significant a concern as many investors think and media people would like you to believe. The ways mutual funds charge is almost as varied as the number of mutual funds in existence. There are, however, some basic methods. Among them are:

No-load funds. Some funds sell direct to the public, for example, using direct mail, and don't carry a sales charge because there are no salespeople. Such funds are called *no-load.* The American Association of Individual Investors publishes an annual guide to no-load mutual funds [for more information, call (312) 280-0170] that defines no-loads as funds with sales charges of 2 percent or less. Bookstores carry books on no-load funds, too.

Low-load funds. Between the extremes of no-load and load funds is a gray area. In recent years, funds whose sales charges fall between the extremes have been given the name *low-load.* We define these as funds that charge between 4 and 6 percent.

Load funds. The remaining funds charge up to the maximum sales charge the Securities and Exchange Commission (SEC) allows, namely, 8.5 percent.

Sales charges are calculated as a flat percentage of the amount of money invested. If a fund charges 4 percent and you invest

$10,000, when you give the fund your money, the fund will keep $400 for its services and invest the remaining $9,600 in your name. When the sales charge is levied at the time you invest, it is said to be a *front-end charge*. A *back-end charge* is when the sales charge is levied at the time of withdrawal. Somewhat similar to the back-end charge is the redemption fee. This is paid when money is withdrawn. The difference between a back-end charge and a redemption fee is that the back-end is a sales commission paid to the person who sold the fund. The redemption charge, which generally goes to the fund, is designed to encourage investors to stay with the fund. As a rule, redemption charges decline over time until they disappear. The redemption charge might be 7 percent the first year and decline 1 percent a year until the eighth year when it no longer exists.

Adding to the confusion is the so-called 12b-1 plan. When a fund firm adopts a 12b-1 plan, it can use fund assets to pay for overhead and marketing expenses, such as advertising and sales commissions paid to brokers. This may be in addition to any load charges the fund levies. Unlike the load charges, which are paid by the investor just once, 12b-1 charges are paid annually. If these charges are 1.5 percent and each year you have $10,000 in the fund, then each year you will pay $150 for these charges.

The reason I pay little attention to loads is that, over time, they lose their significance. If you stay in a fund from 5 to 40 years, the commission becomes insignificant. Assume that you invest $10,000 and pay a 6 percent sales commission ($600). By keeping your money in the fund 10 years, the average annual amount of the commission is only $60. Admittedly, you've lost the use of the money during the 10 years, but this is still not important if the fund is a good performer.

More significant are the annual management fees or expenses all funds charge, typically about 1.5 percent a year. Some, though, are as low as one-half of 1 percent, like American Funds. Although American Funds has an upfront commission, it is still cheaper than many no-load funds over the long term because its ongoing management fees are lower. An additional factor is the short track records of many no-load funds. These funds became popular during the 1980s when many new ones were created, which means they've never experienced a prolonged bear (down) market. You just don't have any idea how they'll do when the market goes in the tank (which it will eventually do, I believe).

In addition, if you only look at cost when choosing a mutual fund, you'd never pick a foreign stock fund because they have significantly higher costs than domestic stock funds. You'd lose the increased rate of return and diversification foreign stock funds bring to your portfolio.

▼

FAST FACT: It's not what you pay in commissions and management fees that count, it's how well the fund performs.

A fund that provides average returns of 15 percent a year, year after year, is no investment wimp, even if it carries a sales charge. There are funds with such track records that I recommend below.

Let me give you real world examples. A favorite fund of mine is Growth Fund of America, one of the funds sponsored by the American Funds Group. If you invested $10,000 in this fund on the last day of 1977 and still held it on December 31, 1991, and reinvested all your earnings, you'd have $139,976, for a 19.21 percent annual growth rate (after commissions and fees). That's a long time to produce this return, but Growth Fund of America has done it. American Funds' Investment Company of America fund, during this same time, enjoyed a 15.27 percent annual growth rate. On the last trading day of 1977, the Dow Jones Industrial Average stood at 831.17. It reached 3,168.83 at the end of 1991, for an annual growth rate of 10.03 percent. American Funds' products did substantially better than the market and did so over a 14-year period. They have a sales charge of 5.75 percent. That's why I say, don't pay much attention to the commissions— keep your eye on the bottom line. It's where you make or lose money.

When You Need Mutual Funds

You use mutual funds in a variety of ways. They are used for retirement planning, financing a college education, providing income on an ongoing basis, and for other goals as well. I consider mutual funds the most versatile investment vehicle available. That's because they are economical (their costs to the investor are modest), effective (they are professionally managed), and varied (there are hundreds to choose from and many different kinds).

How I Pick Winners

With all these cautions about mutual funds, you're probably wondering how anyone can find a few winners. Actually, it's not that hard. That's because I've whittled down the process to two primary factors.

Long-Term Track Record—What's Hot Is What's Not

First, look at the fund's long-term track record. Over and over I've emphasized the importance of the buy-and-hold strategy in this book. Nowhere is this more true than with mutual funds.

People think I'm crazy when I say they should have investment horizons of 20, 30, even 40 years. That's not off the wall if you're likely to live another 20, 30, or 40 years. Suppose you're 40 years old now. Chances are good you'll be around another 40 years. If your investment horizon is a year or two, what happens when the year or two is over? You're back to square one. You again need places to put your money. If you do that, you'll need to spend all your spare time looking for investments. I find it far more productive—and profitable—to say, "I'm probably going to be around for X number of years, so I need investments that will take care of me that long."

I emphasize the importance of a long-term investment horizon because it directly affects how I analyze mutual funds and how I think you should.

Look at a fund's track record over at least 15 years. I didn't just pick this number because I do well with it in Las Vegas. You need to look at performance over a sufficient period to see how a fund will do over good times and bad. A good 15-year track record limits your risk exposure. You might hold a fund for 20 or 30 years and want to use that as a yardstick, but not many funds have track records that long. So 15 years is a reasonable time frame to get a feel for how a fund will do over the long term.

Trying to use the 15-year period has one difficulty: It's a bit hard to find this information. Ratings of mutual funds, widely published in the popular press, are useless. They focus on just the past year, even the past quarter, which is not only ridiculous, but dangerous. These ratings imply the top fund for the past quarter or past year will be at the top in the future. That's garbage. Market conditions usually cause a particular fund to be the year's stellar performer. Because these conditions constantly change, there's about as much chance of this year's number 1 fund repeating this feat year after year as there is that the federal government will never again run a deficit. Avoid anything that's scalding at the moment. Keep in mind a favorite homily: What's hot is what's not to do. When something's hot, the moment to buy at a good price has already passed.

To find the 15-year track record of a fund, contact the fund itself or ask your financial planner or broker to do so. It doesn't cost anything. You will receive a *hypothetical illustration*. It will take a certain dollar amount (I always request an example where $10,000 was invested as a lump sum), hypothesize investing this amount 15 years ago, and then run yearly calculations up to the present.

I'll shortly recommend several funds. If you want additional funds to choose from, I recommend *The 100 Best Mutual Funds You Can Buy* by Gordon K. Williamson, published by Bob Adams, Inc., Holbrook, Massachusetts. It sells for $12.95 and any bookstore with a good business section should have it or can order it for you. You can buy it direct from the publisher by calling (800) 872-5627. I had been analyzing funds for many years when this book first appeared in 1990, and it surprised me how much our recommendations coincided. I use more stringent criteria, such as the 15-year track record, which Williamson doesn't usually look at (he concentrates on 3 and 10 years), but overall, his recommendations are excellent.

Another important source of information is Morningstar Inc. in Chicago [(800) 876-5005]. It publishes an annual guide, *The Mutual Fund Sourcebook*, for $225, that contains one-page analyses of more than 1,000 equity funds and 1,000 fixed-income funds. It also publishes *Mutual Funds Values*, bound in a looseleaf binder, which reports on over 1,000 funds and is updated every two weeks. An annual subscription to this costs $395, and there's an introductory three-month offer for $55. Your financial planner, broker, or library may have Morningstar's publications.

Management

Mutual funds, more so than any other institution in the financial world, are the creation of a personality, the manager who gives the fund its character. There is in fact a "star" system, where every fund seeks to create (or steal) a star manager in the hope that he or she will produce a great track record and attract investors. Funds even lure managers from competitors with seven-figure annual incomes. If the manager likes the idea of holding cash when things in the market are murky, the fund will often be heavy with CDs and short-term bonds. In the same situation, another manager might go for blue chip stocks. It's a matter of personality.

The role of the manager was never more clearly seen than when the redoubtable Peter Lynch announced his retirement from Fidelity Investments' Magellan Fund, the largest mutual fund of its time. The announcement, made on March 28, 1990, that he would retire two months later made the front pages nationally. It was the *Wall Street Journal's* lead story, which began with the question: "How do you replace a legend?"[26]

This is Wall Street's equivalent of Hollywood. The movie industry pays Michelle Pfeiffer and Arnold Schwarzenegger big bucks on the assumption they'll bring in millions just on their name appeal. It's the same with Michael Jackson in music, Michael Jordon in basketball, and Stephen King in publishing. It works like that with mutual funds, too; stars attract investors.

The problem is that if you invest in a fund with a star at its helm and then the star goes off to greener pastures, what do you do? I agree with an analyst quoted in the *Wall Street Journal* who said, "If the star leaves, the whole track record becomes invalid."[27] When the star leaves, so should you.

In fact, you're better off not putting yourself in this position in the first place. Not all funds rely principally on one person. Some have a committee or modified committee structure. Again, one of my favorites is American Funds Group. Not only does this firm have a superb long-term record (*13 percent a year compounded for 57 years*), but it uses multiple managers as its management structure. Each fund is divided into segments, which have individual managers. Depending on the size and scope of the fund, there are 5 to 12 managers, or as American Funds calls them, counselors, per fund. In addition, the investments of some

MUTUAL FUNDS ▶ 129

segments are the picks of about 20 analysts. This means that if a manager leaves, the management of the whole fund doesn't change. Remarkably, few managers at American Funds leave. Most have been there 20 years or more. Other fund families use committees, where a group of analysts make investment decisions. This can work well also.

I said there were two important factors to consider when analyzing funds. That's true, but I also consider a couple more, and you might want to use them if you decide to do your own analysis.

Turnover Rates

Turnover rates may seem to relate to McDonald's and its revolving door of teenage employees, here today and gone tomorrow. But with mutual funds, turnover applies to mutual funds and is a little understood but important indicator of a fund manager's philosophy.

A fund's turnover rate refers to the number of times the investment portfolio is bought and sold annually. If a fund holds 150 stocks at any time and during the previous year bought and sold 90 stocks, its turnover rate is 60 percent ($90 \div 150$). On average, this fund trades 60 percent of its stocks a year.

A turnover rate of 200 percent in a stock fund is too high. The more a stock fund trades, the more it resembles a speculator rather than an investor. I keep emphasizing the benefits of the buy-and-hold strategy, and this principle applies to mutual fund management as well as individual investors. Some funds, if their investment philosophy is aggressive (and you know this from reading the prospectus), can have a turnover of as much as 150 percent, and that might be okay. For most funds, though, the turnover rate is preferably 30 percent or less.

FAST FACT: You may hold a mutual fund's stock for years, but if that fund is a speculator, so are you. Seek stock funds whose turnover rates are below 30 percent, unless you purposefully are targeting a segment of your portfolio to more risky, speculative investments. In any case, don't go with a fund with a turnover rate over 150 percent.

You may think that because the fund's manager is a "professional," it's okay if he or she trades a lot. They must know what they're doing. Research shows otherwise. A study done in 1987 looked at the 20 stock funds with the highest and the 20 with the lowest turnover rates for the period 1984 to 1986. The 20 low-turnover funds had a compound total return of 50.7 percent for the three years versus 34.1 percent for the high-turnover ones. The low-turnover funds' return was nearly 50 percent higher than those that were speculating.

In 1990, Morningstar Inc. looked at the performance of 278 funds and divided them into four categories based on their turnover rates. Those with the lowest turnover (23 percent each year) had by far the best returns. The ones with the highest turnover (the highest rate was 154 percent) did second best, followed by the group with the second-lowest turnover. Bringing up the rear was the group with the third-lowest turnover. The only group to significantly outperform the average for the entire 278 funds was the one with the lowest turnover.[28]

The Beta

The beta is a statistical technique used to measure a stock or fund's volatility compared with the market as a whole. If the fund has a beta of 1.0, then its price moves in tandem with the market. A 10 percent increase or decrease in the market will result in a 10 percent increase or decrease in the fund's value. A beta of 0.8 says a 10 percent change in the market results in an 8 percent (8 percent is 0.8 of 10 percent) change in the fund. A beta of 1.2 results in a 12 percent change in the fund if the market changes 10 percent. Obviously, the higher the beta, the more volatile and risky the investment.

For mutual funds, this is how I rank betas:

0.8 or less	Low risk
0.8–1.1	Medium risk
1.0 and up	High risk

Morningstar Inc. reports betas. Your library, financial planner, or stockbroker should have Morningstar's reports. You can purchase the firm's mutual fund reports directly as I mentioned earlier.

I discussed in Chapter 5 how to assess your affinity toward risk. If you are a low-, medium-, or high-risk investor, then orient your mutual fund investing to funds with comparable betas. You don't have to follow the betas religiously, however. If you're a low-risk investor, putting some money into higher-risk investments is okay as long as you don't bail out when the market turns against you (as it will). Just use the betas as a guideline.

The Fund's Investment Philosophy

Funds come in many different flavors, focusing on very different kinds of investments, and that's why they fit in everyone's portfolio. Use them to tailor your investments to match your needs. For example, if you need inflation protection, you might buy a gold or real estate fund. Need to diversify outside the country? Try a foreign stock fund. Also, mutual funds are perfect vehicles for dollar-cost averaging because fund sponsors allow shareholders to invest as little as $25 at a time.

You make money in stocks in two ways: dividends (typically cash paid to shareholders that comes from the company's profits) and capital appreciation (increases in the stock's price). The two general categories of stock mutual funds—growth and income—mirror this in their payoffs. Growth funds' investment strategy is to buy the stocks of companies likely to grow and, hopefully, see their stock price grow with them. Stocks in growth-stock mutual funds usually pay small or no dividends. Income funds, on the other hand, seek to provide their shareholders with income now. They like companies that pay sizable dividends, such as utilities, and companies in mature low-growth industries.

There are variations within these categories. Growth funds might invest in established high-tech firms, like Microsoft and Novell. These companies plow their earnings back into research and development rather than paying dividends. Other funds are more speculative. Some, for instance, invest in small-company stocks of young and unproven firms. The fund's prospectus, as well as the write-ups by Morningstar Inc. and Williamson, will tell you what a fund's objectives are.

In addition to stock funds, there are also money market funds, which invest in short-term investments, pay low rates of return, and are very safe in maintaining the value of your principal; bond funds, which invest in government bonds and/or the bonds of major corporations; tax-exempt bond funds, which put their money into municipal and other vehicles that are exempt from federal (and sometimes state and local) income taxes; and balanced funds, which include stocks and bonds in their portfolios.

Many other types exist, including those that invest in foreign stocks, options, limited partnerships, gold, and precious metals.

The one that's right for you depends on what you need to balance your portfolio and the types of risks you are willing to take.

Closed- versus Open-End Funds

Closed- and open-end mutual funds are worth mentioning. Closed-end funds sell a set number of shares at an initial public offering and then these shares trade like common stocks, moving up and down in value with changes in the value of the bond's investments (what they buy with all the money from selling stock). Frequently, closed-end funds sell at less than their true value, or *net asset value*, especially immediately after they are sold to the public. If a fund has assets worth $10 million and has 1 million shares outstanding, each share has a net asset value of $10. It's not uncommon for such shares to sell at less than $10. Never buy closed-end funds at their initial offering because the chances are excellent they'll soon go down in price.

The more common open-end funds lack a finite number of shares. They issue shares when investors buy and redeem shares (buy them back) when investors sell. What investors pay and receive depends on the net asset value of the shares that day. In this case, the price is always identical to the net asset value at the time of the trade. I recommend these.

Bonds and Bond Funds

You can invest in bonds by buying them outright or buying shares of a mutual fund, which, in turn, buys and holds the bonds themselves. As you'll see in the sample portfolios in Chapter 15, only international and Treasury bonds fit into my asset allocation model. All other bonds, such as corporates and municipals, don't optimize an investor's profits given their risks, as the model demonstrates. However, individual bonds are essential for depression/recession protection, and many investors like bond mutual funds. Bonds are sufficiently popular so that it's worth mentioning some important points about them here.

Interest rates are the most important determinant of bond prices. An increase in interest rates results in decreased bond prices, with the reverse being true. This is simple to understand. First, remember that when you buy a bond, the issuer agrees to pay you a fixed interest for a fixed amount of time, at the end of which you get your initial investment back (the principal) plus all interest not paid over the term of the bond. Also remember, however, that you can sell a bond at anytime over its term, with the price you get determined by market conditions, which include interest rates.

A $1,000 bond that pays 8 percent when the market as a whole is paying 8 percent will have the same price it had when issued. It's paying $80 a year. $1,000 × 8% = $80.

If interest rates go up, then investors can get more interest either by buying a new bond at the new higher rate or in comparable investments. Assume rates reach 10 percent. For your original 8 percent bond, investors will pay you only $800 because they receive only $80 in interest each year. At $80, only a price of $800 gives the investors the market rate of return (10 percent): $800 × 10% = $80.

But suppose interest rates fall to 6 percent Then the price of the 8 percent bond will rise to $1,333. An 8 percent $1,000 bond pays $80 in interest. That's the same as a $1,333 bond that pays 6 percent, because 6 percent of $1,333 equals $80: $1,333 × 6% = $80. These prices are, admittedly, approximations.

In addition to interest rates, bond prices move according to how close the bond is to its maturity date. This is the date the bond expires and investors receive the principal back. The principal is what the original investors paid for the bond, typically $1,000. If a $1,000 bond pays 8 percent interest, and the market rate at this time is 6 percent, normally the bond would sell for $1,333. Suppose the bond matures next month. At that time, investors will receive only $1,000 from the company. They won't pay a premium over $1,000 because they'll only get the higher interest rate (8 percent) for a short time. The bond will trade for about $1,000 as a result. The closer the maturity date is, the more it influences the bond's price.

Many bonds have call features, which allow the company or agency that issued the bond to call, redeem, or cash in the bond at a certain date before its maturity for a certain price. If a bond pays 10 percent and the current market rate is 6 percent and the bond is callable, the issuer will, whenever possible, call the bond and immediately turn around and sell new bonds at the lower (6 percent) rate. This is analogous to a homeowner refinancing his mortgage when interest rates drop significantly. A bond sold with a call usually is priced as though the maturity date *is* the call date. If the bond matures in 17 years but is callable in a year, investors will look at the bond as though it matures in one year because they can't count on getting the interest rate for the full 17 years.

One last important factor on bond prices relates to rating. Moody's and Standard & Poor's are the big bond rating services. Bonds are debt. Bondholders lend money to the company or government agency issuing the bond. This differs from stocks, which are equities. If you own stock in a company, you have an equity (ownership) interest in the company. The company doesn't have to pay you anything, although many firms disburse profits to stockholders by paying dividends. Not so with corporate bonds. Bondholders are like banks. They lend the company money, and the company agrees to pay interest at set times (usually every three months) of a set amount and return the money originally paid for the bond on a certain date.

The reason there are rating services for bonds but not stocks is because the services study the issuing companies or agencies to determine the likelihood the interest will be paid on a timely basis over the life of the bond and the principal returned at maturity. There's nothing like this to study with stocks, because stocks don't promise interest or the return of principal. For bonds, the lower the rating, the greater the chance the bond will default on its interest payments and principal. To compensate for this higher risk, the higher the interest rate the company issuing the bond is forced to offer to attract investors. If the bond has a low (or no) rating when issued, it will come out with a high interest rate. Companies or agencies whose credit worthiness has dropped since they first issued long-term bonds will find their bonds reflect the lower ratings by selling for low prices, which, of course, translate into higher yields for investors who are taking more of a risk and need to be compensated for that at a higher rate than if the company were rock solid. (See the appendix at the end of the book for an explanation of bond ratings.)

Investors often think that sound companies have sound bonds. That's true for a time, but may not be true forever, which is why it's important to monitor ratings and how the issuing organization is doing financially on an ongoing basis. Let me give you an example. Olympic & York Developments Ltd. is the world's largest commercial office building developer with major holdings in New York, Toronto, and London. One of its properties is 55 Water Street, a very large Manhattan office building in the Wall Street area that was built in the early 1970s. In May 1986, Olympia & York issued $435 million worth of 10-year bonds on 55 Water Street, yielding 8¼ percent and selling at $1002.50 per bond. At the time, the building was full, Wall Street was doing incredibly well, the New York real estate market was extremely strong, and the prospects for Olympia & York selling the building at a profit within 10 years looked good. The investment community liked the bonds, and Olympia & York got its money on favorable terms.

Six years later, with market interest rates lower than in 1986, the price of the bonds should have increased. Instead, in May 1992, the bonds were selling for $430 and had a yield-to-maturity of 37¼ percent. What happened? For one thing, parts of Olympia & York went into bankruptcy. For another, the New York real estate market collapsed. The building depended on attracting and keeping brokerage firms as its primary tenants. However, between 1986 and 1992, many of its brokerage tenants either went out of business, moved, or consolidated. The overall going rate for space in Manhattan declined so that even those companies who stayed as tenants got leases at lower-than-expected rates. The building was seen as outmoded, lacking the sophisticated wiring and open floor spaces that financial firms need in the 1990s.

In 1986, there was probably no real estate firm in the world more respected and considered more secure than Olympia & York. Six years later, it was a mess. This is the kind of thing that can happen to most any firm and why no corporate bond can ever be considered absolutely secure.

Bond Issuers

Corporations issue bonds, as do public agencies (e.g., school districts, sewer districts, and airport authorities), state and local governments, and the federal government. The interest on municipal bonds (issued by cities or towns or their agencies) is usually free of state and federal income taxes if the bondholder is a resident of the state where the bond is issued. Federal bonds issued by the Treasury (Treasury bills are short-term bonds—30 days to one year; Treasury notes are medium-term bonds—two to 10 years; and Treasury bonds are long-term bonds—30 years) are free of state income taxes.

As we learned in Chapter 3 on depression/recession protection, Treasury bonds are excellent for bulletproofing. But as I mentioned in Chapter 5 on risk, all bonds really do carry some risk. The bulk is interest-rate risk, the risk that their yields won't keep up with the yields of other investments. It's not enough for a bond to pay its interest promptly and repay the principal when due. If the bond doesn't perform as well as other investments, you lose money.

Price movements also can produce losses. If interest rates rise or a bond's rating falls, its price will drop. So even if the bond pays its interest, bondholders may come up short if they are forced to or choose to sell the lower-priced bond before its maturity. Those who buy mutual funds made up of federal government bonds often get a rude shock. Their stockbroker sold them the fund saying they were guaranteed not to lose money. After all, the federal government is certain to pay its debts. That's true. But if interest rates rise, the prices of bonds fall, and that includes Treasury bonds. A government bond mutual fund trades bonds, buying and selling freely across terms and only rarely holds bonds to their maturity. These trades can result in losses not because the bonds renege on their obligations, but because of market conditions that depress their market value. Fund holders who try to sell during these times end up with losses, although they invested in government bonds "guaranteed" not to default.

Bonds are bought through financial planners and stockbrokers. They trade on the exchanges and usually have liquid markets.

Using a Private Money Manager for a Personalized Mutual Fund

A number of my clients use private money managers. A good one is much like a mutual fund manager: someone who invests your money in a number of stocks. In fact, picking a money manager is largely like picking a mutual fund manager: Look at his or her track record.

In addition, the private money manager must have a personality that's comfortable for you. Mutual funds can have tens of thousands of investors, so the likelihood of you talking to a fund manager is slim. One of the advantages of having a personal money manager is you can personally communicate with him or her. That's why your personalities must be compatible.

Money managers tailor your investment program to your needs and goals. However, they typically limit the investments they work with (usually just U.S. stocks and U.S. corporate bonds), so it's unlikely a manager can provide complete bullet-proof protection. You'll still have to do some investing yourself.

Most managers won't take on clients with total assets of less than $300,000. As their fee they charge one-quarter of 1 percent to 1 percent annually of the total portfolio they manage. The larger the portfolio, the smaller the percentage. Morningstar Inc. has a listing of money managers. Ask friends and colleagues for references and check each manager's performance. It's important, too, to talk to several of his or her clients.

What to Buy

We've been talking up to now about how I pick mutual funds. Now I'll recommend several worth buying.

American Funds Distributors
333 South Hope Street
Los Angeles, CA 90071
(800) 421-0180

American Funds and Templeton are my two favorite fund groups. Just about any fund sponsored by American Funds is worth investing in. I particularly like the following:

The U.S. Treasury Money Market Fund of America

Date founded: 2/91

Average annual total return from 12/31/76 to 12/31/91: n/a

Approximate annual turnover rate: n/a

Beta: n/a

Investments in portfolio: U.S. Treasury securities maturing in one year or less.

Minimum initial investment: $2,500

Minimum subsequent investment: $50

Investment objective: Provide shareholders with a way to earn income on their cash reserves while preserving capital and maintaining liquidity.

Comments: This is an excellent fund to park your cash temporarily until making subsequent investments, as well as a place to put the cash portion of your portfolio.

Growth Fund of America

Date founded: 1/1/59

Average annual total return from 12/31/77 to 12/31/91: 19.21%

Approximate annual turnover rate: 26%

Beta: 1.04

Investments in portfolio: According to the company, this fund "invests in a variety of companies characterized by superior growth potential." About 81 percent of the portfolio is in stocks, 4 percent in bonds, and 15 percent in cash.

Minimum initial investment: $1,000

Subsequent initial investment: $50

Investment objective: Growth of capital rather than current income.

Comments: A fund with a wonderful long-term record. When used with asset allocation, keep in mind it keeps about 20 percent of its assets in cash.

Washington Mutual Investors Fund

Date founded: 7/31/52

Average annual total return from 12/31/76 to 12/31/91: 15.4%

Approximate annual turnover rate: 19%

Beta: 0.91

Investments in portfolio: This fund is always fully invested in solid stocks and in some instances in convertible securities of U.S. companies.

Minimum initial investment: $250

Minimum subsequent investment: $50

Investment objective: Growth of capital while being fully invested.

Comments: Good long-term track record. This fund fits well in asset allocation because it is virtually fully invested in common stocks at all times.

Investment Company of America

Date founded: 1/1/34

Average annual total return from 12/31/77 to 12/31/91: 15.27%

Approximate annual turnover rate: 17%

Beta: 0.83

Investments in portfolio: The fund is about 81 percent invested in stocks, 13 percent in bonds, and 6 percent in cash.

Minimum initial investment: $250

Minimum subsequent investment: $50

Investment objective: Long-term growth of capital and income using primarily common stocks.

Comments: Famed for performing well no matter what the economic climate, Investment Company of America is another of American Funds' star long-term performers—this fund has been a star since 1934.

Bond Fund of America

Date founded: 5/28/74

Average annual total return from 12/31/76 to 12/31/91: 10.67%

Approximate annual turnover rate: 112%

Beta: 0.78

Investments in portfolio: This fund invests in a diversified portfolio of bonds and other fixed-income obligations. At least 60 percent of its assets must be invested in government-issued securities, corporate bonds rated A or better, and money market instruments.

Minimum initial investment: $1,000

Minimum subsequent investment: $50

Investment objective: With at least 60 percent of the portfolio in high-grade straight debt securities, the fund looks for a high level of current income and preservation of capital.

Comments: As mentioned in Chapter 15, which contains the sample portfolios, many of my clients who are a bit uncomfortable investing in stocks first put their money into this fund and gradually shift their funds in a diversified mix of stock funds. For those who lack much investment experience, this fund is a good place to start.

Templeton Funds
700 Central Avenue
St. Petersburg, FL 33733
(800) 237-0738

John Templeton is one of the shining lights of the investment world and has been for decades and with good reason. He and his funds are winners year after year. Despite the funds carrying his name, he's got professional managers who work with each fund. This is not a firm, therefore, based solely on the star system of management. Here are my Templeton favorites:

Templeton Income Fund

Date founded: 9/24/86
Average annual total return from 9/24/86 to 12/31/91: 8.9%
Approximate annual turnover rate: 117%
Beta: 0.20
Investments in portfolio: Globally diversified bond fund.
Minimum initial investment: $500
Subsequent initial investment: $25
Investment objective: High current income.

Comments: Excellent international bond fund that works well in the international bond segment of our asset allocation model.

Templeton Foreign Fund

Date founded: 10/5/82

Average annual total return from 10/5/82 to 12/31/91: 18.5%

Approximate annual turnover rate: 8%

Beta: 0.61

Investments in portfolio: About 80 percent of this fund's investments are in stocks in foreign companies located around the world. The remainder of its portfolio consists of bonds and short-term securities.

Minimum initial investment: $500

Subsequent initial investment: $25

Investment objective: Long-term capital growth rather than income.

Comments: This fund has performed well since its inception and fits into our asset allocation model because it is a pure play in foreign stocks.

Templeton Growth Fund

Date founded: 11/29/54

Average annual total return from 12/31/77 to 12/31/91: 17.15%

Approximate annual turnover rate: 13%

Beta: 0.88

Investments in portfolio: Primarily invests in common stock, but it will also invest in preferred stocks and debt securities such as convertible bonds and bonds selling at a discount.

Minimum initial investment: $500

Minimum subsequent investment: $25

Investment objective: Long-term capital growth.

Comments: The granddad of all international funds, and one of the best at combining both domestic and foreign stocks.

Templeton Real Estate Securities Fund

Date founded: 9/12/89

Average annual total return from 9/12/89 to 12/31/91: n/a

Approximate annual turnover rate: n/a

Beta: n/a

Investments in portfolio: Real estate investment trusts.

Minimum initial investment: $500

Minimum subsequent investment: $25

Investment objective: Long-term capital growth.

Comments: Excellent diversification of different kinds of real estate and in different places in the United States. Great fit with our sample portfolios.

MFS Financial Services
500 Boylston Street
Boston, MA 02116
(800) 654-0266

MFS Worldwide Governments Trust

Date founded: 2/25/81
Average annual total return from 1/1/82 to 12/31/91: 15.5%
Approximate annual turnover rate: 280%
Beta: 0.30
Investments in portfolio: U.S. and foreign government bonds.
Minimum initial investment: $1,000
Minimum subsequent investment: $50
Investment objective: Preservation and growth of capital with moderate current income through international fixed-yield securities and currencies.
Comments: A good blend of both domestic and international bonds.

MFS Managed Municipal Bond Trust

Date founded: 12/16/76
Average annual total return from 12/16/76 to 4/30/92: 9.38%
Approximate annual turnover rate: 316%
Beta: 0.94
Investments in portfolio: Various municipals.
Minimum initial investment: $1,000
Minimum subsequent investment: $50
Investment objective: Current income exempt from federal taxes.
Comments: If you want a tax-free fund, this is one of the best. Like corporate bonds, U.S. municipal bonds do not fit the asset allocation model.

Franklin Funds
777 Mariners Island Boulevard
San Mateo, CA 94404
(800) 342-5236

Franklin Gold Fund

Date founded: 5/19/69
Average annual total return from 12/31/76 to 12/31/91: 17.31%
Approximate annual turnover rate: 4%
Investments in portfolio: Mining companies, primarily those engaged in gold mining, and related businesses.
Minimum initial investment: $100
Minimum subsequent investment: $25
Investment objective: Capital appreciation and international diversification.
Comments: The nonexistent turnover rate makes it an excellent hedge fund and does a great job of fitting our asset allocation model.

Eaton Vance Distributors
24 Federal Street
Boston, MA 02110
(800) 225-6265

Income Fund of Boston

Date founded: 6/30/72
Average annual total return from 12/31/76 to 12/31/91: 10.7%
Approximate annual turnover rate: 70%
Investments in portfolio: Below investment-grade/junk bonds
Minimum initial investment: $1,000
Minimum subsequent investment: $50
Investment objective: Current income.
Comments: If you need high income for applications such as a charitable remainder unitrust, this might be a good way to get there. Be alerted that this does not fit our asset allocation model.

Van Eck Securities
122 East 42nd Street
New York, NY 10168
(800) 221-2220

Van Eck Gold/Resources Fund

Date founded: 2/15/86
Average annual total return from 2/15/86 to 12/31/91: 2.33%
Approximate annual turnover rate: 3%
Investments in portfolio: Primarily gold stocks.
Minimum initial investment: $1,000
Minimum subsequent investment: $100
Investment objective: Growth.
Comments: A well-diversified precious metals fund. Like Franklin's gold fund, there is almost no turnover rate. This fund is unique in that it has no South African stock in its portfolio. While its annual return is low, that's okay. What we want here is an investment that moves opposite to the majority of other investments. Not everything goes up all the time. The asset allocation model leverages off the tendency of certain investments that usually move in opposite directions. This fund does exactly that, which is why it works so well in our asset allocation model.

Pioneer Funds Distributor
60 State Street
Boston, MA 02109
(800) 225-6292

Pioneer Three

Date founded: 11/12/82
Average annual total return from 11/12/82 to 12/31/91: 12.93%
Approximate annual turnover rate: 15%
Investments in portfolio: Small capitalization stocks.
Minimum initial investment: $1,000
Minimum subsequent investment: $50
Investment objective: Long-term growth and income of securities

of companies with market capitalization of less than $750 million.

Comments: Good asset allocation fund because it's well diversified and highly invested (few assets are kept in cash).

Our Five Model Families

FAMILY 1: A COUPLE SAVING FOR THEIR RETIREMENT

Because Jackie and Bob are saving for their retirement and therefore have tax deferral as a primary concern, they'll use annuities rather than mutual funds. However, since there is not a good variable annuity available with *a small-cap fund,* we will buy the small-cap fund on a taxable basis from Pioneer Three. The model calls for 7 percent, which comes to $1,750.

PORTFOLIO	
30-year Treasury bonds	$2,500
Cash and cash equivalents	1,000
Franklin Valuemark II Real Estate Securities Fund	3,250
Franklin Valuemark II Precious Metals Fund	3,000
Pioneer Three	**1,750**

FAMILY 2: A SINGLE MOTHER SAVING FOR HER CHILDREN'S COLLEGE TUITION

Marilyn will be using mutual funds. Ten percent of her assets should go into a U.S. stock fund, with Washington Mutual Investors the one I recommend. Instead of putting the money directly into the fund, we'll dollar-cost average, so we put in $1,000 (10 percent of the $10,000 she already has saved). Our asset allocation model calls for this medium-risk investor to have 24 percent of her assets in international stocks, so we'll take $2,400 (24 percent of $10,000) and invest it in the Templeton Foreign Fund. Another 20 percent ($2,000) goes into international bonds, and we'll use the Templeton Bond Fund. Finally, we'll put 7 percent ($700) into the Pioneer Three. After these initial investments, we'll invest $50 a month as dollar-cost averaging, putting the money in the various funds to maintain our proper proportions. This completes Marilyn's portfolio.

PORTFOLIO

30-year Treasury bonds	$1,000
Cash and cash equivalents	400
Templeton Real Estate Fund	1,300
Franklin Gold Fund	1,200
Washington Mutual Investors	**1,000**
Templeton Foreign Fund	**2,400**
Templeton Bond Fund	**2,000**
Pioneer Three	**700**
Total	$10,000

FAMILY 3: A COUPLE SAVING FOR THEIR FIRST HOME

After the Santangelos have their bulletproofing investments in place, they should then add to the remaining portions of their portfolio. Because they are dealing with small amounts of money, they invest according to the minimum of each mutual fund. The Santangelos' portfolio is now complete.

PORTFOLIO

Treasury strips	$1,400
Templeton Real Estate Fund	4,000
Pioneer Three	**5,200**
Washington Mutual Investors	**3,000**
Templeton Foreign Fund	**6,400**
Total	$20,000

FAMILY 4: A COUPLE WANTING TO MINIMIZE THEIR TAXES

The Jordans want to cut their taxes to the bone, so they won't be using mutual funds for the remainder of their portfolio but will use annuities instead. There's one exception, namely, with regards to their small-cap investment (or investment in a company with a market capitalization of less than $750 million). Because of the lack of a good variable annuity with small-cap stocks, we use the mutual fund Pioneer Three for 7 percent of the portfolio.

PORTFOLIO

Franklin Valuemark II Zero Coupon Fund Maturing 2010	$120,000
American Funds U.S. Treasury Money Fund of America	84,000

Franklin Valuemark II Real Estate
   Securities Fund   156,000
Franklin Valuemark II Precious Metals Fund   144,000
Pioneer Three   **84,000**

FAMILY 5: A RETIRED COUPLE

Like the Jordans wanting to minimize taxes, the Moriartys will also use annuities.

PORTFOLIO

Cash and cash equivalents	$175,000
30-year Treasury bonds	85,000
Franklin Valuemark II Real Estate Securities Fund	100,000
Gold bullion coins	50,000

--- H I G H L I G H T S ---

Mutual fund benefits: An easy way to diversify and maintain balance within your portfolio between assets whose prices move opposite each other. They are easy to cash out of so they are highly liquid, and they provide a source of income via dividends.

How to choose a mutual fund:

- Look at the fund's long-term track record, preferably about 15 years.
- Look at the fund's management; try to use the "star" system of management.
- Go with funds having a 30 percent asset turnover rate if you want low risk and up to 100 percent turnover if you want high risk.

The fund's beta:	0.8 or less	Low risk
	0.8–1.1	Medium risk
	1.0 and more	High risk

9

ANNUITIES:
Tax Delayed Is Money Made

A well-known comedian's famous lament is, "I don't get no respect." If variable annuities could talk, they'd probably say the same (though with better grammar). About 40 million people hold shares in mutual funds, nearly twice as many as have annuities. In my opinion, that's cockeyed. The ratio should probably be reversed.

Most who hold mutual funds should have variable annuities instead.

Don't get me wrong. Mutual funds are often wonderful investments, which is why I spent the entire last chapter talking about them. They can't be beat in tax-sheltered situations, such as individual retirement accounts (IRAs) and pensions. Plus, they are very liquid so, if you suddenly need money, getting it from a mutual fund isn't much harder than taking money out of a savings account. It's just that their near cousin, the annuity, offers advantages that mutual funds can't equal. There's a time and a place for each.

This chapter is a quick introduction to variable and fixed annuities—what they are, their benefits, their varieties, the best ones, and how to use them. In a few pages, you'll have all the information you'll need to use annuities—specifically variable annuities—effectively in your financial planning for the rest of your life.

What Are Annuities?

Here is a brief discussion of the two types of annuities; they are discussed in more detail later in the chapter.

Fixed Annuity

A fixed annuity is, in effect, a loan you make to an insurance company. In return, the insurance company guarantees the return of your principal but generally does not guarantee the amount of interest you'll receive. (Sometimes there's a guaranteed return, but it's generally just for a limited period, such as one year.) You have no say as to how your money is invested; the insurance company makes all the decisions. The interest earned is tax deferred until withdrawn. You can invest in a fixed annuity by making monthly payments or in a single lump-sum payment. Withdrawal options are varied. I do not recommend fixed annuities for reasons I'll soon explain.

A Variable Annuity

A variable annuity is like a tax-deferred mutual fund. They're purchased from insurance companies because they have a small amount of life insurance, which allows the annuity to offer tax-deferral benefits. Like a mutual fund family, a variable annuity allows you to choose among various investments, such as government bonds, U.S. stocks, foreign stocks, and gold. Also, like a mutual fund, your principal is not guaranteed. How well you do financially depends on how well your investments perform. A variable annuity is not a loan to an insurance company, and the money you invest is kept in a separate account that's not subject to the insurance company's creditors. If your insurance company gets into financial hot water, you stay cool because your money can't be touched by the insurance company's creditors.

The Insurance Component

It's worth noting that, besides providing tax deferral benefits, the insurance portion of variable annuities provides two additional benefits as well. First, it provides a modicum of life insurance that guarantees the principal if you die while the annuity is in force (with a fixed annuity, the principal is guaranteed even if you withdraw the money before you die). Second, it makes sure the annuity continues to pay you the amount specified in the annuity for as long as you live, even if that's to age 105 or more.

The fact that there is an insurance component is a big plus—which is the variable annuity's enormous advantage over mutual funds—in that the money you pay into the annuity accrues tax free until you start taking it out. Many, late in life, have less income than when they were younger and so are in a lower tax bracket. This means they pay less of their accumulated gains back to the government as taxes. So the longer they hold off paying taxes, the more they gain. In fact, even if their income and tax bracket rise, they still come out ahead because of those years of tax deferral.

Some wrinkles exist with the annuity not found with a mutual fund. The annuity functions somewhat like a nondeductible IRA (the kind where you are not eligible to deduct contributions from your taxable income), with such features as tax deferral and early withdrawal penalties (you get taxed at a higher rate by the IRS for sums withdrawn prior to age 59½ and the annuity's sponsor will pay you less, too). Yet, one important advantage of an annuity over an IRA is that there's no maximum contribution you can make to an annuity, unlike the IRA's $2,000 yearly limit. (See Chapter 12 for more information on IRAs and other tax-deferred investments.) In fact, the IRS will hit you with a penalty of 10 percent (plus taxes owed at your tax rate) for any sums withdrawn before age 59½, which is the reason most annuities begin paying out no earlier than this.

Because of IRS and sponsoring company penalties, use this investment only for the long term—more than seven years. The appropriate use of variable annuities is for retirement planning or sheltering income on investments. There is rarely an appropriate use of fixed annuities, as discussed shortly.

What makes variable annuities generally better than mutual funds? Tax considerations. As we discussed earlier, the best way of investing is in (1) tax-deductible and tax-deferred investments, (2) tax deferred, and (3) taxable investments. IRA investments are both tax deductible and tax deferred, because the former means you can deduct any IRA payment (up to $2,000/year) from your gross income before you pay taxes on it. So a $2,000 IRA payment made in a year when your gross income was $40,000 means you pay tax on only $38,000. That same money (and everything else that accumulates in your IRA) is also tax deferred in that you don't pay any taxes on its appreciation or the interest until you begin taking money out. While annuities are tax deferred (you pay taxes only when you begin to receive payouts), with mutual funds, you pay taxes as you go along according to the interest and dividends you earn and capital appreciation when you sell. This gives annuities preference over mutual funds. Over time, tax-deferral compounding is very, very powerful, as Table 3 in Chapter 6 demonstrated.

A mutual fund can create tax liabilities even if the value of the mutual fund *falls*. In declining markets, mutual fund managers often sell their investment winners to lock in gains and hold onto their losers hoping they'll turn around. Taxes are due on realized gains. These can't be offset by unrealized losses (losses in stocks that have dropped but not yet sold). The gains plus dividends paid often mean investors have a tax liability even if the fund's value has dropped. If something like this happens within an annuity, you don't suffer because the gains are tax sheltered.

Early withdrawal charges are the biggest downside to annuities compared to mutual funds. With variable annuities, this typically means you'll pay 5 to 7 percent of the accrued value of the annuity the first year or so if you take out your money, with this

SPEND SMART: Most annuity holders will never use the life insurance that comes with annuities. But here's a situation that makes the insurance useful. Now retired, you want to leave all the money in your annuity to your heirs. To leave as much as possible, you want to become a very aggressive, risk-taking investor. If your investments work out, your heirs get more money than if you had been conservative. However, you're concerned about losing money. Don't be. If you suffer losses, the insurance guarantees that when you die, your heirs get all the money you originally put into the annuity. There cannot be any loss of principal. Put another way, *the insurance covers any losses.*

figure dropping 1 percent a year until the seventh year, after which there are no withdrawal fees. Because you should keep your money in an annuity for longer than seven years anyway, I don't consider early withdrawal fees a major consideration.

About 95 percent of all variable annuities have no sales charge (what you pay to start up), while the average annual fee for overhead expense runs about 2.25 percent, according to Variable Annuity Research & Data Service. As with mutual funds, you shouldn't worry about costs—it's the bottom line that counts. If the annuity pays a good return, who cares what its charges are?

Fixed versus Variable Annuities

Fixed Annuities

As noted, fixed annuities guarantee you will never lose your principal. They also have the image (promoted by the insurance companies) that they guarantee a fixed rate of return. This usually is not the case. Interest can vary from year to year depending on how well the insurance company's investments do. When there is a guaranteed fixed rate of return, it's usually for a limited time, typically not more than a year. You can frequently spot such a "fixed annuity" because the promised rate of return is unusually high, significantly higher than the current market rate. After that, the insurance company can pay whatever it wants (down to a minimum if the policy has a minimum).

Avoid fixed annuities. Here's why:

- *Lack of safety.* A fixed annuity is a loan by you to an insurance company. The insurance company mixes your money into its own general accounts. I don't want to loan them anything because many are struggling financially, and neither should you. In today's climate of floundering insurance companies, I'd hate to try to guess which ones will be left standing 10, 20, or 30 years from now. You don't need this risk, and there's no reason you should take it. Because of investors' concerns with safety, insurance companies have tried to camouflage the product, calling it a "special interest account," "guaranteed account," and even the non sequitur "variable-rate fixed annuity." Don't be fooled.

- *No bulletproofing.* They can't be used to bulletproof your portfolio because the insurance company chooses the investments. Inflation can turn your fixed annuity into a near worthless piece of paper by the time it starts paying out.
- *Bad fit.* They do not fit into our asset allocation model (described in detail in Chapter 15).
- *No control.* Because your money is combined with the insurance company's general accounts, the insurance company decides how it's invested. You have no control, yet you are counting on this money to provide financial security during your retirement years. Annuities are too important to your financial well-being for you to give up all control to an insurance-company bureaucracy.
- *Draconian penalties.* All annuities carry their fair share of penalties. None are worse than those of fixed annuities. I've seen some that have 20 percent penalties if you withdraw any or all of your money within the first 10 years. Others start with a 20 percent early withdrawal penalty that declines 1 percent for *20 years.* That's crazy. You may intend to keep your money in the annuity for 20 years, but you need the flexibility to withdraw it earlier if need be and without getting hit for a big loss years after you opened the account. I've seen penalties on fixed annuities two to four times those found on variable ones.

For these reasons, avoid fixed annuities.

However, there is one exception in which using a fixed annuity makes sense. In a pension plan or a taxed-sheltered annuity, if a fixed annuity is your only choice, then use it. Using a fixed annuity is better than not using a pension plan at all. Be sure to keep watching the rating of your insurance company. If it falls below an acceptable level, your best bet is to leave your money there so you don't incur any withdrawal penalties, but stop contributing.

Variable Annuities

Variable annuities, as we discussed before, are variable in every sense. They are annuities that make no guarantees. They don't guarantee you'll get back your principal nor earn any particular rate of return. View them as essentially tax-deferred mutual funds—tax-deferred investment vehicles where you can make or lose money. But don't worry. The ones I recommend are generally low risk. As long as you pick well-run annuities that put their money in investments you are comfortable with, the risk level of a variable annuity will match your personality. These annuities have a number of benefits, including the opportunity for you to make good money safely while bulletproofing your portfolio and enjoying the power of compounding that comes from tax deferral. With variable annuities, you decide where your money goes (limited, of course, to the alternatives offered by the issuing company). Your payout depends on how well your investments do during the life of the annuity.

The investment choices available with a variable annuity are nearly as diverse as with mutual funds. In fact, many mutual fund companies offer annuities (through insurance companies) that are typically much like the companies' mutual funds. They are different only in that the annuities typically started later than the fund and therefore have some different investments, even if their investment philosophy is the same as the fund's.

Some of the benefits of variable annuities are the following:

- *Safety.* If your insurance company crashes, your financial future doesn't. Unlike fixed annuities, variable annuities put investors' money in accounts separate from the insurance company's general funds. No matter what happens to your insurance company, your money is safe. Today, especially, that's important.
- *Bulletproofing.* Because you can choose from a wide variety of investments, it's possible to use variable annuities to protect against severe recession or depression and runaway inflation. For example, Franklin annuities, issued by North American Life & Casualty, offers funds that invest in precious metals securities, real estate securities, U.S. government securities, foreign government and corporate securities, utility stocks, as well as zero coupon bonds (strips). Nearly complete bulletproofing is possible here.
- *Encourage long-term investing.* We've discussed throughout this book the desirability of using the buy-and-hold investment strategy. Admittedly, sticking to it can be hard. The market drops, we panic, so we sell. Or we worry about

fluctuations and trade a lot. All annuities carry significant penalties for early withdrawals—imposed by both the insurance company and the government. This gives investors a strong motivation to stay in an annuity for the long term. I call this a blessing in disguise. You want to hold onto your investments, and annuities encourage you to.

- *Control.* A company offering a wide range of annuities provides you with a lot of control over your investments. But the company must offer two things for this to work for you. First, you need a company that offers a wide variety of investments, and second, when need be, you have to be able to exercise control freely by switching your investments between the funds. If you pick the right annuity company that offers a broad product line, and you judiciously move your money around when you need to (to maintain balance in your portfolio), you've got just about all the control you need. Moving money around inside an annuity is just like moving money among various mutual funds to balance your portfolio, which I discussed before. If your portfolio doesn't need balancing, you probably shouldn't be moving in and out of annuities—just sit and hold.

Contributions

To get started with an annuity requires a minimum contribution, typically between $1,000 and $5,000. American Fund's annuity has a starting minimum of $1,500; Franklin's is $5,000. After that, you can pay in at any time you wish. The minimum amount of later contributions varies. For instance, Franklin's minimum is $2,000, whereas American Legacy's is only $25.

As with mutual funds, you can transfer your money among the family of funds offered. This is typically free and done without tax penalty. Franklin allows 12 such transfers a year free of sales charges and transfer fees. More transfers than that means you have to pay. You would transfer your money in order to maintain balance among your investments. If your international-stock annuity does particularly well and now represents a higher percentage of your portfolio than you want (Chapter 15 tells you what the percentages are for each type of investment), then you would sell some of your shares in the international-stock annuity and spread the money between the other annuities.

Choosing an annuity is much like picking a mutual fund. You want to study the management, its investment philosophy, and its track record. The easiest way is to look at the track record of the annuity's comparable mutual fund. Yes, just as with computers and hit movies, annuities sport clones. Many mutual fund firms have their regular funds and then funds cloaked within annuities. (These mutual fund firms work with insurance companies.) American Funds calls their annuity funds American Legacy II; Templeton Funds calls theirs Templeton Investment Plus Annuities. The investments and philosophy of the mutual fund and annuity fund are not identical, but they're frequently similar.

Why not just look at the track record of the annuity? Because few variable annuities have been around long enough to have long-term track records. The 1950s saw the first issues of variable annuities (fixed annuities date back to 1812), but it was the Tax Reform Act of 1986 that really made these products popular. That's not very long ago, so you use as a form of proxy the long track record of the mutual fund of which the annuity is a copy.

To learn which "mother" a specific annuity has sprung from, just ask. The mutual fund firm will tell you the annuity's mutual fund proxy. Then you evaluate the original fund as you would any other mutual fund, remembering the criteria of Chapter 8.

Miami-based Variable Annuity Research & Data Service (VARDS) is a research firm and publisher that follows 85 annuity companies responsible for 97 percent of the assets now in annuities, according to the company. VARDS publishes monthly and quarterly reports that track rates of return and other information. For more information, call (305) 252-4600.

With New York-based Financial Services Week (FSW), VARDS publishes the semiannual VARDS/FSW National Variable Annuity Almanac for $49.95. It includes profiles of several dozen annuities. Unfortunately, they're listed by insurance company, so you need to know which insurance company your investment advisor is using. For instance, American Funds, whose investment advisory arm is called Capital Research and Management Company, uses Lincoln National Life Insurance Company in Fort Wayne, Indiana. To learn about American Funds' annuities, you have to look under Lincoln National. Each profile includes such information as the minimum premium you can deposit, sales charges, early withdrawal penalties, annual charges, the availability of dollar-cost averaging, the ratings of four of the five major ratings services (unfortunately, the one missing is Weiss), rates of return for periods up to five years, and other information. To order the almanac, call (212) 227-1200. VARDS does not sell annuities; it makes its money through the sale of information and publications.

What to Invest in

One of the beautiful aspects of variable annuities, providing you are with a company that offers a wide range of investment options to choose from, is the ability to use them to create a balanced portfolio, including bulletproofing, without current taxation. As I noted earlier, some variable annuities have such varied funds as precious metals, real estate, Treasuries, and zero coupon bonds.

We've talked before about what to invest in and how to keep your portfolio balanced. Working with an annuity is like working with conventional investments. Chapter 15 provides sample portfolios including tax-deferred ones that use annuities. There you can find specific annuities to invest in.

When to Use Annuities

Just to recap, you use annuities most anytime you have the opportunity, recognizing that getting out of them is not as easy as other investments, such as mutual funds. In our sequence of investing model, the ideal is investments that offer both tax deductions and tax deferrals. Annuities fit in the second level, because they offer only tax deferrals. This is still better than investments that offer neither tax deductions nor tax deferrals, such as mutual funds.

Annuities work wonderfully for those who are retired. They can also work well for those who live off their investments, as we'll see in the next section.

Cut Your Taxes 78 Percent—That's No Exaggeration!

Annuities can be real tax savers. Here's an actual example using a technique I call a *modified split annuity strategy* (don't let the name scare you), which gives you steady income while cutting your taxes to the bone. It's ideal for the retired individual or couple living off their investments and therefore has wide application to anyone worried about financing their retirement— most everyone!

The strategy works like this:
You have X amount of dollars. Your goals include

- Maintain as much principal as possible while enjoying the income you need.
- Make sure you don't outlive your income.
- Minimize your taxes so as to maximize your after-tax income.

My strategy allows you to achieve these goals simultaneously. You only need to put your money into two types of investment vehicles.

1. Put part of your funds in an annuity, and let them accumulate tax deferred, which maximizes the principal.
2. Put the balance of your funds into a conventional, non-tax-deferred investment and withdraw funds at a rate to provide the income you need.

Structured in a certain way, the funds in the annuity will grow to be equal to the original total at precisely the same time as the funds in the conventional investment run out. The reason this strategy dramatically cuts your taxes is that most of the money you withdraw from the conventional investment is principal, and you don't pay taxes on principal, only on interest.

Let me illustrate with an example. Assume you're 65 years old. You want your investments to generate $9,000 a year in income for as long as you live; you are in the 35 percent tax bracket and have $100,000 to invest.

With the modified split-annuity strategy, you put 35 percent of your money into a conventional bond fund and 65 percent into an annuity. How you divide this up depends on your needs. I typically use this strategy for a five-year period. So when I set this up for a client, we leave enough money outside the annuity to generate the amount of income needed. The remainder goes into the annuity. I'll compare this strategy to one that puts all your money into a taxable vehicle, such as a conventional bond fund.

Conventional strategy: Put $100,000 into a bond fund. It pays $9,000 (9 percent) a year in interest.

All the income is taxable. Assuming a 35 percent tax rate, the tax liability is $3,150, leaving you with an after-tax income of $5,850. This never varies from year to year (assuming the interest and tax rates remain the same). At the end of the five years, you've got your $100,000 and you generated $29,250 in after-tax income.

Modified split-annuity strategy: Put $35,006.86 (35 percent of $100,000) into a bond fund and $64,993.14 (65 percent) into an annuity.

If you put $35,006.86 in a bond fund that pays 9 percent and take out $9,000 per year (the same income as with the conventional strategy), at the end of five years you've got nothing left. I picked the number $35,006.86 because it allows you to take out $9,000 a year income and at the end of five years have nothing. It's like calculating the principal and interest payments on a mortgage. Any amount of money and number of years can be analyzed in the same way using a financial calculator.

The remaining $64,993.14 is put in an annuity (perhaps an annuity's bond fund) that also grows at 9 percent a year. At the end of five years, this annuity, which enjoys the power of tax-deferred compounding, grows to $100,000.

After five years, with *both* strategies, you have

- $100,000 in assets.
- You've received $9,000 a year in income.

The difference is that all the income generated from the bond ($9,000 a year) is taxable. If you pay 35 percent total for federal, state, and local taxes, you're left with $5,850 in annual income.

With the annuity strategy, part of the $9,000 is a return of the principal you put in. The rest is interest. You only pay taxes on the interest earned. In the first year, $3,150 is taxable, $5,850 is not. Assuming the same 35 percent tax rate, your total tax bill the first year is $1,102.50 (35 percent of $3,150), leaving you with $7,897.50 after taxes. This compares with after-tax income of $5,850 by using a non–tax-deferred vehicle like a conventional bond fund. With my strategy, your disposable income the first year is *35 percent greater* than with the traditional approach.

And it gets better. Each year, more and more of the $9,000 you take out is principal, so less and less is taxable interest. Your tax bite gets smaller each year. In the first year, your taxes are $1,102.50. In the fifth, they will be down to only $284. In that year, your spendable income will be $8,716, while it will remain at $5,850 using the conventional approach with a certificate of deposit. In that last year, your spendable income will be *49 percent higher* than with the conventional approach. During the five years of the plan, you've cut your tax bill a whopping 78 percent with the modified split-annuity strategy!

The graph in Figure 3 uses these numbers to show just how much money in taxes is saved with this strategy.

I used this strategy with one of my clients and had an even more dramatic effect than with the above example. The year before I put her into a split-annuity strategy, she paid a total of $46,250 in income taxes. The next year, with the strategy in place, her income the same, and her principal growing, her tax liability was $5,000. She cut her taxes *89 percent*.

▶ FIGURE 3

Tax Advantages of Modified Split Annuity Strategy.

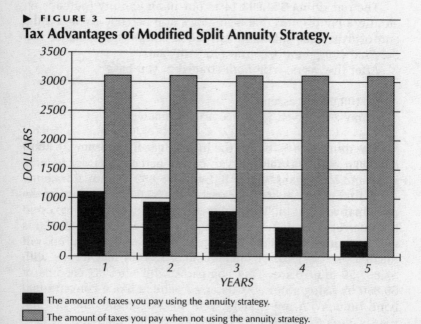

The amount of taxes you pay using the annuity strategy.

The amount of taxes you pay when not using the annuity strategy.

Depending on your situation, there may be a perfect balance between the amount spent generating income and the amount to which the annuity rises, or there may not. My experience says that most people have income needs that are small enough so they end up with more money at the end of this strategy than they started with.

Easy to do and highly effective, this is a strategy everyone should consider.

How to Get Out

When you buy a variable annuity, what you're really buying is units (like shares) of the variable annuity taken as a whole. The more money invested, the more units you receive. The payout at maturity is a fixed percentage of the units' value. Payouts can keep up with inflation if the value of the units increases. The value of the units in turn depends on the assets in the annuity. If it's a stock annuity and the prices of the stocks the annuity is invested in go up, the value of the units increases. The reverse holds, too. This is just like a mutual fund.

Assume the yield is 10 percent, you invest $100,000, and a unit when you first invest is worth $10. You receive 10,000 units ($100,000 ÷ $10) and the payout per unit is $1 a year (10 percent of $10). The first year you receive $10,000 (10,000 units × $1).

Suppose the following year was good for the annuity's investments and the value of the units increased to $12.50. You still have 10,000 units and the payout rate is still 10 percent, but you now get $1.25 (10 percent of $12.50) for a total of $12,500. This is how your payout increases with an annuity and how it helps you keep up with inflation.

The withdrawal terms vary with the annuity. You determine what you want, and likely, there's a product to fit your needs. Among the most common options are the following:

Life annuity. Beginning on a set date, these annuities provide a monthly payout until you die. If you die five months after you started collecting, for instance, you only receive five months' worth of payments. Because it stops paying when you die, it generally provides the highest monthly payout. These are available *only* as fixed annuities. You should avoid life annuities unless you have no one you wish to leave your money to.

Life income with guaranteed payments. If you want an income for your entire life (starting at a predetermined date), while guaranteeing your heirs get something if you die prematurely, this option could be for you. It's like the life annuity option, only with a guarantee payout period, usually for 10 or 20 years. Die two years into a 10-year payout period annuity and your heirs collect the eight remaining years of the payout period. This being less risky than the life annuity option, the monthly payments are less.

Joint and survivor. This flavor of annuity covers you and someone else you appoint (usually your spouse) and keeps paying until both die. Since two people are more likely to collect for longer than one, payouts for this type are less than with life and life income with guaranteed payments annuities.

Lump sum. You can get an annuity that pays you a lump sum on a certain date. You are then free to use the proceeds as you wish. Be aware that if you take out your money in a lump sum, the IRS might slug you with a heavy tax hit. Spreading your withdrawals over time could place you in a lower tax bracket than taking your money out all at once.

Many variations on these themes exist. Instead of a guaranteed payout period, for instance, you may get an annuity that pays a flat sum upon your death. In a joint-and-survivor arrangement, the surviving person might only get two-thirds the monthly payment received when both beneficiaries were alive. Like most insurance instruments, annuity types are limited only by the creativity of their issuers.

Which Annuities to Invest in

Three firms that have excellent mutual funds are also noted for annuities. I recommend you set up an annuity with any of these.

American Funds
300 South Hope Street
Los Angeles, CA 90071
(800) 421-0180

American Legacy II International Fund

Date founded: 5/1/90
Average annual total return 5/1/90 to 12/31/91: −1.76%
Approximate annual turnover rate: 8.2%
Beta: n/a
Investments in portfolio: Domestic and foreign stocks.
Minimum initial investment: $1,500
Minimum subsequent investment: $25
Investment objective: Seeks long-term growth of capital by investing primarily in securities of issuers located outside the United States.
Comments: Excellent fund for asset allocation due to its good diversification between countries. It keeps a good balance of foreign stocks, which allows us to use it for foreign stocks in our asset allocation model.

American Legacy II Growth Fund

Date founded: 2/8/84
Average annual total return 2/8/84 to 12/31/91: 14.82%
Approximate annual turnover rate: 9.8%
Beta: n/a
Investments in portfolio: Domestic stocks.
Minimum initial investment: $1,500
Minimum subsequent investment: $25
Investment objective: Seeks growth of capital.
Comments: Well diversified in the U.S. market. It works well in the U.S. as part of our asset allocation portfolio.

Franklin Valuemark
777 Mariners Island Boulevard
San Mateo, CA 94404
(800) 342-3863

Franklin Valuemark II Zero Coupon Fund Maturing 2010

Date founded: 3/14/89
Average annual total return from 3/14/89 to 12/31/91: 27.22%
Approximate annual turnover rate: 180%
Beta: n/a
Investments in portfolio: Treasury strips.
Minimum initial investment: $5,000
Minimum subsequent investment: $500
Investment objective: Conservative alternative to fixed-income securities.
Comments: Excellent substitute for Treasury bonds in the medium-risk asset allocation model because they have one maturity date and investments don't change.

Franklin Valuemark II Real Estate Securities Fund

Date founded: 1/24/89
Average annual total return from 1/24/89 to 12/31/91: 24.84%
Approximate annual turnover rate: 6%
Beta: n/a
Investments in portfolio: Real estate investment trusts.
Minimum initial investment: $5,000
Minimum subsequent investment: $500
Investment objective: Capital appreciation.
Comments: Excellent asset allocation vehicle for the real estate part of your portfolio. Well diversified between all real estate markets.

Franklin Valuemark II Precious Metals Fund

Date founded: 1/24/89
Average annual total return from 1/24/89 to 12/31/91: 8.9%
Approximate annual turnover rate: 10%
Investments in portfolio: Domestic and foreign mining stocks.
Minimum initial investment: $5,000
Minimum subsequent investment: $500
Investment objective: Capital appreciation.
Comments: Good precious metals fund with low turnover rate. It is well diversified between various countries. It fits well in our high-risk portfolio.

Templeton Funds
700 Central Avenue
St. Petersburg, FL 33733
(800) 237-0738

Templeton Investment Plus Bond Fund

Date founded: 8/88
Average annual total return from 8/88 to 4/30/92: 7.7%
Approximate annual turnover rate: n/a
Investments in portfolio: Foreign and domestic corporate and
    government bonds.
Minimum initial investment: $1,000
Minimum subsequent investment: $25
Investment objective: Seeks high current income.
Comments: Provides diversification between all markets using
    both government and corporate bonds.

Our Five Model Families

FAMILY 1: A COUPLE SAVING FOR THEIR RETIREMENT
    For Jackie and Bob, we'll use the following: 24 percent of their
$25,000 ($6,000) goes into American Legacy's II International
Fund, which is international stocks. Our asset allocation model
calls for 10 percent in U.S. stocks so we'll put $2,500 into Ameri-
can Legacy II Growth Fund. These can both be purchased inside
American Legacy II. The model calls for 7 percent, which comes
to $1,750. For the international bond portion of the portfolio,
we'll use Templeton Investment Plus Bond Fund and invest 20
percent ($5,000). This completes this couple's portfolio.

PORTFOLIO	
30-year Treasury bonds	$2,500
Cash and cash equivalents	1,000
Franklin Valuemark II Real Estate Securities Fund	3,250
Franklin Valuemark II Precious Metals Fund	3,000
American Legacy II International Fund	**6,000**
American Legacy II Growth Fund	**2,500**
Templeton Investment Plus Bond Fund	**5,000**
Total	$25,000

FAMILY 2: A SINGLE MOTHER SAVING FOR HER CHILDREN'S COLLEGE TUITION

Marilyn's portfolio is complete. She does not use annuities.

FAMILY 3: A COUPLE SAVING FOR THEIR FIRST HOME

The Santangelos' portfolio is complete. They do not use annuities.

FAMILY 4: A COUPLE WANTING TO MINIMIZE THEIR TAXES

Because minimizing taxes is the goal, annuities play the most important role in the Jordans' investments. For the U.S. and international stock portions of their portfolio, we use American Legacy II and for international bonds, Templeton Investment Plus Bond Fund.

PORTFOLIO	
Franklin Valuemark II Zero Coupon Fund Maturing 2010	$120,000
American Funds U.S. Treasury Money Fund of America	84,000
Franklin Valuemark II Real Estate Securities Fund	156,000
Franklin Valuemark II Precious Metals Fund	144,000
Pioneer Three	84,000
American Legacy II Growth Fund	**120,000**
American Legacy II International Fund	**288,000**
Templeton Investment Plus Bond Fund	**240,000**
Total	$1,200,000

FAMILY 5: A RETIRED COUPLE

With the Moriartys, we'll use the split annuity strategy discussed in this chapter, where one portion of their portfolio is subject to taxes and the other accumulates tax free. The goal is to provide $35,000 a year in income for five years, with investments yielding 9.5 percent (low risk). To achieve this level of income with this yield, they need to set aside $134,000. They want to be extra conservative so they will put the $134,000 into the American Funds' U.S. Treasury Money Market Fund of America. This will cost them a bit more in taxes compared with an annuity but makes them feel comfortable. We put 18 percent into international bonds found in Templeton Investment Plus Bond Fund ($90,000). This completes their portfolio.

PORTFOLIO

Cash and cash equivalents	$175,000
30-year Treasury bonds	85,000
Franklin Valuemark II Real Estate Securities Fund	100,000
Gold bullion coins	50,000
Templeton Investment Plus Bond Fund	**90,000**
Total	$500,000

─────────── H I G H L I G H T S ───────────

Annuities are mutual funds with an insurance component that provides tax benefits.

Annuities are a better investment than mutual funds for many investors.

Annuities are used primarily for retirement planning and should be considered only as a long-term investment.

Use *only* variable annuities; their payouts vary with how well the annuities perform.

Do not use fixed annuities.

Annuities can cut your taxes dramatically.

10

HARD ASSETS
Tangibles That Provide Real Protection

Up to now, I've talked about investment instruments that come largely from the brains of financial artists and Wall Street wizards, such as mutual funds, annuities, stocks, and bonds—abstract stuff, concepts, paper. In this chapter I'm going to discuss tangibles that you can put in your pocket, stand on, hold, and admire. These are called *hard assets.*

Everything from baseball cards and beer cans to gold and diamonds comes under the hard-asset label. In this chapter, I'll touch on the most important of the hard assets. First, let's discuss their use in financial planning.

The Uses of Hard Assets

Hard assets, besides being tangible, have another even more important common characteristic—the predictable way their value changes under different economic conditions. That's why I place them all in one chapter. Their use in financial planning in general and bulletproofing in particular is the same, whether it's gold or real estate or Chinese porcelain that you're buying.

Hard assets are inflation hedges, which merely means that they protect your financial future when prices in general are rising sharply, namely, in times of high inflation. In Chapter 4 on inflation bulletproofing, I estimated how these assets respond to different rates of inflation. These numbers are worth repeating:

Inflation rate of 10 percent: Inflation-protection investments increase 13 percent.

Inflation rate of 20 percent: Inflation-protection investments increase 30 percent.

Inflation rate of 100 percent: Inflation-protection investments increase 200 percent.

Inflation hedges come to your rescue the worse the economy gets. The higher the inflation rate, the more investors find themselves in hotter and hotter water, watching the real value of their money dramatically dropping. So investors rush to move their money into hard assets. The beauty of inflation hedges like hard assets is that as everything else is falling apart, these increase their value *in real terms* because of this rush.

This might seem like magic, but behind it is an easily understood logic. There's a flight of investors' money to hard assets when inflation skyrockets, and that puts greater and greater upward pressure on the prices of those assets, which, after all, come in limited quantities. There's only so much desirable real estate in a given area, so much gold mined in a year. During inflationary times, desirable, productive investment opportunities are hard to find. CDs and money market funds get decimated because their profit is in their interest rates. Sure, the interest rates on bonds and CDs rise during times like these, but usually not as fast as inflation is eating away at that rise. Besides, interest is merely money, and it's money that rapidly loses value in inflationary times. Bond prices fall because interest rates rise. Stocks usually suffer because inflation hurts corporate profits.

What's left? Hard assets. The hotter the inflation rate, the fewer the options for investors. They flee to hard assets, driving up prices at ever-increasing rates. That's why the prices of hard assets outpace the inflation rate, and the higher the inflation rate, the more they produce profits in real inflation-adjusted terms.

Hard Assets and Bulletproofing

Hard assets are essential to bulletproofing, which protects against catastrophe, maximizes returns, and minimizes waste. Hard assets address two of these: They protect against the catastrophe of runaway inflation, and they maximize returns because they perform so well when prices spiral.

They also rank high in our sequence of investing approach, providing tax-deferral protection. Capital gains taxes (taxes paid on an asset's increase in value) are not paid until the asset is sold, so that, as hard assets appreciate, taxes are deferred. Not until you sell hard assets does Uncle Sam get his cut. In fact, you may even get a tax deduction, as can be the case with real estate.

Inflation protection and tax-deferral are, then, two very good reasons to put hard assets in your portfolio. Let's look at the major types of hard assets.

Real Estate

Most Americans own their home, making them real estate owners. Few, though, are real estate investors. When I talk about real estate, I'm referring only to real estate bought for investment purposes. Financial planners call your primary residence "an asset for personal use" rather than an investment because you have to live somewhere, and if you sold it, you'd probably use the money simply to buy another house, not freely applying it to other investments.

Real estate bought for investment purposes is something you can easily buy and sell, using the profits for whatever you want. When you sell stock there's nothing to say you must immediately buy more stock. Likewise, there's nothing to say you have to buy more investment real estate immediately after you sell your present investment real estate. That's not true with one's home.

More than any other popular investment, real estate owns a piece of our psyche. Such phrases as "going back to the land," "live off the fat of the land," and "land of our dreams" all attest to the hold land has on many of us. The American dream is largely a nice house in a nice community, and home ownership is the ultimate financial goal for many. In some cultures, land has mystical qualities, and no individuals own it. It is too important for that. The land is owned collectively or by a higher order.

The emotional aspect of real estate ownership is important because it can color our judgment. The property may not make sense economically, but if we like it for emotional reasons or feel we are not successful unless we own property, we may make poor investment choices. Before buying any real estate, stand back and analyze it purely for its economics. You do this with mutual funds and insurance products. Do it with real estate! There have been many poor investments because sentiment took precedence over business considerations.

Investing in real estate can take several forms.

Direct Ownership

Direct ownership is when you own the real estate itself, holding title to it. It could be income generating: an office building or other commercial property, a farm, a house you rent out, or an apartment house. Or, it could be non-income producing: a vacant lot or a house you use as a second home until its value appreciates.

Direct ownership of real estate is a touchy subject. It can be a great or horrible investment. For some, it is the best investment—of any kind—they can make. Many of the greatest fortunes in the history of this country have come from real estate. For others, it can be their worst investment. I know two men, a man and his son-in-law, who made their money as a construction contractor and manufacturer, respectively. After doing quite well, each decided independently to invest their wealth in direct ownership of real estate, specifically apartment houses. Both men lost practically their entire savings because they didn't know the real estate management business. They were good at what they did. What they weren't good at was managing real estate.

That's the key: management. If you want to manage real estate and are good at it, direct ownership can produce spectacular results. If you don't like real estate management and aren't good at it, bet on losing much or all of your investment, and that doesn't take into account lost sleep. You can't be a passive investor when you own real estate directly. It requires your active involvement.

I'm a licensed real estate broker and, as I've mentioned before, made most of my money through the direct ownership of real estate (condos in the ski resort community of Park City, Utah). Real estate ownership and management is so complex that many books have been written about it. Space prevents going into the details here, but let me offer a key piece of advice many in the industry know and that I can tell you from my own experience is true: *In real estate, you make money when you buy, not when you sell.*

This means your chances for making money in real estate are best when you are a smart buyer. If the market's weak, most real estate owners know to hold (often they have no choice because there are no buyers). Eventually, prices rise, buyers enter the market, and the owners are able to sell. So, being a smart seller is not that hard.

Being a savvy buyer is much more difficult. The best time to buy is when everyone else thinks it's the best time to sell. Going against the conventional wisdom is a struggle for most people, which is why most who invest in real estate have limited success at best.

I talked earlier about devastation dividends. These come when the price of an asset is getting clobbered at a time the underlying value of the asset is strong as happens frequently with stocks. A company is doing well, but during one quarter, its performance hits a snag. The earnings are reported, the market is disappointed, shareholders panic and sell, and the price plummets. That's when the smart investors walk in and pick up the stock cheap. These investors enjoy a devastation dividend—extra profit because of the temporarily depressed stock price.

FAST FACT: Here's a guideline for deciding when a piece of real estate is sufficiently devastated so that you run little risk of losing money and have great opportunities of making money: It is time to buy a property when its price is less than the cost of replacing the building with the land thrown in free. Remember, though, that this is not the only criteria for evaluating whether a specific house, commercial space, or rental property is a good investment!

Real estate is another area where devastation dividends happen frequently. A market goes sour, people scramble to get out, and prices take a free-fall. I've seen it happen time and again. I've made millions in such situations.

I bought several Park City condos for $45,000 apiece; their replacement costs were about $75,000. The buildings were bought at a big discount; the land was free. I sold them for $140,000 each a few years later.

The frequency with which the value of real estate drops into the devastation-dividend range is surprisingly high. As I write this book in May 1992, the *Wall Street Journal* reports that commercial real estate in New York and other cities has dropped as much as 50 percent in value in just the past two years. This means devastation dividends are right now possible in these real estate markets. You must be receptive to them and be willing to act when they appear.

Another recommendation: invest only near your home. You know this market best, and any management problems can be easily handled. If real estate in your area is booming, it may not be the time to buy. You don't have to buy only when real estate offers devastation dividends (though you won't maximize your profits unless you do), but recognize that real estate is cyclical. If the boom's been going for several years, buy other hard assets. A market just getting on a roll, though, could be ripe for picking. However, individual pieces of property are hard to fit into a portfolio based on an asset allocation strategy. That's because of the difficulty in diversifying with individual properties—the cost of which would soon dominate any portfolio if you tried to spread risk by buying different kinds of real estate in varying markets. Real estate investment trusts (REITs) and real estate limited partnerships (RELPs) make it much easier to diversify.

Real Estate Investment Trusts

Think of REITs as mutual funds that specialize in real estate. Typically, the managers invest their pooled funds in dozens of real estate opportunities, just as a mutual fund has its investments in dozens of companies. REITs are corporations. When you buy an interest in one, you become a shareholder, just as if you owned stock in a publicly traded company like IBM. They enjoy special tax status, though. Provided they pay out at least 95 percent of the net income to shareholders each year (95 percent of all the money they make after expenses), there's no corporate income taxes on that profit before it's paid out. Of course, you, the shareholder, do have to pay income taxes on the payouts.

REITs come in three types:

1. *Equity REITs.* This is the mutual fund equivalent of the direct real estate investor. Equity trusts buy property and rent it to others. They invest in office buildings, shopping centers, apartments, and the like. At least 75 percent of their holdings are equity interests.
2. *Mortgage REITs.* These invest in commercial-property mortgages. Their function is to finance real estate development, and so they serve as lenders to developers receiving back interest and principal payments just like a bank after issuing a mortgage. At least 75 percent of their holdings are mortgages.
3. *Hybrids.* These have both direct ownership and investments in mortgages.

There are more than 200 REITs in existence. Of these, almost two-thirds are equity. The rest are about evenly divided between mortgage and hybrid. Some are self-liquidating and others have perpetual life. Perpetual life REITs buy and sell and theoretically go on forever. Self-liquidating ones, sometimes called *finite REITs* (Trammell Crow, the big Texas-based developer, has some), have predetermined life spans of between 5 and 35 years, with 8 to 10 years being the most popular. All properties are held until the trust is liquidated, at which point everything is sold and the proceeds of the sale distributed to the shareholders. These REITs mimic bonds. Early on, they trade at values dependent on their rates of return. But the closer to the liquidation date, the more their share value depends on their liquidation value. Perpetual REITs far out number self-liquidating ones.

One other important difference: Equity REITs enjoy unlimited upside potential, whereas mortgage REITs do not. If the value of an equity trust's properties goes sky high, the trust fully benefits. A mortgage trust only holds fixed-rate obligations, representing the fixed interest rate the trust charges the developer on principal lent him. The property's owner benefits if the property's price increases because of inflation or increased demand, but the mortgage holder has only a loan paying the same interest rate no matter how much the property appreciates.

Both types of trusts can suffer dramatically if the real estate market drops. In 1990, REITs as a group fell 17.2 percent in value.[29] Equity REITs suffer because the value of their holdings drops. Mortgage REITs go down because in bad economic times, when leasing or selling property is tough, owners of real estate default on their mortgages. They don't pay their mortgage to the REIT, which can't pay it out to you.

By the way, hybrids can be the most dicey of the REITs. Some hybrids became hybrids against their will, so to speak. They were mortgage REITs and became property owners and managers when the mortgage holders defaulted.

The volatility of REIT prices varies with the trust's leverage, that is, how much of its assets it has lent as mortgages. The more leverage (money borrowed), the more volatile. The more volatile, the more inflation protection. At the time of this writing, the debt-to-equity ratio of REITs averaged about 2 to 1. I would say that a 3-to-1 debt-to-equity ratio or more is a highly leveraged REIT.

My recommendation on REITs: Use *only* equity REITs if you are buying directly into a single REIT. Even better than individual REITs is to invest in good REIT mutual funds, which are simply mutual funds holding a wide range of REITs as investments. If you want more information on individual REITs, including tips on how to analyze them, please see the appendix at the end of this chapter. For most investors, a REIT mutual fund is the way to go. The two REIT funds I recommend, run by Franklin and Templeton, are discussed in Chapter 8.

Real Estate Limited Partnerships

As with many securities, you can buy RELPs either when they're first issued, called the *primary market*, or at any time after that (the *secondary market*) as people who bought at the issuance resell their shares. You should only buy RELPs in the secondary market, after their initial public offering, for then they can be dynamite investments.

To understand a RELP, consider that when two people get together and start a business and don't incorporate, they have a partnership. Many professional practices, such as law firms, are partnerships. The income and losses of a partnership pass down to the partners without tax liability. That's their advantage over a corporation, since corporations must first pay taxes on their income before paying dividends to shareholders. A partnerships' disadvantage is their unlimited liability. If sued, each and every partner is fully liable, no matter what percentage of the business the partner owns. With a corporation, there's limited liability in that shareholders can only lose what they've invested.

Limited partnerships, in which a sponsor or general partner has unlimited liability and all other partners have liability limited up to the value of their investments, have the best of both partnerships and corporations. Profits and losses go directly to the partners, but liability is limited to the amount invested. A $5,000 investment in a RELP can produce no more than a $5,000 loss.

A sponsoring organization, which, hopefully, has management experience in the area in which the partnership will invest, organizes a limited partnership. Initially, it sells a fixed number of shares at a fixed price to investors who want to put their money in the assets the sponsor chooses. With a RELP, that's real estate. (There are limited partnerships that invest in many different kinds of assets, from oil to cattle, but I like only RELPs and only those in the secondary market.) The person or organization who puts the deal together (the general partner) and runs the RELP collects fees for its responsibilities, which include collecting the money, investing it and managing the properties until the partnership is dissolved.

The trouble with RELPs when first issued lies largely with the general partner. I consider RELPs a license to steal for the general partner, whose up-front fees frequently are 20 percent of the money collected and can be more. The general partner also gets fees each year as compensation for his or her management efforts (as much as 10 percent of the cash flow—not of the initial investment) and may even get a hefty chunk of the profits (assuming there are any) when the properties are sold and the monies distributed to the limited partners. So you, the limited partner, buying in at the initial offering for $5,000, may spend $1,000 just to get in, plus several hundred dollars more for the first year for fees, leaving you less than $4,000 in real investment.

Fees aren't the only problem with RELPs. They're highly illiquid. Because I recommend you buy and hold, this isn't necessarily a major problem. Yet it can become one, because these partnerships often perform so poorly you want to cut your losses by getting out early, but you can't.

Further, there's frequently self-dealing between the general partners (there can be more than one), in which they trade properties back and forth between different RELPs, taking fees (like a broker's commission for buying and selling stock) for their efforts. It's not uncommon for an organization to be the general partner of two or more RELPs, buying and trading between them for its own benefit, in that it reaps a fee from both RELPs for a single transaction.

If you buy into a RELP at its initial offering, you don't know what it will invest in. (This also applies to newly issued REITs.) The general partner may make good investments or poor ones, but you won't know until the RELP is well established and the investments are made, which may take several years. General partners at times make poor investments because they're in a hurry. The faster they speed up the investment process, the quicker they get the fees the investments generate. Further, you don't know how well the general partner will manage the properties.

However, RELPs bought in the secondary market (once they have been sold to the public) are often excellent investments. Every stock was once an initial public offering. Immediately it began trading (some who bought originally want to sell their shares while others want to buy in), and this trading is always in the secondary market. The New York Stock Exchange is a secondary market except for those few stocks each year that come out as initial public offerings. RELPs trade on a secondary market, too, and, just like stocks and bonds, at prices different from the initial offering depending on market conditions.

Another aspect of RELPs is noteworthy: Like closed-end mutual funds, these often trade below their fair market value.

Here are criteria for choosing a RELP from the secondary market:

- It should provide you with good cash flow. At the time of this writing, this was 10 percent, up from 8 percent in the late 1980s/early 1990s. If you invest $10,000 in a RELP, a

10 percent cash flow means you'll get $1,000 as your share of the profits each year. The change was primarily due to the fall in prices of RELPs as the real estate market fell in many places around the country. Regulators didn't help. They made it more difficult for market makers (brokerage firms that specialize in RELPs and create markets for them by finding buyers and sellers) to develop and maintain markets, which pushed up returns. Just like a riskier company must offer a higher interest rate on its bonds to attract investors, RELPs must offer a higher return in a depressed market.

- If you are a low- to moderate-risk investor, buy nonleveraged RELPs, those that pay for their properties entirely in cash. As I noted earlier in the discussion on risk, the more leverage (or debt), the greater the risk. If you are a risk taker, you might want to invest in RELPs with lots of leverage. A highly leveraged RELP can be as much as 80 percent leveraged. It's like putting down 20 percent for your house and borrowing the rest. If the RELP has $20 million in assets, then an 80 percent-leveraged RELP will have $100 million worth of real estate in its portfolio, whereas a zero-leveraged one would have $20 million.

- Buy RELPs that sell for between 60 to 80 percent of their fair market value. If their assets are worth $100 million and they have 10,000 limited partnership units (the number the sponsor originally sold), then the fair market value of each unit is $10,000. To be in our desired range, the price of these units would be $6,000 to $8,000.

- Study the general partner's track record. Is this his or her first RELP? What kinds of returns have its limited partners received from cash disbursements and on a one-time basis when the RELPs have been liquidated?

- Don't pioneer. This means don't buy a RELP whose management is new to RELP investing. During the past couple of years, with apartment and commercial property taking a beating, some general partners have looked to other markets, such as retail, to create business for themselves. Others that focused on a specific geographic area are now investing nationally because their traditional market is devastated. Don't buy RELPs from general partners such as these until they've proven themselves in their new markets.

• Understand the investment risk that comes with RELPs. If the money the limited partners have invested in the RELPs is invested in fully tenanted properties, it's less risky than if invested in property still to be developed. The more leveraged, the more risky, too.

All RELPs have finite lives. They end at a specified time unlike a stock, which goes on in perpetuity. Typically, they are designed to last 7 to 10 years. Because of the poor real estate market in many areas in the early 1990s, some of the RELPs designed to dissolve within this time frame are still with us, waiting for the market to turn around before selling their assets.

Purchase RELPs (like REITs) through financial planners and stockbrokers. The cash flow is usually easily determined by asking the general partner, though it might be difficult to know the likelihood that the cash flow will continue at its present rate. The information on leverage is typically available from the RELP's annual report. The fair market value is more difficult, because it depends on a recent appraisal. The general partner probably has this information. You can contact the general partner directly or ask your financial planner or broker to do so. If he or she recommends a RELP, he or she should have all this information readily available. The *Stanger Report*, discussed below, reports appraisal values.

I'm not aware of anyone who rates RELPs. The most complete source of information about them probably comes from Charter Financial Publishing Corporation. It doesn't sell RELPs but publishes the monthly *Stanger Report*, which covers just about every aspect of the RELP market, including recent prices on the secondary market, the track records of about 800 RELPs in terms of their cash distributions and cumulative returns, and the appraised values of their assets, when available. The publication also rates the fee levels and risk of investment for new issues (RELPs first being offered to the public). A one-year subscription to the *Stanger Report* costs $447. If your financial planner or stockbroker does much investing in RELPs, he or she should have this publication available. To order, call (908) 389-3600.

Charter Financial also has a 900 telephone line. Investors and financial planners can call this line and talk to someone about specific RELPs. The cost is $5 per minute. The telephone number is (900) 786-9600.

For more information on Charter Financial and its products and services, contact

Charter Financial Publishing Corporation
179 Avenue at the Common
Strewsbury, NJ 07702
(908) 389-8700

Collectibles

Even more so than direct ownership of real estate, collectibles require active interest. For most people, collectibles are not a viable investment vehicle. The one exception is gold coins, which I'll discuss more fully next. Those willing to become immersed in a collectible, though, can enjoy enormous rewards. The financial profits can be huge. And so can the psychological ones. There's great satisfaction in learning about something, trading in it, meeting people with similar interests, and creating a collection of objects that may have beauty as well as value.

Three problems limit the usefulness of collectibles for most people:

1. Collectibles absolutely require you to know what you're doing. Whether it's prints or stamps or political campaign buttons or impressionist paintings, if you don't know what you're doing, those who do will eat you alive. The learning process can be expensive because of the mistakes you'll make. It can be time-consuming. It can be difficult. If you're willing to put up with all of these, collectibles can provide wonderful rewards.
2. Profits are hard to come by with collectibles. Unlike real estate, for example, you generally buy collectibles at retail and sell at wholesale. If you bought a print for $1,000 from a dealer and immediately turned around and sold it back, you'd probably get about $500. The wholesale price has to double just for you to break even. So even if you know what you're doing, it can sometimes be hard to make a buck.
3. Marketability can be a major problem. If you can't market the collectible—meaning you can't find a buyer—you're stuck. The collectibles market isn't like the New York

Stock Exchange, which has lots of buyers and sellers, as well as specialists who make sure there's a market for each stock. You may buy a collectible but, when you're ready to sell, find there's no one interested in buying it from you.

Although I encourage few of my clients to invest in collectibles, I know personally how much fun and how profitable they can be. I'm a collector of Maxfield Parrish prints. Parrish was an American illustrator and painter (1870–1966). During the 1930s, he was among the most popular artists of the time, primarily because his paintings were made into prints that were enormously well liked. I now have a few dozen of his prints. They're not particularly expensive, with many selling for a few hundred dollars apiece. But it takes some knowledge to collect them intelligently. It was a couple of years before I could quickly spot a quality Parrish print (done at the time of his greatest popularity) from a cheap one (done long after).

Effective collectors have this level of knowledge. Also, collectibles do not work well in our asset allocation model. If you find immersing yourself in a field is appealing, consider collectibles, but don't go into them until you've given it careful thought. Most investors, though, should steer clear. The only collectible we include in our asset allocation model is graded gold coins, which we discuss in the next section. For these, you don't need to be an expert—there's a ready market, the dealer markup is reasonable, and they fit into our model.

Gold

Gold has had an almost mystical hold on the imagination since early recorded history. It was possibly the first metal used by humans. Many have attributed magical powers to it, including some modern-day investors. Medieval alchemists took base metals such as lead and tried to turn them into gold. Gold stimulated the European exploration of the New World. Gold has been special to humans for millennium, and though it has lost some of its investment luster during the past decade or so, it still ranks as an important, valuable hedge against inflation.

Gold can be held in a variety of forms. Gold bars—bullion— is one way. Bullion is as convenient to an investor as a Corvette is to a family of eight. A Vet can ultimately get the entire family where it wants to go, but there are lots of inefficiencies. Bullion must be assayed (tested for weight purity) when bought and again when sold. This takes time and costs money. It must be stored. This is inconvenient and pricy. Not many people want bullion, so it's not very liquid. I never recommend that clients buy bullion, though bullion coins can be good investments.

Gold stocks are a possibility. They can be quite volatile, which is what you want for inflation protection. If a mining company breaks even when gold sells for $400, and gold is selling for $405 per ounce, its profits are $5 per ounce. But if gold's price moves up 2 percent to $415, the mining company's profits per ounce go to $15. That's a 200 percent increase. The reverse is also true, which is why gold mining companies' stock prices often swing with the frequency of monkeys on a tree limb.

My usual recommendation to clients is not to buy gold stocks individually but, as with common stocks in general, to buy mutual funds that hold gold stocks. Here you get diversification and professional management. In Chapter 8, I recommended two gold mutual funds: Franklin Gold and VanEck Gold Resources. As with most mutual funds, brokerage firms and financial planners sell them. For those who want gold in their portfolio, this is one of two forms of gold I recommend.

The other is gold coins. Coins can be used in two ways:

1. *Bullion coins.* These are coins whose value is almost entirely based on their gold content. The better-known gold coins (and the ones I recommend) include the Canadian Maple Leaf, the Chinese Panda, the American Eagle, and the South African Krugerrand. Each of these contains an ounce of gold (the Panda comes in smaller sizes, too). You buy them from coin dealers. Generally, you'll pay the current spot price of gold plus 5 to 15 percent. If gold is selling for $400 an ounce on the spot market (which is what gold is selling for today, not in the future with futures and options), then expect to pay between $420 and $460 per coin.

2. *Numismatic coins.* These are gold coins that have value because of rarity or beauty beyond just the value of the material in the coin itself. This "additional" worth is called *numismatic value.* A Frank Lloyd Wright house has value as a house but also as a work of art by an acknowledged master. The value of the Wright house above and beyond its practical value as a residence

is comparable to the value of numismatic coins above and beyond the value of their materials.

Because of this additional value, numismatic coins provide two ways for investors to win. The first is in the material in the coins. The second is how they fare in the numismatic market. A gold numismatic coin can increase substantially in value even if the price of gold doesn't move. The numismatic value alone can drive up its price.

I like numismatic coins as an inflation hedge because of the double play you get. The straight gold bullion coins depend almost entirely on the price of gold for their return on investment. In recent years, that's been pretty poor.

The biggest risk with numismatic gold coins is getting what you pay for. Historically, buying a coin was like buying a print or diamond: You had to know what you were doing or you'd likely get taken by the seller. The coin industry during the 1980s tried to overcome this problem by standardizing the grading of coins.

Several grading companies sprung up, the best known (though not necessarily the "best") being Professional Coin Grading Service and the Numismatic Guaranty Corporation. These two services grade a coin on a scale of MS1 to MS70 (MS being mint state), with the higher the number, the better the quality. Investment-grade coins are those with ratings between MS60 and MS70. Once graded, the service puts the coin in a tamper-resistant plastic holder called a *slab*. Such coins are now referred to as "slabbed." *Never buy a coin that's not slabbed.* If you do, count on not getting what you paid for.

The price of coins within a given grade can vary as much as 20 percent, because even within a grade, there are differences in quality. My advice is that if you don't have someone you can trust and who is expert at grading coins, buy the cheapest coins you can in the particular grade you want.

Being slabbed is not a 100 percent guarantee the grading is accurate. There's a lot of subjectivity to grading and much in the way of questionable practices. In 1990, the Federal Trade Commission went after the Professional Coin Grading Service, charging that it did not always provide objective and consistent grading and made false and misleading claims. The Professional Coin Grading Service signed a consent decree without admitting or denying the charges and agreed not to imply its service eliminated all risk in coin investing. Although the grading services are not perfect, they're the best thing we have. Shop around and look at the same coin with the same grade to get a feel for what is a good specimen for that grade.

Don't buy coins from mail-order dealers. The industry is generally sleazy, and nowhere more so than among the high-pressure mail-order dealers who pitch their wares over the telephone. Ignore claims that rare coins have been the best long-term investment for the past 20 years. Such claims are based on a survey of 20 coins done by the Wall Street investment banking house Salomon Brothers. Using the performance of these 20 rare coins to predict the future value of a coin the average investor will buy is like looking at how well impressionist paintings have done in the past decade and saying this is proof that your $49.95 Salvador Dali or Erté print is sure to appreciate in a similar manner. So abused was Salomon's survey by coin dealers that the firm announced in 1991 it would no longer do the survey. If any coin dealer quotes you the results of the survey, take your business elsewhere.

Attend local coin clubs. Ask the members who are the most reputable local coin dealers. Call the Better Business Bureau. Use dealers who are members of the Professional Numismatists Guild or the American Numismatic Association. Expect to pay a 15 to 20 percent markup on a numismatic coin. Once you have the coins, put them in a safe deposit box and forget about them.

Which coins should you buy? Look for coins whose value is at least 25 percent based on its gold content, with 50 to 60 percent being the ideal. If gold is trading for $400 per ounce and the coin has one ounce of gold, a coin that would fit the criteria I just mentioned would sell for roughly $650 to $800 as the ideal (50 to 60 percent of its value is its gold content) on up to $1,600 (that's 25 percent of its value in gold). This puts a "floor" under its value. Even if the coin's numismatic value declines sharply, its gold value will hold up its price, provided the price of gold doesn't collapse. I think it unlikely gold will ever drop dramatically unless there's a sudden run-up as happened in the early 1980s when gold nearly doubled in price in a few months and then plummeted.

If you want to use gold coins as an investment, consider buying the U.S. $20 gold piece, a St. Gauden, which has a grading of

MS63. This coin has a bit less than an ounce of gold, is readily available, is well known, has a relatively liquid market, and the MS63 grading makes for a good mix of gold content and numismatic value. Expect the gold content to account for 50 to 60 percent of this coin's price.

Our Five Model Families

We've already allocated to each of the families the correct amount of hard assets they need.

Appendix: How to Analyze Individual REITs

In general, buying REITs directly is the least risky way to invest in real estate (except for buying REITs via a mutual fund). The reasons are similar to why mutual funds are the least risky means to invest in stocks and bonds. Both benefit from diversification (in the case of REITs, this is seen in the number of properties they own, the types of properties, and the geographic disbursement of the properties) and professional management.

With REITs, there's an additional factor. Compared to other ways of investing in real estate (direct ownership and RELPs), REITs are unusually liquid. About 70 percent of all REITs trade on the New York Stock Exchange (e.g., Burnham Pacific Properties and Rockefeller Center Properties) and the American Stock Exchange (e.g., Arizona Land and Royal Palm Beach), as well as the over-the-counter market. (The remainder trade privately, which means that selling these can be difficult.) Also, the shares of REITs are rarely expensive, so investors of all incomes can afford them.

Some REITs specialize. Meditrust and Nationwide Health Properties (both of which trade on the New York Stock Exchange) invest in health-care properties, while Storage Equities (New York Stock Exchange) invests in miniwarehouses.

Analyzing REITs is very difficult. Read the annual report and ask your broker for information. Among the things you want to know are the following:

- The track record of management. The annual report should discuss how the REIT has fared over time; if it doesn't, that might be a red flag that management doesn't have much to brag about.

- The track record of the REIT's share price (your broker can supply this).
- The REIT's portfolio:
  - Where are the properties?
  - Are these markets depressed or overbuilt?
  - What types of properties are in the portfolio?
  - How many of the properties cover their costs and make a profit and how many are struggling?
- The REIT's projected cash flow (income the properties generate): Is it enough to cover the REIT's yield? Most REITs at the time of this writing had yields of between 7 and 11 percent; of the 20 largest REITs, their yield averaged 7.8 percent with a range of 4.8 percent to 10.1 percent. You want to look at net income plus depreciation, in other words, funds from operations or "cash flow." Sometimes cash is raised through the sale of assets or the sale of more stock. Selling an asset is a one-time event, so you don't want your yield to be dependent on such sales. The sale of more stock can be detrimental by diluting the investor's holdings.
- How much will be left to disburse to shareholders? Remember that REITs must pay out almost all their earnings to shareholders to avoid paying taxes.
- Are dividends covered by cash flow (which you want) or by the one-time sale of property (usually a bad sign)?
- Is dividend growth consistent?
- Is the REIT trading below fair market value (also called *net asset value*)? This means that if you take the fair market value of the trust's assets and divide it by the number of shares, this amount is more than the price of the REIT. Such a situation is comparable to that frequently found with closed-end mutual funds, where if all the stocks in the fund were sold, there would be more money left per share than what the shares are currently trading for.
- Management ownership: You want management to have a stake in how the REIT does. If it takes out a big salary, owns little or no stock, and has few or no stock options, keep away. If management owns stock that represents a sizable portion of management's net worth, then management has a strong incentive to have the REIT be a star performer.

Don't get too excited if you find a REIT with a high yield, such as 11 percent or more. The market is probably telling you something: Management isn't performing, the dividend is threatened, or growth potential is questionable.

Also, although it may be good to find a REIT trading below its fair market value, that may also be a signal by the market that trouble is brewing. According to Garrison Brothers of Houston, which analyzes the 20 largest capitalized REITs, in early 1992, these 20 traded at an average of 109 percent of what Garrison calculated was their net asset value, nearly 10 percent over fair market value, signaling that they had no need to offer higher interest and so were probably very sound.

In terms of asset allocation, the more diversified a portfolio, the lower the risk. This holds for REITs. Those that specialize in a certain type of property or geographic area are more volatile than those widely diversified. A geographically concentrated REIT, for instance, will be largely dependent on the health of the real estate market in its area. If the market does very well, so will the REIT, but if the market falls apart like a lean-to in an earthquake, then expect the REIT to collapse.

As with all real estate and other investments, view REITs as long-term investments. You probably won't make any money with them for several years. An investment horizon of from 7 to 10 years is reasonable.

Do not buy a REIT at its initial public offering. That's because they tend to trade below their offering price shortly after the offering (though there are exceptions). The market discounts the share price by the amount of the offering that went to pay the offering's fees. These fees typically run 6 to 12 percent. If an offering comes out at, say, $10 and the fees were 10 percent ($1), the stock will likely trade at $9 shortly after the offering.

To buy REITs, see your financial planner or stockbroker.

The National Association of Real Estate Investment Trusts publishes the annual *REIT Sourcebook*. It costs $500 and contains a write-up of each REIT, its portfolio, and other information. The association also puts out a membership directory ($195) and a monthly newsletter that tracks REIT prices ($75). For more information about the association or about REITs in general, contact:

The National Association of Real Estate Investment Trusts
1129 20th Street, N.W., Suite 705
Washington, DC 20036
(202) 785-8717

--- HIGHLIGHTS ---

The value of hard assets increases faster than inflation.

Hard assets are ideal inflation-protection hedges and are therefore essential for bulletproofing.

Real estate:

> Direct ownership of real estate is good, but only if you are willing to take a hands-on approach.
>
> *Real estate investment trusts:* Hard to analyze but overall, the least risky of real estate investments; better to buy them in mutual funds than individually.
>
> *Real estate limited partnerships:* Poor investments when initially offered; excellent when bought on the secondary market.

Collectibles are only for those willing to do the work of learning about what they are buying.

Gold: Buy numismatic or bullion gold coins or gold mutual funds, not bullion or individual gold stocks.

11

COLLEGE TUITION:
Smart Answers to Tough Questions

You look at your son or daughter entering first grade and you're proud. A good education can provide a better life. In the back of your mind, though, is a troubling thought: How are you going to pay the mountainous cost of a college education? How many of us can afford to send one child to college at today's prices? A family with several children may have to make some hard choices about which colleges it can afford and for how long. After retirement worries, paying for a child's college education is the most common financial concern of my clients. Even wealthy families are nervous and rightly so. College is expensive.

The most important action you can take to cover college financing is to start saving now. Getting an early start here is more important than in any other area of your financial life. The "window of opportunity" is short. Come age 18, your child is ready for college, even if your wallet isn't. You can postpone retirement, put off estate planning, wait to start budgeting (though you shouldn't procrastinate on any of these), but you can't hold off on your child's educational development. Your child may decide not to attend college or wait awhile, but that is beyond your control. You have to assume your child will go to college right after graduating from high school. That requires planning.

What College Costs

The College Entrance Examination Board says tuition and fees at four-year public colleges for full-time, in-state students averaged $2,137 for the 1991–1992 academic year, and room and board averaged $3,351, for a total of $5,488. At private colleges that year, tuition and fees averaged $10,017, and room and board, $4,386, for a total of $14,403. Conservatively, I add $2,000 to these figures for such incidentals as books, spending money, and travel between home and school.

Roughly, then, it costs $7,500 to put a student through one year at a public college in today's dollars and $16,500 at a private one. College costs over the last several years have increased an average of about 7 percent annually. Assuming costs increase 7 percent a year in the future, a four-year college education at a

▶ TABLE 4 _____

How Much You'll Need to Save Monthly for Your Child's College Education

(1) Child's Age Now	(2) Amount Needed at Start of College	(3) Monthly Amount You Need to Save
Newborn	$168,997	$ 315
1	157,941	330
2	147,609	346
3	137,952	365
4	128,927	385
5	120,492	409
6	112,610	437
7	105,243	469
8	98,358	508
9	91,923	555
10	85,909	614
11	80,289	690
12	75,037	790
13	70,128	930
14	65,640	1,141
15	62,083	1,509
16	57,780	2,206
17	53,500	4,277

public college totals $33,300 and $73,259 at a private one or about $50,000 for an average price. This assumes your child entered college in the fall of 1991.

How much will you need to save to have $50,000 when your child, at some point in the future, is ready to get a higher education? Table 4 gives you a quick estimate. It assumes: Your child will enter college at age 18; you want $50,000 in today's dollars when he or she starts college; college costs increase 7 percent a year; and you'll earn 9 percent on your investments after taxes.

Column 1 is your child's age now.

Column 2 assumes you want $50,000 in today's dollars when your child enters college. If college expenses increase 7 percent a year and your child is 10 years old today, you need $85,909 in eight years when your child enters college.

Column 3 shows how much you need to save each month depending on your child's age. For example, if your child is now 10, you have eight years to save. You must save $614 per month to have the amount needed ($85,909) by the time he or she enters college.

As this table vividly shows, the earlier you start, the easier it is to have enough for your child's education. If you have a newborn, you must save $315 a month. For a 10-year-old, almost twice this amount is needed to meet the goal in half the time.

Investments to Use

Throughout this book we've talked about various types of investments, such as mutual funds, Treasuries, collectibles, and others. Use these for college planning. Risk, though, is more of a consideration here than in other areas of your financial planning. Why? Your time is limited.

Here's what I recommend:

- If your child is less than 7 years old now, be aggressive, but always within your comfort limits. The more time you have, the more time available to make up for market fluctuations. If an aggressive portfolio fails (which is more likely compared to a conservative one), you can make up for it before your child enters college if the child is very young. The advantage of being aggressive is the opportunity to earn larger returns than if you are conservative. (It's the risk–reward ratio at work.) If you are a risk taker, use the high-risk portfolio outlined at the end of the book. Low- to medium-risk takers should aim toward the moderate-risk portfolio outlined in the last chapter. Recommendations: growth mutual funds and leveraged real estate.

• If your child is between 7 and 15, be more conservative. High-risk takers should move down to the moderate-risk portfolio. Moderate-risk takers stay at the moderate level or move down to low risk. Those comfortable with only low risk should stick with the low-risk portfolio. Again, for a detailed look at appropriate investments, see the portfolios in Chapter 15. Recommendation: intermediate-term bonds.

• If your child is older than 15, you want to preserve capital. Safety is the main concern because there's no time to make up losses. This is not the time for risk, not even for those who like to take risks. Recommendations: short-term CDs or money market mutual funds.

Emphasize growth, not income, because you don't need money now, but later. You're looking for your money to grow as quickly as possible. Also, growth vehicles, such as growth stocks, provide tax-deferral benefits. This fits in with our sequence of investing, when you want to put your money into tax-deferred investments before taxable ones.

For this very specific purpose, many financial planners recommend Series EE government bonds because of their tax advantages. I don't, because they offer a poor return, but I'll briefly discuss them because they are popular. Series EE bonds provide deferred income until cashed. They also can provide tax-free income under certain conditions, such as when they are redeemed specifically to pay for college or vocational-school tuition and fees. To get the full tax exemption in 1991 (if you redeemed at that time), your adjusted gross income could not exceed $62,900 for joint filers and $41,950 for single filers. The exemption declines as incomes rise and disappears at $94,350 for joint and $57,700 for single, at which point they're taxed at their full value. Annual adjustments are made to these limits to account for inflation. Quite simply, though tax-deferral and possible exemption may sound good, the fundamental investment is not. EE bonds are not high payers. Their interest is only

85 percent of the average yield on five-year Treasuries, although one worthwhile feature is that EE bonds are guaranteed to pay no less than 6 percent if held for five years or more. Because they have such a poor rate of return they rarely keep up with the rate that college costs increase, let alone provide you with real (inflation-adjusted) gains, which is the point of this whole exercise. At the time of this writing, they paid just over 6 percent, while college costs were increasing by at least 7 percent.

Several states now offer special zero-coupon college savings bonds. From Chapter 3 you'll remember that zeros (also called strips) sell at a steep discount from their maturity value, pay no interest, and pay the maturity value at the date of maturity. They are exempt from federal income tax and state and local taxes if you live in the issuing state.

If Your Child Is a Teenager

If your child is now a teenager, it's not too late to ease the financial burden. Have him or her enroll as soon as possible in college-level courses. Most high schools offer such courses for good students, and these are typically free. Or your child might take courses at a local college. While these will probably cost some money, they have the advantage of spreading the cost of tuition over a longer period than the usual four years of college. The idea behind this approach is that by getting college credits while still in high school, your child can graduate from college sooner than the traditional four years and thus save you money on tuition, housing, and so on.

▼
═══════════════════════════════════════

SPEND SMART: Several colleges and state university systems now offer "pay now, study later" prepayment plans. You deposit a certain amount of money now, depending on your child's age, and when he or she enters the college, part or all tuition is paid for. If your child decides to go to college elsewhere, usually these plans will return your original deposit, but not any earned interest. Generally, I discourage clients from participating in these plans. They limit a child's choice of college, there's risk (namely, that the child won't attend that college), and their return on investment usually isn't very good.

When your child chooses a college, consider buying a condominium near it. This could save on rent (roommates could pay at least part of the mortgage), provide tax deductions, and also has the potential for capital gains if the real estate market in the area increases while your child is studying. You might spread the risk by purchasing the condo with other parents whose children attend colleges in the area.

How Your Child Can Contribute

The ways your child can contribute to his or her education are many and varied. A child who works during his or her high school years 15 hours per week, earning minimum wage, for 40 weeks a year plus eight weeks during the summer full time (40 hours) can earn each year after taxes one-third to one-half the one-year cost of tuition and room and board at a public university.

Your child might also go to an in-state public university and perhaps can attend a college close by so he or she can live at home. Many students (and parents), however, find this unacceptable since this is usually an age when young adults want to gain some independence.

SPEND SMART: If you own an unincorporated business, your child can work for you until age 18 and take the standard deduction on his or her tax return. Meanwhile, the parent can write off the child's income as an expense on the parent's Schedule C form. The parents do not have to pay Social Security taxes for the child. In addition, any interest income earned on the income from the business is not subject to the "kiddie tax" limitations.

Don't turn up your nose at the idea that money earned at high school jobs can make a real contribution to paying for college. Let the child put all his or her earnings in a savings account or mutual fund, while you provide spending money. This is a form of forced savings for both the child and you, and the wages earn interest until withdrawn. Tax laws allow up to the first $1,000 of a child's unearned income to be taxed at the child's income tax rate. When income is received from sources other than work, such as dividends and interest, it's considered unearned income. If the child earns more than $1,000 in unearned income, this is taxed at the parent's rate until the child reaches 14.

Because the goal is to minimize taxes, you get the maximum advantage toward reaching this goal if your child doesn't earn more than $1,000 in unearned income in his or her own savings account. How much in assets are needed to generate $1,000 in interest or other unearned income? If the assets earn 9 percent, it takes a bit over $11,000 to generate $1,000 of unearned income. Beyond this amount, there are no tax advantages.

There are disadvantages to having even this much in the child's name. You lose some control because the assets are now in your child's name, not yours. And when the child is about to enter college and applies for financial aid, the college may require much of these savings be used for college. The college or government entity providing the financial aid expects a larger slice of the student's needs to come out of any savings in the student's name (or any income he or she earns) than from the parents. The fewer financial resources the student has, the more financial aid he or she can get. Generally, keep money for a child's education in an account in the parent's name.

Sources of Financial Aid

A Co-op Education

Cooperative education, where work and education are combined in a formal program designed to provide students both classroom and real-world experience, is an excellent means of helping finance a college education although many students and their parents seem to be unaware of it. The first co-op program was in the engineering college at the University of Cincinnati in 1906, and engineering probably remains the academic field where co-op education is most widely found. Over the years, though, it has become broadly used. Every type of college, from liberal arts to technical, has co-op programs.

The employers frequently are small firms, but major corporations and public agencies also participate, including Eastman Kodak, Digital Equipment Corporation, General Motors Corporation, IBM, Mobil Corporation, Toys R Us Inc., United Parcel Service, the U.S. Department of Labor, the U.S. Department of Veterans Affairs, and Xerox Corporation.

The National Commission for Co-operative Education (NCCE) estimates that about 1,000 colleges and universities have co-op programs with a total of 250,000 students. At least 50,000 employers participate. Co-op programs typically take one of two forms, requiring either parallel or alternate participation in academics and employment.

In a parallel program, the student attends school part of the day and works part of the day. Parallel programs are found most frequently in community colleges. In an alternating co-op program, the student goes to school full time for three or six months then works for the same amount of time. This alternating pattern continues until graduation. Alternating programs usually add a year to the length of a college education. These types of co-op programs are most typically found in four-year colleges and universities.

The advantages of co-op programs include the following:

- *Money.* While in school, the student earns money. The NCCE estimates that during the 1990–1991 school year, co-op students earned an average of $7,500. That can go a long way toward paying for one's education.
- *Experience.* Co-op employment is usually in the student's academic field. An electrical engineering student doesn't co-op at a McDonald's restaurant, for instance, but in a firm where there is a demand for electrical engineering expertise. By the time a co-op student graduates, usually two years of applicable professional work experience has been acquired.
- *Exposure.* It gives students a chance to try one or more fields to see which they like best.
- *Contacts.* Frequently, employers hire their co-op students on a permanent basis after the student graduates. That makes co-op a way to earn money while at school, gain real-world experience, and get a job when school is finished.

Included among the many universities that offer co-op educational programs are the following:

Boston University
California State University,
  Long Beach
Carnegie-Mellon University
Case Western Reserve University
City University of New York,
  Herbert H. Lehman College
Cornell University
George Washington University
Georgia Institute of Technology
Indiana University, Bloomington
Louisiana State University
Michigan State University
New York University
North Carolina State University
Northwestern University
Pennsylvania State University
Syracuse University
University of Arizona
University of Cincinnati
University of Colorado, Boulder

University of Connecticut
University of Florida
University of Maryland,
  College Park
University of Massachusetts,
  Amherst
University of Miami
University of Michigan,
  Ann Arbor
University of Texas, Austin
University of Vermont
University of Washington
University of Wisconsin,
  Madison
Utah State University
Virginia Polytechnic Institute
  and State University
Washington State University
Washington University, St. Louis
Wayne State University

For more information on co-op educational programs, contact:

The National Commission for Co-Operative Education
360 Huntington Avenue
Boston, MA 02115
(617) 437-3778

Work Study

In work study programs, schools, using public funding, provide students with part-time jobs on campus or sometimes off campus for nonprofit or public agencies. The jobs typically pay a bit above minimum wage. Unlike co-op programs, these jobs frequently have nothing to do with a student's interests or academic major, but simply provide expense money for the student and needed labor for the school or agency. The number of hours available depends on the amount students can earn as determined by the college's financial aid officer.

Grants and Loans

Many opportunities exist for a student to get grants (which don't have to be paid back) and loans (which do). Admittedly, the paperwork and rigmarole surrounding grants and loans can be daunting. The applications are complex and must be filled out precisely. "I've seen a lot of money lost," one college financial officer told me, "because deadlines weren't observed." For most financial aid, the student must attend school at least half-time. Some aid is prorated. For example, the maximum available under Pell Grants is $2,500 per year; for a half-time student, it's $1,250.

> *Pell Grants.* Pell Grants are federal grants for undergraduate education based on need. This means that a student's scholastic or athletic merit has no bearing on the size of aid or even if it is awarded. The student's income and, if the student is a dependent, the student's family's income are what counts. The maximum amount available can change from year to year. During the 1992–1993 academic year, the maximum for a full-time student was $2,500.
>
> *Supplemental Education Opportunity Grants.* This is used as a supplement if the Pell Grant doesn't provide all the money needed. Although it can go as high as $4,000, one financial aid officer told me that because of the limited availability of funds, most of these grants are around $300. Like Pell Grants, these are based on need but, unlike Pell Grants, are administered by individual colleges rather than through the federal government.
>
> *Perkins Loan.* Formerly called the National Direct Student Loan, the Perkins Loan is administered by the individual college or university, and its size varies among schools. Based on need, it carries an interest rate of 5 percent. Repayment begins nine months after the student graduates or leaves school. Students who have completed less than two years of a bachelor's degree or who are enrolled in a vocational program can borrow up to $4,500. They can borrow an additional $4,500 ($9,000 total) after achieving third-year status. A maximum of $18,000 can be borrowed for professional or graduate study, which includes any Perkins amount already borrowed for undergraduate study.

The following chart shows typical monthly payments and total interest charges for 5 percent loans over a 10-year period.

Total Loan Amount	Number of Payments	Monthly Payment	Total Interest Charges	Total Repaid
$ 4,500	120	$ 47.73	$1,227.60	$ 5,727.60
9,000	120	95.46	2,455.20	11,455.20
18,000	120	190.92	4,910.40	22,910.40

Source: U.S. Department of Education.

Stafford Loan. Unlike the Perkins Loan, banks handle Stafford Loans. The student's eligibility is first determined by the school, which generates the necessary paperwork. The student takes the paperwork to a participating bank. Repayment begins six months after the student graduates or leaves school. The interest rate is 8 percent during the first four years of repayment, and 10 percent for the last six years. During the first two years of undergraduate work, the student can borrow up to $2,625 a year. Those in the third and fourth years of undergraduate studies can borrow a maximum of $4,000 per year. Graduate students can take out loans as large as $7,500 per year.

Here are estimated repayment plans for 8 percent/10 percent loans.

Total Indebtedness	Number of Payments	Monthly Payment	Interest Charges	Total Repaid
$ 2,600	64	$ 50.00	$ 614.60	$ 3,214.60
4,000	119	50.00	1,972.48	5,972.48
7,500	120	93.52	3,722.07	11,222.07
10,000	120	124.68	4,961.77	14,961.77
15,000	120	187.01	7,441.17	22,441.17

Source: National Council of Higher Education Loan Programs Inc./U.S. Department of Education.

Supplemental Loans for Students (SLS). How much you get from SLSs depends on how much the school calculates the student's contribution should be and what schools call the "cost of attendance," what it costs to attend that particular school. These loans, which can be up to $4,000 a year, are for independent students (whose parents do not take a deduction for them as dependents on their income tax). Their maximum is $20,000. Their interest rates vary.

Parental Loans for Undergraduate Students (PLUS). PLUS loans are much like SLSs, only these are for dependent students. They too have variable interest rates and a maximum of $4,000 a year to a maximum total of $20,000.

The first step to get federal financial aid is to contact your student's college financial aid office. It must determine eligibility before you can apply to any of these programs.

▼
___

FAST FACT: The federal government runs a free information hot line about its financial aid programs: (800) 4-FED-AID [(800) 433-3243]. The line's services include sending aid applications to callers, providing guidebooks and other printed material, assistance with filling out applications, and determining Pell Grants eligibility.
___

Keep in mind that financial aid packages are frequently based on what an education costs at a particular school (cost of attendance) minus what the school determines is the highest amount the student and his or her family can contribute. There's a widely used methodology that looks at a family's assets and income, as well as the student's, and calculates how much both family and student (assuming the student is a dependent) can contribute toward the student's education. If the calculation says the student and family can contribute $3,000 per year and the college costs $6,000, then the shortfall of $3,000 will be the amount of financial aid available. A school costing $12,000 entitles the student to $9,000 in financial aid, whereas a college that costs $3,000 will result in no financial aid for the student.

ConSern

In addition to the above sources of funding, consider the Consortium of Education Resource Needs, or ConSern. This nonprofit organization, a program of the U.S. Chamber of Commerce, provides long-term educational loans for employees of sponsoring companies and their families. About 21,000 companies participate, from those with a handful of employees to giants such as Kodak, K-Mart, and Sears. If your employer does not participate, you might recommend that it join. To participate, an employer must fill out an application and pay a fee based on the size of the company to become a member of the U.S. Chamber of Commerce.

The loans run for 15 years with no prepayment penalty. The rate is an average of the 30- and 90-day Commercial Paper Rate published in the *Wall Street Journal* plus 4.6 percent. In early 1992, with interest rates low, the rates on ConSern loans were 9.5 percent.

Loans are available up to $25,000 per year for four years. Payment begins within 30 days of receiving the loan. The student has the option of paying only the interest on the loan until leaving school, when he or she must begin repaying the principal, or he or she can begin repaying both interest and principal immediately.

The only requirement is a simple one-page application plus $45 for each loan. With a properly completed application, the loan turnaround time usually runs 7 to 10 days, according to ConSern. The employee's ongoing income secures or guarantees the loan. Like the closing costs of a mortgage, the security feature does cost money, namely, up to 3.5 percent of the loan. However, this amount is amortized or spread out over 15 years, so it is not significant. For example, the security on a $10,000 loan is $23 per year. Minimum family income requirement: only $15,000.

For more information, contact

ConSern
205 Van Buren Street
Herndon, VA 22070
(800) SOS-LOAN/(703) 709-5626

The above sources for grants and work study are the major sources of financial aid. However, there are thousands of other sources. Many service groups, like the Kiwanis Club and 4-H Club, provide scholarships, as do religious organizations, corporations, foundations, special interest groups, and the like. Just about all states provide grants or loans to their residents who attend colleges in their state. The military is also an important source of funding through the Reserve Officers Training Corps (ROTC), the service academies such as West Point and Annapolis, the GI Bill, the Reserves, and the Veterans Administration.

For information on both private- and public-sector financial aid, the best place to start is at the reference desk of the main library at a major university. There you will find many directories and books about financial aid.

Our Five Model Families

Only Family 2, a single mother saving for her children's college tuition, is concerned with the material in this chapter. We've already noted where Marilyn should put her money. I advised her to have her children take college courses in high school to help reduce costs later, to save all of her children's earnings from part-time jobs, and to study carefully the scholarships available.

H I G H L I G H T S

Save early/save NOW.

Investments:

> If your child is younger than 7: growth mutual funds, leveraged real estate.
> If your child is between 7 and 15: intermediate-term bonds.
> If your child is older than 15: CDs, money market mutual funds.

Have your child take college courses while still in high school.
Consider colleges with co-op programs.
Financial aid programs: Pell Grants, Supplemental Education Opportunity Grants, Perkins Loans, Stafford Loans, Supplementary Student Loans, Parental Loans for Undergraduate Students.
Other financing sources: ConSern, organizations, foundations, corporations, the military.
The first step for financial aid information: a major university library.

12

RETIREMENT PLANNING:
Mining the Gold in the Golden Years

Of all the financial concerns facing my clients, the one they most ask about, the one that terrifies them no matter what their income, is that they'll have nothing when they retire. For many, retirement is their worst financial enemy, but it doesn't have to be.

Basketball teams usually practice one of two philosophies. They have freewheeling offenses, hoping to outscore the other team, or they have detailed defensive plans to limit the other team's ability to score. The freewheelers do okay against weaker teams, but from my observations, they crash and burn when confronted by a well-executed defense. True, the better teams can all shoot the ball, but more importantly, they can play defense. It's usually defense that wins basketball games, and it's defense that wins the retirement game, too. Hoping you earn enough between now and retirement to build a tidy nest egg rarely works. Better that you plan defensively now, so that you're sure you have enough when the time comes.

Many of those retired have learned the hard way. Despite a lifetime of work, they don't have enough to make ends meet in retirement. Instead, they must rely on children and other relatives or just do without. And the prospects for those of us yet to reach retirement age are even worse. This worries professional observers. Seventy-two percent of 491 North American actuaries surveyed a couple of years ago believed that no more than 50 percent of the baby boomers who reach age 65 between 2010 and 2028 will have enough for retirement.[30] The rest will be in trouble. Actuaries are insurance company mathematicians who use statistics to calculate the probabilities of certain events, such as a person getting sick. They use this analysis to determine the premiums insurance companies charge so that the money taken in covers the claims by policyholders. Actuaries are always looking toward the future, and when they're worried about the future, as they are about the ability of baby boomers to finance their retirements, then we should all worry.

The problem: We don't know how much to save. Without clear, specific goals of how much to save, many of us end up putting little, if anything, aside. It's much easier to find the determination to save when your goal is specific and you know how much to save and the precise benefits you'll receive. That's what this chapter is about.

Our approach to retirement planning is simple to understand and easy to put into practice. You need two skills to create a workable retirement nest egg—planning and determination. Without planning, you can't shrewdly invest your retirement nest egg. Without determination, you'll never save regularly, which means you're unlikely to save enough, ever.

To focus your planning efforts, ask yourself the following:

- How much income will I need?
- How much income will I have?
- Will my income last?
- What can I start doing now to make sure I have enough later?

As we saw in Chapter 2 on financial planning, a plan requires specific goals. The first question—How much income will I need?—is a goal. I'll discuss shortly how to determine your needs on the day you retire, because creating a plan is just not possible unless you know how much you want and when.

Retirement income comes from a variety of sources. Usually, Social Security, pensions, and investments provide the bulk of retirees' earnings, although wages and inheritances can also be important. Income sources will be discussed in detail in a moment.

Will my income last? This is an often-overlooked question. Income runs out because inflation's insidious effects have been ignored. It's not enough to have a nest egg sufficiently large to cover your expenses on retirement day. You need enough—or to earn enough during your retirement—to increase your income sufficiently to offset inflation.

Table 5 shows the destructiveness of inflation over time.

As can be seen, between ages 65 and 79, the purchasing power of every dollar of income drops by half, even when inflation runs at a "moderate" 5 percent a year. Put another way, you need $2 of income at age 79 for every dollar of income you had at 65 just

▶ TABLE 5 ——————————————————————————

Inflation's Effects on Retirement Income[a]

Age	Nominal Value of Income	Purchasing Power Income	Income Required to Maintain Value
65	$1,000	$1,000	$1,000
66	1,000	952	1,050
67	1,000	907	1,103
68	1,000	864	1,158
69	1,000	823	1,216
70	1,000	784	1,276
71	1,000	746	1,340
72	1,000	711	1,407
73	1,000	677	1,477
74	1,000	645	1,551
75	1,000	614	1,629
76	1,000	585	1,710
77	1,000	557	1,796
78	1,000	530	1,886
79	1,000	505	1,980
80	1,000	481	2,079
81	1,000	458	2,183
82	1,000	436	2,292
83	1,000	416	2,407
84	1,000	396	2,527
85	1,000	377	2,653

[a]Assuming an inflation rate of 5 percent.

to *maintain* your life-style. If you live to 85, you'll need close to $3 of income for every dollar you had when you started retirement. That's why your plan must generate increasing income during your retirement years.

Where Do You Start?

What you can start doing now is really what this book is about. Client after client has sat before me in wonderment: Where has the time gone? they ask. They remember when they were 25 and just starting a family. Now they're 45 and can't believe how quickly 20 years have passed. And they worry about the next 20 years, because that's all the time they have left to create a retirement nest egg. Twenty years now seems so little. Fortunately, there's still time left to save.

These people aren't lazy or spendthrifts. They have expenses and these took precedence over their retirement. Immediate needs, such as a child's college tuition, drowned out the postponable—money put away for retirement.

One couple had an annual income of $300,000—and virtually no retirement cache. Putting two children through Ivy League colleges was propelling them toward the poorhouse, they claimed. A high income wasn't enough; they still didn't save. Sure, they had a bushel full of unavoidable expenses, but they did have enough left over to put aside for a rainy day. Like so many, their problem wasn't a lack of money, but the lack of a plan. No plan, no savings. I put them on a plan, and their entire financial future changed abruptly even though their income remained the same.

If you get nothing else from this book but the motivation to start running your finances according to a plan, then I consider this effort a great success. Nothing is more important than creating and following a financial plan, and no planning is more important than retirement planning.

In this chapter, I'll discuss the various investment vehicles designed particularly for retirement. The investments we've discussed earlier are those you'll want to use with your retirement plan to serve related purposes, building a portfolio to meet immediate, ongoing, and long-term needs.

Goal: How Much Will I Need?

To get an idea of how much you'll need when you retire, think of your needs now. How much would you need if you retired today?

Needs change over time, so you'll have to make accommodations. If you have children, they'll eventually go off on their own (really!). The expense of feeding and clothing them will disappear. Your house will be paid for. Some personal expenses will probably decline because you're no longer working. Other expenses will increase. Medical bills typically climb with age. There will be grandchildren to shower with gifts. Vacations become more frequent.

The biggest change, of course, isn't on the expense side of the ledger, but the income side. We no longer work. Or if we take a job, it's part-time and at a lower wage than we earned before retirement.

Picture yourself in retirement. Here are some questions to ask:

- How much will you travel?
- How many grandchildren are you likely to have?
- Will you work part time during retirement?
- Will you keep your home? Will you sell it and rent? Will you owe anything on it by retirement? Will you never own your own home and always rent?
- Where do you want to live? How does its costs compare with your current hometown?
- What situations could force you to take money out of your nest egg before retirement (paying for a child's education, buying a second home, starting a business)?
- Will you want to pursue costly hobbies? How will you fill your time once you stop working?
- Will you want to take college courses? Courses are now widely available for the retired, many of which require travel. The tuition may be modest, but the cost of travel and accommodations can make them pricey.

Take your current income, add the expenses likely to increase (medicine, travel), deduct those likely to decrease (housing, child care), and you have an idea, in today's dollars, how much money you'll need when you retire.

> **FAST FACT:** If all of this hypothesizing befuddles you, I have an easy rule of thumb: For your pretax income, you need 75 percent of the pretax income you now earn.

Table 6 illustrates this fast fact.

Now you know, in today's dollars, what you need in annual income when you retire. What you will need in your initial retirement year (20 years hence, say) would be easy if it weren't for inflation. Because inflation, at some level, is probably here to stay you have to project what today's annual income will need to be in Year X (the year you retire).

▶ **TABLE 6**

Annual Income Today before Taxes	Annual Income You Need for Retirement
$ 30,000	$ 22,250
40,000	30,000
60,000	45,000
80,000	60,000
100,000	75,000
150,000	112,500
200,000	150,000
300,000	225,000
400,000	300,000
500,000	375,000

There's a quick and dirty way to figure out how much you need to save each month for retirement. (There's a more exhaustive way, which are the calculations I do for my clients.) Simply use the easy method I gave you in Chapter 2, the chapter on financial planning. Here it is again.

1 Time (years)	2 Current Investments	3 Growth Factor	4 Assets Would Grow to This Amount	5 Amount Needed to Reach Goals	6 Difference	7 Monthly Investment Factor	8 Amount to Invest Monthly
5	$_____	× 1.5 =	$_____	$_____	$_____	÷ 74	$_____
10	$_____	× 2.6 =	$_____	$_____	$_____	÷ 184	$_____
15	$_____	× 4.2 =	$_____	$_____	$_____	÷ 287	$_____
20	$_____	× 9.6 =	$_____	$_____	$_____	÷ 593	$_____
25	$_____	×17.0 =	$_____	$_____	$_____	÷ 2,000	$_____

Let me quickly work through an example so you can see how easy it is to use this table.

We'll assume you want to retire in 25 years, now earn $60,000, and, as a goal, want to use the standard 75 percent of current income as the income you want your assets to generate. We'll also assume that you have $10,000 in assets now that can be used for retirement and you'll earn 9 percent after taxes on your assets when you retire.

In the last line of the above table, the one for 25 years, you would put in Column 2, $10,000. The calculation would be $10,000 × 17.0 = $170,000.

You want to earn 75 percent of your current income, which is $60,000. Seventy-five percent of $60,000 = $45,000 (0.75 × 60,000). Because we assume you'll earn 9 percent on your investments, you'll need $500,000 when you retire to generate $45,000 a year in income (9 percent of $500,000 = $45,000). So in Column 5 you write in $500,000.

You need $500,000, but your current assets will only grow to $170,000, leaving you a shortfall of $330,000. In the table, this is just subtracting Column 4 from Column 5. The answer, $330,000, goes in Column 6.

The final calculation is quite simple. You need $330,000 in 25 years and want to know how much you need to save each month so that you will have this amount on retirement day. That's where the monthly investment factor (Column 7) comes in. You divide Column 6 ($330,000) by Column 7 (2,000), and you find you must put aside $165 each month for your retirement ($330,000 ÷ 2,000 = $165). These few calculations provide a retirement plan that will take care of you for life. (Where you should put the $165 each month is discussed in detail in Chapter 15.)

Retirement Planning for Those Who Are Employees

Social Security

Nearly everyone in this country who receives a wage, salary, or income pays into Social Security. For years, Social Security has been subject to much skepticism. Many believe the Social Security system won't be around when they stop working. Rather than helping them during their postwork years, they think Social

Security will be bankrupt. They view Social Security as the government's equivalent of a Ponzi scheme, where those who get in early make out like bandits and those who come later are left holding the bag.

This fear is not unfounded. The early birds have already gotten their payouts. Baby boomers like me may find only worms. What's the problem? Social Security, despite what people think, is not conventional insurance that just happens to be required by the government.

If you buy term life insurance or medical insurance or auto insurance, your insurance company estimates what it will have to pay out during the term of your insurance policy based on probability tables and charges you accordingly. By studying past mortality records, let's say, they might have found that housepainters are likely to die young, costing them more money. This is because the company won't have the painters' premiums for a long enough time to generate sufficient profit to cover the payouts as the painters die. Consequently, if you want to be insured and are a housepainter, you'll pay higher premiums to cover the company's higher risk. What you pay is what the insurance company and its actuaries think you will cost it. The insurance company uses assumptions founded on experience.

Another example: Someone in good health and aged 25 is not as likely to die as someone who is ill and aged 75. Not surprisingly, the insurance company charges the older person more than the younger one. Male drivers under age 25 get into more accidents than female drivers of the same age, so their auto insurance premiums are higher.

This is not how Social Security works. You don't pay into it as an investment that is returned to you when you retire, with your premiums based on actuarial studies of how long you're likely to collect. Rather than being actuarially based, Social Security is cost based. You pay to cover Social Security's expenses *now*. It's a pay-as-you-go system. Your taxes go not for yourself in the future, but to those on Social Security today. Your children will pay *your* Social Security, not theirs.

That's why there is so much talk about the declining number of people supporting those on Social Security. There's some controversy about this on the actual figures. However, even conservative estimates say the ratio of active workers per retired worker will fall dramatically. Today it's about 4 to 1, by 2025, expect it to decline to 2.8 to 1.[31] There were a lot of babies born during the baby boom, and far fewer afterward. Those few who came after the baby boom will have to support those many born during it. The fewer available to support retirees, the harder for the system to keep up with the needs of the retirees.

The current Social Security rate is 6.20 percent of wages up to $53,500. Add another 1.45 percent for Medicare, which applies to wages up to $125,000, for a combined rate of 7.65 percent. This shows up on your paycheck under FICA (Federal Income Contribution Act). Employees and employers each pay this amount. The self-employed pay double this, 15.30 percent, but can deduct half from their adjusted gross income on IRS Form 1040.

One of the first steps when beginning your retirement plan is to check with the Social Security Administration. Make certain its records of your payment history are accurate. If the Social Security Administration has your income at less than what it was, your benefits when you retire will probably be less than you deserve.

In 1987, the General Accounting Office reported that $58.5 billion in contributor's earnings between 1978 and 1984 had apparently been left out of Social Security records. Employers reported these wages to the Internal Revenue Service but not to Social Security.[32] That represents a lot of Social Security benefits deserving people won't get.

FAST FACT: Checking your Social Security record is easy. Call (800) 2345-SSA [(800) 234-5772] and ask for a Request for Earnings and Benefit Estimate Statement.

It takes two to three weeks to receive the Request for Earnings and Benefit Estimate Statement. Filling it out takes a couple of minutes. It asks for your Social Security number, date of birth, name, address, sex, last year's earnings, this year's estimated earnings, the age you plan to retire, and your estimated future average yearly earnings. When you send the completed form back, the Social Security people will calculate your estimated benefits and send back the Personal Earnings and Benefit Estimate Statement in four to six weeks.

The information you receive includes a year-by-year statement of your taxed earnings and the Social Security taxes you paid. This is broken down further between Social Security and Medicare for every year since 1966 (when Medicare began). It then breaks down your retirement benefits based on:

- The year you think you'll retire.
- The earliest age at which you can receive unreduced retirement benefits.
- The benefits you'll receive if you wait until 70 to start collecting Social Security.

Mistakes can happen. Now is the time to check your Social Security records. Don't wait until retirement to see if there are errors. By then, it may be too late to make corrections because of bankrupt former employers or missing records. Everyone should check their Social Security records, and do so every few years when it is easier to find errors and make corrections. Besides, it doesn't cost anything except a couple of minutes of your time.

The most important thing you need to know about Social Security is that it will not provide for all your retirement expenses. It was never designed to. Don't get complacent if you have a high income. On a percentage basis, the more you earn, the less Social Security provides for your needs. That's because there's a cap on how high Social Security benefits go. On the other hand, the more you earn, the higher the standard of living you will probably want to maintain during retirement. Of retirees with at least $20,000 in annual income, the Social Security Administration estimates that a mere 21 percent of that comes from Social Security benefits. Investments provide 34 percent, earned income 24 percent, pensions 19 percent, and the remaining 2 percent is from other sources.[33]

How much will Social Security provide you? Some estimates are given in Table 7.

While Social Security has a cost-of-living clause—it rises in tandem with the Consumer Price Index—my guess is it will never pay much more of a retiree's total income needs than it does right now and may well pay less. Ask any retiree today and you'll hear that Social Security is not much help providing a decent retirement living standard, as Table 7 illustrates. So far,

▶ TABLE 7

Approximate Monthly Benefits If You Retire at Full Retirement Age and Had Steady Lifetime Earnings

Your Age in 1991	Your Family	Your Earnings in 1990				
		$20,000	$30,000	$40,000	$50,000	$51,300 Or More
45	You	$ 863	$1,124	$1,263	$1,392	$1,422
	You + spouse	1,294	1,686	1,894	2,088	2,133
55	You	783	1,014	1,106	1,181	1,195
	You + spouse	1,174	1,521	1,659	1,771	1,792
65	You	725	926	982	1,021	1,022
	You + spouse	1,087	1,389	1,473	1,531	1,533

Source: Social Security Administration, "Retirement" (pamphlet).

Social Security has been a sacred cow, remaining untouched by Congress. If the budget deficits continue or the economy goes haywire, pressure will descend on Congress to reduce Social Security benefits. Social Security will be there when you retire, I believe, but don't bet everything on it.

One of the major areas of financial stress on older people is the cost of medical care. Social Security, with its Medicare program, helps older Americans deal with these costs. Don't confuse this with Medicaid, which is for the poor. If you are 65 or older and eligible for Social Security, you can get Medicare.

Medicare covers inpatient hospital care, skilled nursing facility care, some home health care, and hospice care. It does not cover prescription drugs, routine foot and dental care, most nursing home care, and "custodial care," which is care a person not medically skilled can provide, and is for helping people with daily living chores. Examples include help with walking, bathing, and dressing.

According to the Social Security Administration, "Medicare provides **basic** health care coverage, but it can't pay all of your medical expenses, and it doesn't pay for most long-term care" [emphasis theirs].[34] Like Social Security itself, Medicare helps, but I wouldn't rely on it too much. You'll have to cover much of your medical expenses when you retire, either with insurance above and beyond Medicare or by paying for the care directly.

View Social Security and Medicare like you do automobile air bags. These devices can save your life, yet you don't rely on them solely for safety when driving. You make sure your brakes work well, your tires are in good shape, your seat belt is fastened, and your driving is defensive. You augment air bags with other safety precautions.

Most of my clients don't want Social Security counted at all as part of their retirement calculation. They don't believe it will be there when they retire. If it still exists, they believe it will provide about the same protection as an umbrella in a hurricane. I'm a little more optimistic. My recommendation is to discount Social Security 5 percent for each year you are younger than 40. If you're 33 now, for example, you're seven years younger than 40, so discount your Social Security benefits by 35 percent.

Individual Retirement Accounts

The sequence of investing we've been following dictates this priority: (1) invest where you get a tax deduction and tax deferral; (2) invest where taxes are deferred; (3) as a last resort, invest in taxable investments. For those who qualify, individual retirement accounts (IRAs) give both tax deductions and tax deferrals. IRAs have been around since the mid-1970s. IRAs were hot for a while because just about everyone qualified for both the tax deduction and deferral. Since 1987, when Congress limited the IRA's tax deduction, they've resided in the backwaters of retirement planning.

Many who started IRAs when they were fully tax deductible have let them languish. That's not smart. This money can make your retirement easier. If you are 40 years old today, have $15,000 in an IRA, can earn 9 percent a year, plan to retire at age 65, and never add another cent to the IRA, it will provide a nest egg of almost $130,000 when you retire.

The IRA's golden years came between 1982 and 1986, when everyone could put as much as $2,000 in an IRA and deduct it from their taxable income. Plus, the money in the account grew tax deferred until withdrawn for retirement. (You had to be at least 59½ to withdraw without penalty; if younger, the penalty was 10 percent, plus standard income taxes.)

What turned people off to the IRA was the 1986 Tax Reform Act. This limited the full deduction to single workers who earn less than $25,000 (partial deductions apply up to $35,000) and married workers whose family incomes came to less than $40,000 (partial deductions apply up to $50,000). Those not covered by pension plans could get the full deduction, too, no matter what their income. Everything else about the IRA remained the same.

Because of the changes in the tax law, most people with IRAs should maintain and manage them (carefully monitoring their performance) but shouldn't make any more contributions. If you've never had one, it's probably smart not to start one now. There are more generous tax breaks in 401(k) and 403(b) plans, which I'll discuss shortly.

I recommend IRAs to clients whose family incomes fall below $50,000. However, that could change, because Congress is always considering rules changes. For instance, there's been talk of going back to those times when everyone was eligible for IRA income deductions.

SPEND SMART: Combine all IRA accounts into one. Any annual fees are for each, so one account costs less than three or four. Also, with larger amounts of money to invest, you make bigger stock and bond trades. The larger the trade, the smaller the commission as a percentage.

Don't ignore your IRA account. Small differences in returns really add up over the long term. If you have $15,000 in your IRA today and earn 7 percent a year and retire in 25 years, you'll have $81,411 on retirement day. However, if you earn 9 percent during those 25 years, you'll have $129,346 when you retire. That "little" 2 percent difference increases the amount you'll have by nearly 60 percent.

Tax-deferred vehicles, like annuities, don't go into IRAs. Also, never ever put your IRA funds into tax-exempt investments, such as municipal bonds and tax-exempt money market funds because tax-exempt securities pay lower yields than non-tax exempts. You might as well get the higher yields of conventional securities because the IRA is deferring the tax. Worse, and this is hard to fathom but believable because the IRS created it, when you take money from a tax-exempt security out of an IRA, you'll pay taxes on it. (For example, if you have a municipal bond in an IRA and sell it and take the money out, you pay income taxes on it.)

401(K) Plans

Established in 1980, 401(k) plans (used in the private sector) and their near twin, 403(b) plans (used in the public sector), gain in popularity every year. Named for the U.S. tax code sections that established them, these plans are excellent retirement vehicles for those who work for firms that offer them. Some firms use 401(k)s exclusively, whereas others add them to pension plans.

Only your employer can set up a 401(k). A private administrator, bank, or insurance company administers the plan. As an employee, you authorize your employer to place part of your salary into a special savings/investment account, which reduces your taxable income. This feature is why 401(k)s are often called *salary reduction plans.*

You have some leeway in how you invest your money, but there's usually only three to five choices. Complete bulletproofing is therefore impossible within 401(k) plans, so some of your funds must go outside the plan.

The maximum contribution each year is $7,000 based on 1987 dollars. Each year the ceiling rises with the Consumer Price Index. At the time you read this, the ceiling will probably be around $9,000. Take out the money before age 59½, and you'll pay a 10 percent penalty, just like an IRA. Also like an IRA (for those eligible), the amount placed in a 401(k) is deducted from your pretax income. If you earn $40,000 and put $5,000 into a 401(k), you're taxed on $35,000. You do have to pay Social Security on that amount up to Social Security's income limit. Earnings accumulate tax free until withdrawn—just like an IRA. Also like an IRA, money withdrawn is subject to tax as ordinary income.

A major difference between the 401(k) and the IRA is that the employer must set up the 401(k). Also, the contribution limit is different (it is $2,000 for the IRA).

Employers often partially match the employee's contribution. It's been estimated that nearly two-thirds of large corporations match employee contributions to some degree,[36] such as 50 cents for every dollar contributed by the employee. Some firms match employee contributions dollar for dollar, although limited by a cap, such as 6 percent of an employee's annual income. Without exception, if your employer contributes, so should you. If you don't, it's the same as turning down a pay raise.

Lump-Sum Distributions

With many firms "downsizing" (shrinking, to put it bluntly), tens of thousands of workers and managers are losing their jobs. Others are offered "early retirement." Often, employees can keep their money in the company's pension plan or take it out as a lump sum. Others move on to better jobs. The amounts of such lump sum payments can be significant, frequently hundreds of thousands of dollars.

An employee leaving a job might ask: Should I leave my money in the pension plan or take it out? If the answer is to take it out, then a second question arises: What do I do with the money I receive? The second question is easy, since that's what we've been discussing at length in this book. The first question, though, requires some thought.

For many, getting laid off is the most important time of their life to make good financial decisions.

FAST FACT: If given a choice of taking a lump-sum payment or leaving it, *take it*. This works in probably 95 percent of the situations I see. Get the money and roll it over into an IRA so you don't pay taxes on it until you use it. If you are irresponsible and likely to squander the money, leave it where it is. That's the only time you don't take it with you.

When offered a lump-sum payout, most people are better off getting their hands on the money. I'm assuming they're not irresponsible and won't spend it on something frivolous. Also, five-year forward averaging (a way of reducing taxes by estimating what you would pay if the money was received over five years rather than in a lump sum) is available to most people, but only if they take a lump-sum distribution.

Why You Should Take the Money and Run

- First, most pension plans offer limited investment opportunities and many of these are not desirable. The mutual funds available, for instance, may be mediocre funds. With the money in an IRA, you can invest in the best funds.
- Second, not only are the opportunities limited, they aren't what you want. In particular, you usually can't bulletproof your portfolio in a pension plan. To protect against severe recession and depression, for instance, you need Treasuries or Treasury strips. Few, if any, pension plans offer these. Inflation protection is difficult, if not impossible, because inflation-protection investments, such as real estate and hard assets, are also not available. (However, these can be bought in your IRA.)
- Third, your investment risk is usually higher in a pension than outside one. That's because diversification is more difficult. Limited choices are the problem, making it hard to achieve diversification. For example, domestic stock funds might be available, but not foreign stock funds.
- Finally, pension plan offerings are often poor investments. For instance, they may have an annuity that provides x number of dollars per month for the rest of your life, with nothing left when you die. You have no estate from your pension to pass on to your children.

Retirement Planning for Business Owners, Professionals, and the Self-Employed

The Simplified Employee Pension Plan/Individual Retirement Account

Pensions come in a variety of forms, but for the small business person, the professional, and the self-employed, the Simplified Employee Pension Plan/Individual Retirement Account (SEP/IRA) is a great tool for retirement planning. These provide solid pension coverage while subjecting employers to moderate administrative costs and minimal complications.

You know about the IRA. The SEP part is a Super IRA. SEP/IRA rules allow employers to contribute to their employees' IRAs rather than using the more complicated and expensive pension plan alternatives, such as Keoghs (see below).

Setting up a SEP/IRA is simple. The employer adopts a SEP/IRA program and helps employees set up their own IRAs. No minimum number of employees need participate. The employer may contribute up to 15 percent of an employee's annual earnings to a maximum of $30,000 (the employee therefore has to earn $200,000 to reach this maximum). The employee can contribute up to, approximately, $8,500 if the employer also sets up a SAR/SEP, but the maximum, including employee contributions, cannot exceed $30,000. The SEP/IRA works for the self-employed, such as doctors and writers, and for small business owners who want to offer their employees a pension plan.

All qualified employees and the business owner must receive the same percentage contribution. For example, if the employer gives 10 percent, the contribution for an employee earning $50,000 a year would be $5,000. An employee who earns $20,000 must receive a contribution of $2,000. The employer may not have had more than 25 employees the year before establishing the SEP/IRA to be eligible for this program. Employers like SEP/IRAs for a variety of reasons: Among them are:

- Low administrative costs ($10 per year per employee).
- The ease of administration.
- The avoidance of liability exposure, because employer contributions go directly into each employee's IRA account, which the employee manages and thus is solely responsible for any losses.
- The ability to exclude some employees from participation, including those who work less than 17 hours a week, those who have not worked at the firm for part of at least three separate years, foreign nationals, and anyone under the age of 21.

Employees like these plans because

- They gain direct control over their own pension investments.
- They are vested immediately.
- It is possible to take money out of a SEP/IRA before leaving a job (subject to an early withdrawal penalty).

- Significant money can be contributed to their plan each year (up to 15 percent of their earnings to a maximum contribution of $30,000).

Keogh-Type Retirement Plans

In 1962 Congress passed the Self-Employed Individuals Tax Retirement Act. The act created Keogh plans, named for Representative Eugene Keogh of New York, the guiding light behind the legislation. Keogh plans have gone through untold permutations while other retirement vehicles have come to resemble Keoghs. As a result, financial planners typically refer today to "Keogh-type" plans. For simplicity, I'll just say Keogh plans.

These are retirement plans that can be structured so that contributions of a set percentage (up to 10 percent of your salary) are made, called a *money purchase plan*, or contributions come from a profit-sharing plan (up to 15 percent of your salary). The money purchase plan requires that the contribution be made each year without fail, whereas the profit-sharing plan does not. The two plans can be used simultaneously so that a maximum of 25 percent is contributed. Keogh plans allow the self-employed, professional, and small business owner to build tax-favored retirement funds in ways similar to those offered by large corporations to their employees.

SEPs, Keoghs, and IRAs share several attributes:

- A maximum contribution of $30,000 a year (for SEPs and Keoghs) is allowed.
- Contributions reduce taxable income by being tax deductible.
- The money in your account grows tax deferred.
- You can begin withdrawals without penalties starting at age 59½ and must begin withdrawals no later than 70½.
- Withdrawals before age 59½ are subject to a 10 percent penalty.
- The monies withdrawn can be taken in a lump sum or installments.
- The money withdrawn is taxed as ordinary income.
- Both plans can be purchased from the same companies, such as insurance firms, banks, financial planners, and brokers.

- The maximum contribution is 25 percent of your annual income (for Keoghs).

These benefits help make Keoghs popular with employees.

It is possible to be a full-time employee with a pension plan and still have a Keogh. If you're employed full-time (say as a graphic artist at an advertising agency), as well as self-employed (you free-lance as an artist), you can have a pension with the ad agency and a Keogh for your self-employed free-lance income.

Further, the Keogh requires withholding a fixed-percentage (up to 10 percent) of your income every year, the money purchase plan. The percentage is fixed when initially set up and doesn't vary afterward. Also, a lump sum withdrawal from a Keogh plan has tax advantages (usually five-year forward averaging) unavailable with an SEP/IRA.

If you change jobs, you have three choices of what to do with the money in your Keogh plan. First, you can take it out as a lump sum. Because this exposes you to both taxes and IRS penalties, it is usually the worst choice. Second, if your new employer has a Keogh, you can roll the money over into your new employer's plan. This is a mediocre solution because it avoids the IRS, but it can make it difficult to use our bulletproofing strategy. The third solution is generally the solution of choice. Here you roll the money over into an IRA. The IRS lets you do this tax- and penalty-free, and because you have complete control over the investments in your IRA, you can easily incorporate our bullet-proofing strategy.

By law, all employees (other than the owner's spouse) with more than three years tenure must be offered the opportunity to join the Keogh. Not only that, but the percentage contributed must be the same for each employee and must be the same the employer holds out for him- or herself. If the business owner takes out 25 percent for him- or herself, then 25 percent must be contributed for each employee who is a part of the Keogh. Obviously, this can significantly increase an employer's expenses, which the owner should be aware of before establishing the plan.

The money can be invested in most anything except directly into hard assets—you can't buy rental property, for example. The employer can manage the money in the account personally or invest it in an annuity or mutual fund.

Keoghs are justifiably popular, with cost usually being their greatest drawback, particularly the completion of IRS Form 5500, which must be filled out each year. (The forms used for the self-employed are easy. But if you have employees, you'll probably want to use a tax professional.) Plus, there are costs and liability exposure if the employer manages the account. Using a plan created by a third party, such as an insurance company's annuity or a mutual fund, controls costs and largely eliminates liability exposure.

Keogh plans can be wonderful instruments for creating a financially comfortable retirement. If you contribute $7,500 a year for 20 years and earn 12 percent a year, for instance, at the end of 20 years you'll have $540,000. Table 8 demonstrates how powerful a Keogh plan can be in providing for your future.

▶ TABLE 8

Keogh Plan Accumulations

	Rate of Return (percent)					
	9		12		15	
Annual Contribution:	$7,500	$15,000	$7,500	$15,000	$7,500	$15,000
Years						
10	$113,947	$227,894	$131,616	$263,231	$152,278	$304,556
20	383,701	767,402	540,393	1,080,787	768,327	1,536,654
30	1,022,307	2,044,613	1,809,995	3,619,990	3,260,589	6,521,177

▼

FAST FACT: When do you use SEP/IRAs or Keoghs? If you want to save 13.04 percent or less of your income, use a SEP/IRA. These are easy and cheap to set up and require little ongoing record keeping. If you want to save more than 13.04 percent (20 percent is maximum), use a Keogh. The Keogh costs more to set up and administer but allows up to 20 percent of your income be set aside in a tax-advantaged account for retirement purposes.

C Corporations

If you have a regular corporation, also known as a C corporation, whose profits, by definition, are directly taxed and then taxed again when shareholders declare their share of the profits as income, you can deduct up to 15 percent of your W2 income for a SEP/IRA, and for a Keogh you can deduct up to 25 percent, with the same maximums as self-employed persons listed earlier. However, if you have an S corporation, which is treated for the most part like a partnership in regard to taxes, so that profits are taxed only once when the shareholders receive their share of the corporation's income, and own more than 2 percent of the stock or you're a sole proprietor or in a partnership, you must use the same percentages as those who are self-employed (13.04 percent for SEP/IRAs and 20 percent for Keogh).

Your Investments

In previous chapters we've discussed the types of investments that provide good returns and security and ways to use them in your portfolio. Our basic investment strategy, including bullet-proofing, applies to your retirement plan. But there are a few wrinkles that are specific to retirement planning.

IRAs, SEP/IRAs, Keogh-type plans, and 401(k)s all offer tax advantages. At the very least, they allow interest, dividends, and profits to accumulate tax deferred until the start of withdrawals. Because the overarching plan, whichever it is, offers tax deferral, you don't need to buy securities for it that themselves already offer tax deferral or deductions. In fact, you shouldn't. Annuities, which are tax deferred, and municipal bonds, which are tax free, are both examples of investments unsuitable for IRAs, 401(k)s, and the like.

Why not use tax-advantaged investments in tax-advantaged accounts? Because tax-advantaged investments can come with a price tag—lower yields—precisely because they are tax advantaged.

Annuities have a price tag, too, namely, their fees and the limitations on the withdrawal of your investment. Why pay these prices when you already have annuities' most important benefit—tax deferral—through your pension account? You may want to use them, instead, for money you want to invest over and above the various caps of IRAs and Keogh plans.

Picture yourself at home on a rainy day. You don't walk around inside with an umbrella. Your roof protects you, making an umbrella unnecessary as well as inconvenient. When you step outside, though, you immediately put up the umbrella. That's when you need its protection.

The tax-advantaged account is like a roof, and the tax-exempt security is like an umbrella. When inside the tax-advantaged account, you've plenty of protection from the rain (taxes). Outside is where additional protection is worthwhile.

That's why you put safe predictable investments into IRAs and such. Investments that you would otherwise have to pay tax on are appropriate. Treasuries are a favorite of mine. Bonds and dividend-paying stocks are also good. You put in investments sure to make you money.

Outside tax-advantaged accounts, it's a different story. Now you need shelter from the tax man. My favorite investment vehicle here is variable annuities, discussed earlier.

If you're a risk taker and you have assets other than pensions, keep your risks *outside* tax-advantaged accounts. These are investments, such as options, gold mutual funds, and other risky opportunities with a fairly high probability of losses. You want these outside your pension account because if you have losses, you can benefit from their tax write-offs. A loss in a bond mutual fund, for instance, can offset a gain in a stock. A loss in an investment under a SEP/IRA umbrella, for instance, brings no benefits because any gains in the SEP/IRA are already tax protected.

SPEND SMART: The way you win with taxes: delay, delay, postpone, postpone, put off, put off, defer, defer, until you die. You win by dying before you pay Uncle Sam. Tax delayed is money made.

Another smart step is to use up assets outside a pension fund before using those in it. One of my clients had enough common stock and cash in CDs to live on for about two years. At the time aged 60, he wanted to retire at 63. I suggested he use the money from the sale of the stock and CDs for living expenses for as long as it lasted. When it was gone, he and his wife would then turn to the money in his pension.

This strategy offers significant benefits, including minimizing taxes. Only the part of the stock that is capital gains is taxed. The cash in the CDs, of course, has already been taxed, so there's no additional tax liability now. His tax liability during the time he lives on his stock and CDs will be very small. Also taxed are any dividends from the stock. By selling the stock now, he minimizes his tax exposure.

At the same time, his pension is growing tax deferred. The compounding he gets from keeping this money in this tax-sheltered situation is substantial. That's why it's best to keep your money in tax-favored vehicles, like pensions, for as long as you possibly can. Only when you absolutely need the money should you take it out.

These are the basics for setting up a retirement plan. You can now create a secure, desirable financial future for you and your family. As I said at the beginning of this chapter, you need two things to get your retirement years on order: a plan and determination. You've now got the plan. You just need the determination to make your plan a reality.

Our Five Model Families

Retirement affected two of the families we are following, Family 1, a couple saving for their retirement, and Family 4, a couple wanting to minimize their taxes. Family 5, the Moriartys, have already retired, and the other two families are concerned about paying for college and saving for a downpayment for a home. The investments for Families 1 and 4 were covered in previous chapters, particularly Chapter 9, about annuities.

The only additional planning any of the families should do relating to retirement concerns Family 4, the Jordans, who want to minimize their taxes. I had this client start a pension plan for his business and to use the pension plan for himself as well as his employees, because the plan provides both tax deductions and tax deferrals. The basic investments he used were outlined in the previous chapters.

───────────── H I G H L I G H T S ─────────────

A financially secure retirement requires planning, determination, and specific goals.
For retirement you need 75 percent of the pretax income you now earn.
Don't count on Social Security to provide much income when you retire.

Use IRAs, 401(k)s, and any other available pension opportunities.
If offered a lump sum for early retirement, almost always take it.
Business owners and the self-employed should consider setting up
  SEP/IRAs or Keoghs.
Start saving for retirement now.

13

SPECIAL SITUATIONS:
Tax Savings, Divorce, Windfalls, and Disasters

Life holds lots of surprises, things we can't plan for, both good and bad. This chapter deals with three of these surprises.

Trusts

What a position to be in. A 28-year-old woman was about to sell a screenplay for well over $1 million, and she had come to me for advice about investing her sudden riches. This was our first meeting—and our last.

I recommended that she give the money away. Every last penny. And do so in such a way that she could never get it back. And I told her to do it as soon as possible.

She never did become a client. Like many, she couldn't accept the strategy I and other tax experts recommend. It was too extreme, too unbelievable, too good to be true, while going against her long-held beliefs about what to do with her money.

I was being truthful. In 1969 the IRS gave the American people one of the greatest financial gifts since the abolition of pauper's prisons. The gift was the deferred-giving trust and in particular, the charitable remainder unitrust. Though known by the horrible-sounding acronym, CRUT, these financial vehicles are music to the ears of every tax planner. They represent the single most powerful tax strategy in existence.

Just like a corporation is a legal entity that is a result of our laws, a trust is a legal entity created by the IRS. Essentially, it is a depository for assets, such as stocks, real estate, collectibles, and most anything else of value (including the rights to a screenplay). Its function is as a management device, a way to manage assets until they are disbursed to a person or organization. A charitable trust is a trust whose assets go to a designated charity. Likewise, a charitable remainder unitrust, when dissolved, has its assets go to a charity. Its income, during the life of the trust, goes to an appointed beneficiary, which could be the charity but is usually you, the donor. Thus, you put your money in a CRUT and earmark it for a charity, but you collect the income (such as dividends and interest) the money generates. CRUTs are a tax strategy typically used to avoid capital gains taxes, though they have uses in retirement and estate planning.

I later heard the screenwriter chose the conventional route of taking all the income and paying taxes on it. Had she taken my advice, she could have enjoyed a tax deduction, additional assets to generate income, a way to have those assets accumulate free of income tax for the rest of her life, a means for avoiding estate taxes, a tool to provide her favorite charity with a gift, and so on. With CRUTs, you can have your cake and eat it and eat it—five times, actually, as I'll soon demonstrate.

Remember the sequence of investing. Choose investments with both tax deductions and tax deferrals first, then investments with only tax deferrals, and last, and only last, investments that are taxable.

CRUTs go right to the top of our priorities. They provide both tax deductions and tax deferrals, making them an important investment vehicle for just about everyone's portfolio. An important note: As a rule, CRUTs only make sense if you have over $100,000 to put in them.

Situations Perfect for CRUTs

CRUTs are wonderfully flexible and work well in numerous situations. Among them:

- *Avoiding capital gains tax.* Many people have assets that have highly appreciated, such as stocks or real estate held for many years. When sold, the profits on these assets are immediately subject to capital gains taxes. If placed in a CRUT, the capital gains taxes are avoided entirely. A neighbor of mine frequently bought and sold businesses. He put them in a CRUT so he wouldn't have to pay capital gains taxes on the profits he made with this trading.
- *Diversification.* If you have a major asset that is the majority of your net worth, you may be reluctant to sell it and diversify because of the taxes you'll pay on the profits of the sale. Put the asset in a CRUT, and you can sell without tax consequences and use the money to become fully diversified.
- *Income tax deduction.* The deduction is calculated in ways only the IRS can compute (and even that's problematic), so you need a professional to let you know the size of your deduction. More easily understood are the factors that affect the deduction. The IRS lets you take a tax deduction today, although the charity probably won't see a cent from your contribution for many years. To compensate for this, the IRS uses the "present value" of the future gift. If the CRUT is set up to last the lifetimes of you and your spouse, the IRS looks at life expectancy tables and says, "Oh, the charity probably won't receive this money for 40 years (or whatever the number is). A dollar today will be worth x cents 40 years from now." That, in part, is how much you can deduct today. In addition, the IRS considers how much money you'll be taking out. The more you take out over the course of your lifetime, the less the charity gets. Suppose you put $500,000 in the CRUT and you want $100,000 a year in income from it. The CRUT has to earn a hefty 20 percent on its investments just to break even. It's very possible that to meet your needs ($100,000 yearly), part of the principal will have to be used in some years, making it even more difficult in later years to meet your demands. The bottom line is, there may not be anything left when you die and the trust ends. Compare this to someone content with only $25,000 a year. This requires a very modest 5 percent a year return on investment. Chances are good that in this situation, not only will the trust have no trouble meeting

your needs ($25,000), but will likely grow since it will generally earn more than 5 percent a year. The more money likely to be left in the trust (meaning, the more money you end up giving the charity), the larger the tax deduction allowed. In sum, the factors affecting the size of your deduction are the size of the contribution; your age or if you use a set period for the CRUT, the length of that period; and the size of the distribution you choose.

An example: If you put $100,000 in a trust, you are 50 years old and your spouse is 45, and you want a 9 percent distribution, your tax deduction will be about $5,000. If you take out only 5 percent, then the deduction increases to about $18,000. If you and your spouse are 60 and 55 and want 9 percent, the deduction rises to about $11,000, and if you want 5 percent, the deduction is $28,000. The deduction is higher when you're older because the chances are good the charity will get the money sooner because you're likely to die sooner.

For a one-life trust, just you or your spouse, the time it takes before the charity gets the money is likely to be less than for a two-life trust. Thus, the deduction is higher. A 50-year-old who wants 9 percent of the trust's assets as annual income gets a deduction of $14,000, while a 60-year-old in the same situation gets a $24,000 deduction. These numbers may change from year to year. Your financial planner, tax attorney, or accountant can tell you how much of a deduction you'll receive.

The Uses of CRUTs

CRUTs can be used for a number of purposes, the most popular being the following:

- *As a part of a retirement strategy.* I'll discuss this shortly.
- *To benefit your heirs.* When the trust ends, the assets can be placed in a charitable foundation that can be kept under the control of your heirs.
- *To benefit society.* You can designate a favorite charity, such as a university, museum, medical research organization, or religious organization, to receive the money from the trust and thus make a contribution to society.

The Advantages of CRUTs

CRUTs provide numerous benefits to you as the donor. Among them are the following:

- You and/or family members can receive payments for as long as you live or for a specified time.
- You specify the size of payments. You also decide who gets the trust's income.
- You can be the trustee, thus maintaining control over the assets.
- You choose the charity that eventually receives the assets.
- Donors usually receive more income from a CRUT than they would receive from the assets before the donation as well as getting the principal returned.
- Heirs may get more money than if the assets never went into a trust in the first place. However, this may involve life insurance and other financial-planning strategies.
- Lower estate taxes frequently result because the assets in the trust may no longer be part of the donor's estate.
- Capital gains taxes can be completely avoided.
- An immediate income tax deduction is usually possible.
- You can put as much as you want in a CRUT initially and add as much as you want during its life.
- CRUTs are surprisingly flexible. There's virtually no limit to the types of investments they can have, and there's lots of flexibility with payout terms, acceptable trustees, and eligible charities.
- Worthy charitable organizations receive your assets and know years ahead they are getting these assets; however, you don't have to tell them in advance. (Some people don't like to draw the attention of the charity or have it question how the trust is managed.)

The Disadvantages of CRUTs

As with any investment, CRUTs have disadvantages. Among them are the following:

- You give up ownership of the assets as they are now owned by the CRUT. This means you can't sell the assets and pocket the proceeds. If any of the assets are sold, the money received stays in the CRUT.

- CRUTs are complex. If not created properly, the IRS may declare the trust invalid and make you subject to a hefty tax liability. Expect to pay upward of $1,000 for an experienced advisor's services. However, by choosing a charity ahead of time and telling it you want to leave it money, chances are good that it will pick up the legal fees.
- CRUT income is not guaranteed. If the value of the assets falls, so will the income payout. Even if the payout is a fixed percentage, if the assets don't earn at least this percentage over the long run, they eventually will become depleted and the trust will have no assets to generate income for you.
- CRUTs are irrevocable. Once you set one up and put assets in it, you can't take them back. Nor can you change the payout terms once established.

Because of their complexity, I strongly urge you to use a professional experienced with trusts to create your CRUT.

SPEND SMART: With a CRUT, you can pass the income on to a second generation, usually your children. This significantly lowers your tax deduction because the IRS bases the deduction, in part, on the life expectancy of the beneficiaries; the longer it takes for the charity to get the money in the CRUT, the lower the tax deduction. With a second-generation CRUT, the IRS will base life expectancy on your children. If you have teenagers, the IRS might say the life expectancy of the CRUT is 60 or more years. That's a long time and makes mincemeat out of your tax deduction. There's a way around this. In the document creating the CRUT, include a statement that you have the right to disinherit your children in your will. With this statement, the children lack guarantees they'll get the CRUT's income, so the IRS may, in some cases, base life expectancy on your life, not your children's.

CRUTs Used for Retirement

Here's a way to maximize the value of a CRUT to get a high level of income during your retirement. From the time you set up the CRUT until you retire (a period when you're earning a living and don't need income from the CRUT), you, as trustee, might invest the trust's assets in investments providing little or no income but good growth potential, such as zero coupon bonds, growth stocks with low dividends, and non-income-producing real estate. The goal at this time is maximizing the trust's assets. When retirement comes and you want income, reinvest the assets in high-yield investments, such as stocks with high dividends, bonds, and income-producing real estate. This strategy minimizes CRUT income when you don't need it and maximizes it when you do (after you retire).

Let's assume you really could use a tax deduction now but won't need income from the CRUT until you retire. Your goals: maximize the tax deduction today, minimize income during retirement, and receive no income in between. As I discussed earlier, the larger the percentage of income you take out, the lower your tax deduction. Assume during retirement that you need 9 percent. You're 45 years old and put $500,000 into a single-life CRUT. Your tax deduction today would come to about $50,000. You'd like a higher deduction, but you know that in 20 years when you retire, you'll want that 9 percent.

I suggest you do the following. Take a 6 percent payout. Your tax deduction doubles to $100,000. Structure your CRUT so it doesn't pay any money until you retire. During the 20 years between now and when you retire, you pile up credits—the amount of money you can take out but don't. If the CRUT earns 12 percent a year then, at the end of 20 years, the CRUT has about $4,800,000. During this time, you were entitled to 6 percent a year. This comes out to $2,150,000, total. Then, when you retire, you withdraw the money as credits up to the maximum amount of the credits. Assume you continue to earn 12 percent each year. You get the 6 percent as your standard withdrawal, plus 6 percent to make up the credits. You continue to withdraw the credits until you've taken out the entire $2,150,000. If one year your CRUT does particularly well, earning 35 percent, for example, you can take out 35 percent, providing you have enough credits to cover the extra withdrawal. What you give up is the income during the period between when you create the CRUT and when you start your withdrawals.

An Example

To get a better idea of CRUTs, here's an example of one at work. Let's say you have a stock you bought 20 years ago for $100,000. If it grew at the 12 percent a year average the stock market has during the past half century, it's now worth close to $1 million. Assume it's a stock in one of America's smokestack industries. The company is in a low-growth industry and has poor prospects for the future, and its stock dividend yields a measly 3 or 4 percent (and may be dropped because of the firm's poor financial showing). The stock has minuscule upside potential.

You want out so you can get a higher yield and an investment with better growth prospects. The answer seems obvious: Sell the stock and put the money into a superior investment. That's fine except for one consideration: taxes. You'll have $900,000 in profits subject to taxes if you sell. Assuming you're in the 35 percent bracket, that's over $300,000 going to Uncle Sam before you spend a cent of it. Instead of having $1 million to reinvest, you've got about $700,000.

Let's assume you set up a CRUT, with the stock placed in it and you the trustee and beneficiary of the trust's income. Of course, what you've lost by doing this is the $1 million, which eventually goes to a charity.

Here are our assumptions:

- You place $1 million in the trust.
- These assets will yield 12 percent annually.
- You are the recipient of the trust's income.
- You are to receive 9 percent of the value of the trust's assets each year.
- Your tax rate on this income is 35 percent.
- Your one-time income tax deduction is $70,000 (7 percent), which results in an income tax savings of $24,500 (35 percent of $70,000).

Table 9 includes the following information:

Column 1: The year.
Column 2: The value of the trust's assets.

▶ **TABLE 9**

The Growth Rate Of Income with a CRUT

(1) Year	(2) Value of Trust's Assets	(3) Income from Trust	(4) Assets Added to Trust	(5) Income to Beneficiary	(6) Aftertax Income	(7) Total Aftertax Income	(8) Income Growth outside CRUT
1	$1,000,000	$120,000	$30,000	$ 90,000	$ 58,500	$ 83,000	$ 650,000
2	1,030,000	123,600	30,900	92,700	60,255	149,729	700,700
3	1,060,900	127,308	31,827	95,481	62,063	223,471	755,355
4	1,092,727	131,127	32,782	98,345	63,924	304,826	814,272
5	1,125,509	135,061	33,765	101,296	65,842	394,444	877,785
6	1,159,274	139,113	34,778	104,335	67,818	493,029	946,253
7	1,194,052	143,286	35,822	107,464	69,852	601,337	1,020,060
8	1,229,874	147,585	36,896	110,689	71,948	720,189	1,099,625
9	1,266,770	152,012	38,003	114,009	74,106	850,470	1,185,396
10	1,304,773	156,573	39,143	117,430	76,329	993,135	1,277,857
11	1,343,916	161,270	40,317	120,953	78,619	1,149,219	1,377,530
12	1,384,233	166,108	41,527	124,581	80,978	1,319,836	1,484,977
13	1,425,760	171,091	42,773	128,318	83,407	1,506,190	1,600,805
14	1,468,533	176,224	44,056	132,168	85,909	1,709,582	1,725,668
15	1,512,589	181,511	45,378	136,133	88,487	1,931,416	1,860,270
16	1,557,967	186,956	46,739	140,217	91,141	2,173,208	2,005,371
17	1,604,706	192,565	48,141	144,424	93,875	2,436,593	2,161,790
18	1,652,848	198,342	49,585	148,757	96,692	2,723,339	2,330,410
19	1,702,433	204,292	51,073	153,219	99,592	3,035,352	2,512,182
20	1,753,506	210,421	52,605	157,816	102,580	3,374,689	2,708,132
21	1,806,111	216,733	54,183	162,550	105,657	3,743,573	2,919,366
22	1,860,295	223,235	55,809	167,426	108,827	4,144,398	3,147,077
23	1,916,103	229,932	57,483	172,449	112,092	4,579,754	3,392,549
24	1,973,587	236,830	59,208	177,622	115,455	5,052,429	3,657,168
25	2,032,794	243,935	60,984	182,951	118,918	5,565,437	3,942,427
26	2,093,778	251,253	62,813	188,440	122,486	6,122,027	4,249,936
27	2,156,591	258,791	64,698	194,093	126,161	6,725,706	4,581,431
28	2,221,289	266,555	66,639	199,916	129,946	7,380,250	4,938,782
29	2,287,928	274,551	68,638	205,913	133,843	8,089,760	5,324,008
30	2,356,566	282,788	70,697	212,091	137,859	8,858,620	5,739,280

Column 3: Income from the trust, which is assumed to be 12 percent annually.

Column 4: Assets added to the trust, which is 3 percent a year (the 12 percent the trust earns less the 9 percent you take out). This amount is added to the number in Column 2 and becomes the trust's assets the following year.

Column 5: Income to beneficiary (that's you): This is the designated 9 percent of the value of the assets.

Column 6: Aftertax income: Take the number in Column 5 and deduct 35 percent (the tax rate) to come up with this figure.

Column 7: Total aftertax income: This is the amount of aftertax income as it accumulates year by year. This reflects the aftertax income generated by the money inside the CRUT, as well as the aftertax income earned by the funds that are accumulating outside the CRUT. The initial year has the $58,500 earned from the assets in the CRUT plus $24,500, which is the money saved from the tax deduction that came with setting up the CRUT.

Column 8: Income growth outside CRUT: If you don't use a CRUT, this is how your assets will accumulate.

Within 10 years of putting your money in a CRUT, you get it back, as Table 9 shows. By year 15, you are at the same place had you not used a CRUT. You double your money in about 16 years and triple it in 19; in 30 years, you have about nine times the amount you started with. And this doesn't count what's been accumulating within the CRUT.

Future Generations

Not only do you and your spouse benefit from a CRUT, but so can your children and even your grandchildren. The income passes on to your children before the assets go to the charity. When your children die, you can have the assets go into a foundation, whose trustees are your grandchildren. While they can't directly get the income from the assets as can you and your children, they can earn salaries for their work by sitting on the board of the foundation and managing its affairs. Their children and succeeding generations do the same. A CRUT can create a legacy lasting generations.

In the above example, we'll assume a generation lasts 25 years. At the end of the second generation, the amount of money that will have accumulated outside the CRUT is $47,730,503, or nearly double the amount ($25,777,016) if you didn't use a CRUT.

Have Your Cake and Eat It Five Times

I promised at the beginning of this chapter to show you how to have your cake and eat it five times. Here's how:

Cake 1: You put $1 million into a CRUT but get back more than this from the income generated by the CRUT.

Cake 2: For less than the amount of the tax deduction, you buy term life insurance for your children for the amount you placed in the CRUT. This insurance is "free" because of the deduction. Your children receive an amount equal to your initial investment at the time of your death.

Cake 3: Arrange the CRUT so the income passes to your children. Over their lifetimes, they get more money than you originally placed in the CRUT.

Cake 4: The money you collected from the CRUT (which was more than you originally put in) goes to your children, who, in turn, earn more from it than the amount you placed in the CRUT.

Cake 5: Your grandchildren sit on the board of directors of the foundation that gets the CRUT's assets upon the passing of the second generation. You specify that a majority of the board must be direct descendants. They receive salaries for their work on the foundation.

That's how to return your initial investment five times over.

Divorce

With divorce imminent, most people head for their friendly lawyer. Lawyers are usually necessary, but they're not the only professionals you should see. After dependent children, finances are the most important area of contention and concern in a divorce. Lawyers deal with legal problems; if you face a divorce and have assets worth fighting over, seek the advice of a financial professional.

Your financial aim in a divorce is to get aftertax assets, where taxes have already been paid or for which there are no taxable gains. If you have several stocks to divide up, for example, get those that have the least gain or, even better, losses.

Let's say you and your spouse bought 1,500 shares of American Express when it was $30 a share and 500 shares of Microsoft when it was $50. At the time of your divorce, American Express trades at $25 and Microsoft at $75. The 1,500 shares of American Express and the 500 shares of Microsoft are both worth $37,500. At first glance, both stock holdings seem equally valuable.

However—and this is the key—with American Express, you have a loss (ignoring commissions) of $7,500 ($5 per share loss times 1,500 shares) and with Microsoft a $12,500 gain ($25 per share gain times 500 shares). You are much better off taking the American Express stock because it does not expose you to any tax liability. In fact, if you have other gains that can offset the loss, you actually save more than $2,500 in taxes (assuming you're in the 35 percent tax bracket). If you take the Microsoft, you'll be immediately subject to a tax liability, which, if you're in the 35 percent tax bracket, will come to about $4,400. So you can save, say, $2,500 in taxes with American Express and pay out $4,400 in taxes with Microsoft, making the difference in total value between the two stocks $6,900 ($2,500 + $4,400).

Keep in mind that pension plans carry different tax liabilities, too, just like an appreciated asset. Let your spouse have the pension plans while you take the assets that don't require you to pay taxes on them today or tomrrow.

You can also use CRUTs with divorce settlements. You put a highly appreciated asset, such as a stock or house, in the CRUT so that when you sell you have no tax liability. As long as you think you'll be alive more than 15 years, you'll at least break even using the CRUT, as we saw in the CRUT example earlier. If you live longer than 15 years, you come out ahead. (Let me also say that a CRUT protects your assets from anyone else ever getting access to them, such as a future spouse.)

If you were instrumental in your spouse's success, such as a wife who put her husband through school, provide the court with future-value calculations on what the spouse's income will be over time. Factor this into any alimony and/or child support payments. On the other hand, if you are faced with paying alimony, try to get out of it. Offer more money in a property settlement to avoid alimony. That's because alimony can be modified in the future as your income rises, which is not good for you. Generally, if alimony hasn't been awarded in the first place, it won't be awarded later, even if your income rises appreciably.

The bottom line in a divorce is to pay attention to the bottom line. Finances are an enormously important source of contention in divorces, which is why sophisticated financial advice is so valuable when you and your spouse go your separate ways.

Windfalls and Disasters

Sometimes things go well for you, sometimes they don't.

Let's assume your ship has come in. Your dream has come true. The sun, the moon, and the earth are all working in your favor, and yes, you have won the lottery. What do you do? First, don't spend it all in one place. Second, well, you already know what to do. It doesn't matter if you earn $40,000 a year or won a lottery that pays you $40,000 a month for the next 20 years, you invest just as we've talked about throughout this book, namely, choose your risk level and pick the portfolio that matches this level. It's all summarized in the last chapter.

Sometimes, though, things go bad. Disaster strikes, and the only thing you can do is start selling off your assets to meet your obligations. I hope you're never in this situation, but if you ever are, these are the priorities by which you start selling until you have nothing left:

1. Use cash and cash equivalents, such as Treasury bills, CDs, and money market funds first. These are generally low-yielding assets that provide little or no tax advantages.
2. Use assets not in pensions or annuities and that therefore do not entail any penalties when you cash out. These should be liquidated in the following order:
   (a) Bonds, which compared with stocks, have lower price fluctuations and smaller commissions.
   (b) Stocks.
   (c) Investments used to protect against depression and inflation, such as Treasury bonds, gold, and real estate.
3. Pension plan assets are the last to go because of their negative tax consequences and penalties. Liquidate these assets in the same sequence as those outside of pension plans,

that is, cash and cash equivalents, then bonds, then stocks, and finally protection investments.

─────────── H I G H L I G H T S ───────────

CRUTs are estate- and tax-planning devices that allow a person to give away an asset in a way that's tax beneficial and receive the income from the asset for up to two generations.

CRUTs fit into the top of an investor's sequence of investing: They provide tax deductions and tax deferrals.

CRUTs are flexible. There's no limit to the value of assets placed in them, the investments allowed are varied, and the payout terms are diverse.

CRUTs have many uses: capital gains and estate taxes avoidance, providing income tax deductions, providing tax shelters for the growth of assets, benefits to heirs and society, and as a retirement-planning instrument.

CRUTs let you have your cake and eat it and eat it for generations to come.

Divorce usually carries important financial ramifications, so get good financial advice.

Divorce means you want assets carrying as little tax liability as possible.

Divorce is perhaps a time to use a CRUT, especially if you have a highly appreciated asset.

Windfalls get invested the same as any other asset.

Disasters are liquidated in the following order: cash and cash equivalents, assets outside of pension plans (first bonds, then stocks, then protection investments), and finally assets inside pension plans.

14

PICKING PROFESSIONALS:
Protect Yourself

Bulletproof *Your Financial Future* is about protecting yourself. This includes protecting yourself from the professionals you hire. As we've seen, part of bulletproofing is avoiding the waste of money. Sadly, few investors know how to choose or deal with professionals—lawyers, accountants, financial planners, stockbrokers, and insurance agents—and often squander sizable chunks of their wealth as a result. Getting you to spend smart with professionals is what this chapter is all about.

Financial Planner

A financial planner is someone who works in all areas of personal finance. The advantage of this approach is that one person can provide a comprehensive, all-encompassing strategy for your entire financial situation. A planner should be able to help protect you from problems such as tax liability, recession, depression, and inflation, that can hurt you financially. Once these are identified, the planner can help you pick and choose investments and strategies that minimize the chances of your being hurt.

Frequently, financial planners are inexperienced. Even those who work for large well-known firms often start practicing before they are ready. Whoever you use, be sure he or she is credentialed and has at least five years of full-time experience.

There are two respected professional credentials. One is the certified financial planner from the College for Financial Planning in Denver, Colorado. This is the credential I have. For the names of certified financial planners in your area, contact the Denver-based Institute of Certified Financial Planners: (303) 751-7600. The other reputable designation is chartered financial counselor from the American College of Chartered Life Underwriters in Bryn Mawr, Pennsylvania. Because this school has long been involved with training those in the life insurance industry, chartered financial counselors tend to be more insurance oriented than certified financial planners. For the names of chartered financial counselors in your area, call (215) 526-1000.

Here are key questions to ask before handing over your money:

☐ *Do you sell whole life or universal life?*
If she does, look elsewhere. As discussed before, these are not products that fit into the bulletproofing strategy. Any financial planner who pushes whole or universal life should be avoided.

☐ *What is form ADV?*
This is not a trick question, or at least it shouldn't be. Form ADV is an SEC form financial advisors are required to give to prospective clients before they do business with them. Why is it important? Because it spells out how the financial planner is to be compensated.

☐ *Are you a certified financial planner?*
This is an industry with little regulation. In an attempt to police itself more completely, the industry has the two certification programs just mentioned. While not perfect, having one of these certifications says the planner has a good knowledge of the business and has promised to abide by the rules and regulations set forth by the industry. Use only planners who are certified financial planners or chartered financial counselors. There are a lot of financial planners around. You might as well get the protection certification provides.

☐ *What types of clients do you serve?*
Some planners specialize in serving one or two types of cli-

ents, such as small business owners, high-income professionals, airline pilots, or middle and upper managers of larger corporations. If the planner specializes, be sure it's a category you fit into. Check to see if there are any planners in your area who have experience with clients in your profession.

☐ *How do you charge for your services?*
Some work only on an hourly rate or retainer, others strictly by commission, while most combine the two ways. These may charge a fee plus commissions, where a client pays an hourly fee plus the commissions generated by any trades or products purchased. Others use a fee minus commissions. Here the planner charges hourly fees and deducts any commissions earned. Depending on the nature of a client's account, planners may use different fee structures with different clients. There's nothing inherently better or worse with any of these approaches. Potential conflicts exist with each. Fees and commissions are important, but it's the planner's competence and compatibility with your personality and goals that's most important.

☐ *Is the planner an employee of one financial service company or an agent of many?*
At all costs, avoid planners who sell the financial products of only one company. You can be sure that everything that planner will put you into, whether it's insurance, mutual funds, annuities, whatever, will come from that company. You want an independent planner willing to analyze what's available and pick the financial products best for you.

☐ *Is his or her investment philosophy consistent with yours?*
This is hard to determine. Some financial planners write articles and appear on radio and television. With these planners, it is usually easy to see if their approach to investing matches yours. For the others, ask about their attitudes toward risk, specific types of investments, debt and leverage, and so on. We have already discussed how to analyze your approach to investing; you can use the same techniques for analyzing the planner's.

☐ *Does the planner support your goals?*
You may have goals that the planner doesn't agree with. I had a client who, because of the early deaths of several of his

relatives, didn't think he'd live past age 45, so his goals were quite limited. He wasn't at all interested in saving for retirement. What he was very concerned with was providing for his childrens' college educations. Another client wasn't concerned with his retirement because he wanted to put all his financial resources into caring for his parents, who were in nursing homes. When I work with a client, I never question what they want out of life. I figure that's their decision, and my job is to help them achieve what they think is important. Be sure the financial planner understands and respects your goals.

☐ *Do you like the person?*
Although this is a very subjective question, don't ignore it. If you are to have a productive relationship with a financial planner, it must be long term. For it to last, the two of you must get along. Pay attention to your instincts here, and trust them.

☐ *How can I monitor the person?*
Constantly check the annual rate of return you are receiving on the planner's investments. Check her mutual fund recommendations against recognized authorities. There are a lot of these. Two good ones are Morningstar Rating Service, available in your public library, and the book *100 Best Mutual Funds You Can Buy* by Gordon K. Williamson, which can be found in the library or bookstore. Do *not* use the ratings found in popular periodicals. That's because the magazines place far too much emphasis on a mutual fund's recent performance.

Too many investors pick planners by what the planner charges. An expensive planner isn't necessarily one that charges the highest commissions or the most per hour. The most expensive ones are those that put you into poor investments and cost you money year after year. How much you pay isn't important, it's what you get that counts.

Lawyers

The United States is estimated to have 70 percent of the world's lawyers. With so many, it's not surprising they're so hungry for business. They must be watched carefully. A lawyer dealing with an unsuspecting client may play a Boris Yeltsin to the client's Mikail Gorbachev: The lawyer will first appear as the client's partner and savior but, before the day is out, is found eating the client's lunch. Gorbachev lost nearly everything when Yeltsin "saved" him during the 1991 coup attempt in the Soviet Union; you too can lose nearly everything with a lawyer if you don't watch out.

Use a lawyer properly, which means not as a financial planner. They are not trained in retirement planning, estate planning, or any other types of planning, and few know much about the subject. The proper use of a lawyer is as someone who draws up documents, whether a will, trust, divorce settlement, or real estate agreement. Never forget this when dealing with a lawyer.

To find a lawyer, ask friends and colleagues who have needed legal help in similar matters to make recommendations. If you know someone at a nearby courthouse, ask who is the best lawyer for your situation. When you first meet the lawyer, ask for names of clients. Shop around. Look for reasonably priced legal help, but don't make price the only consideration; cheap, poorly done legal work can, in the long run, be far more costly than expensive competent work. Many legal matters, though, such as a simple divorce or real estate transfer, can be taken care of for little money. If the work is fairly simple, shop around for price as well as competence.

Here are key questions to ask:

☐ *Do I need a lawyer?*
The first question to ask is of yourself, not a lawyer: Do I really need a lawyer? Some alternatives: Do the work yourself; place a dispute in arbitration; use a financial planner, accountant, or other professional who may be more suited to dealing with the situation; go to small claims court or use other civil procedures that don't require lawyers; use a free or low-priced legal clinic run by a local law school. Before entering a lawyer's office, be sure to know exactly what you want. The more vague your goals, the more leeway the lawyer has to run up your tab.

☐ *Have you handled cases like mine?*
Some lawyers do criminal, real estate, or corporate work, whereas others focus on securities law, taxes, or divorce.

Then there are the generalists who dabble in just about all fields of the law. My recommendation, regarding the use of lawyers for personal finance questions, is to use only specialists. With most personal finance questions, you don't need a lawyer at all. But when you do, you need one who really knows the topic, or you can be severely hurt financially. Areas in personal finance where lawyers are useful: creating trusts, reviewing documents for investment real estate, and drawing up documents for estate planning and partnership agreements.

☐ *How do you charge?*
Lawyers usually charge by the hour, on retainer (a down payment), on contingency (a percentage of money collected; if the lawyer loses the case, there's no fee), or by the specific job. Be wary of a lawyer willing to work on contingency. These are typically "slam dunk" cases the lawyer is virtually sure he or she will win. And for winning, they usually take 30 or 40 percent of the settlement. That's way too much. Try to negotiate a flat or hourly fee for the case. In general, the best arrangement is a flat fee for specific jobs like drawing up a trust or a partnership agreement. The next best fee agreement is hourly, provided you closely watch what you're billed for, have a cap on how much the job will cost, and have the lawyer prove the hours billed were actually worked. Be sure to get specific information about how much you'll be charged, billing practices, and any additional costs (photocopying, which can be quite expensive at expensive law firms, telephone calls, secretarial fees, court costs, computer time, etc.). Insist on itemized bills (even with a flat-fee arrangement if you've agreed that expenses can be added to the fee).

☐ *Do you use life insurance trusts?*
If you're contemplating using a particular lawyer to set up a trust for you, this question is a must. It's a credibility test comparable to asking an insurance agent or financial planner if they sell whole or universal life insurance. If the lawyer uses life insurance trusts with whole or universal life, look for another lawyer. Lawyers who promote insurance trusts with whole life may have an axe to grind that doesn't benefit the client.

☐ *Will you do the actual work?*
You may interview a very slick, competent lawyer and pay the big bucks he or she commands, whereas the bulk of the work may be done by a clerk, paralegal, junior attorney, or other lower-level staff member. If you have a simple matter, these lower-level legal staffers may be fine. But you don't want to pay for the hot shot if you just need the worker bee. Complex matters, though, such as setting up trusts or business partnerships, need experienced legal counsel. Be sure you get it and are not just paying big fees for less experienced advice.

☐ *How long will the matter take?*
Lawyers are notorious for working according to a time schedule only they can understand and tolerate. At times they string things out to boost their fees or because they don't know what they're doing and have to spend much time researching your matter (at your expense) or because they are overworked, lazy, or disinterested. Admittedly, sometimes it's not their fault. The court might delay a matter, as might the opposing attorney. Do not settle for a vague estimate of the time (or the costs) for completion.

☐ *How do you work with clients?*
We're dealing here with subjective criteria. You want to know if the lawyer keeps you up to date with everything or just when important matters come up. (You have to decide which you want.) How does the lawyer handle differences of opinion you may have with his tactics? How available is the lawyer? Ask if he will frequently have your questions answered by an assistant. How do you feel if this is the case? How comfortable are you with the lawyer? Does he communicate well, giving you complete, forthright answers, or is the lawyer evasive or uninformative?

☐ *Are you willing to settle disputes by an independent arbitrator not affiliated with the bar association?*
Like a marriage, you don't enter into a relationship with a lawyer thinking there's bound to be trouble, but there frequently is. Get in writing how the lawyer handles lawyer–client disputes. You want the option of going to arbitration,

particularly with an arbitrator not affiliated with the local bar association.

Accountants

Accountants have the image of being boring and often are. But they can also be useful. As with any other professional, there's a proper way to use accountants. Accountants should be used to identify tax deductions you are unaware of and to fill out tax returns. That's their specific role in the financial-planning process. Like lawyers, accountants are not planners. Don't rely on them for retirement, estate, investment, or other financial-planning advice. The only possible exception is tax planning. A few exceptional accountants may recommend ways to minimize your tax exposure, but in recent years, because of liability concerns, fewer and fewer are doing this.

Ask friends, colleagues, and financial planners for referrals. Big accounting firms offer prestige, which might have some benefits for a business. For individuals, however, this prestige usually comes with a big price tag that's just not worth it. Be sure to get client referrals from the accountant and check them out.

Here are key questions to ask:

☐ *Are you a certified public accountant (CPA)?*
To pass the CPA exam requires rigorous training. These are the best-trained accountants. Only CPAs can do certified audits. Always go with a CPA. Period.

☐ *What do you specialize in?*
Like lawyers and surgeons, CPAs specialize. Some specialty areas of accounting are taxes and the audits of small businesses or public corporations. You want a tax accountant. If you have particularly complex taxes—if your portfolio consists of trusts or complicated real estate holdings, for example—then be sure the accountant has experience with these.

☐ *How much do you charge?*
Typically, accountants don't have the room to finagle and bloat fees as do lawyers. But you still want to know what they charge (usually by the hour) and to get a written estimate of what your job will cost including a maximum fee.

☐ *What benefits can I expect from your services?*
This is a credibility test. Beware the accountant that promises riches. And be forewarned if the accountant suggests changes that seem more for his or her benefit than yours. Run from the accountant's office if he or she suggests you withdraw money from pension and other tax-advantaged retirement accounts to put elsewhere; seems more interested in promoting an investment opportunity than doing accounting work—accountants are not investment advisors so don't take their investment advice; proposes an investment that's guaranteed (there is no such thing); recommends an obscure investment that's sure to return huge profits.

☐ *What shall I bring to the meeting?*
More so than with other financial professionals, you can cut your costs with an accountant by providing lots of information yourself and doing your own research. This is particularly true with tax matters. Once you've settled on which accountant you want, ask what materials she will need before your first meeting.

Insurance Agents

While I have certainly said negative things about insurance agents in this book, most are honest, competent, and valuable. The ones I have trouble with are whole life insurance agents. Since we all need insurance, we all need to deal with insurance agents.

Here are key questions to ask:

☐ *Do you sell whole or universal life insurance?*
This is the acid test. If you are in the market for life insurance and the agent sells whole or universal life, hang up the phone immediately.

☐ *What types of insurance do you specialize in?*
If you want homeowner's insurance and 90 percent of the agent's business is life insurance, you're in the wrong place.

☐ *Are you an independent agent?*
If the agent works for one company only, move on. You want an independent agent who represents many companies. Ide-

ally, such agents can pick and choose among the many companies' policies to find the best one for you. Admittedly, this doesn't always work as well in practice as in theory. Some independent agents get higher commissions from some companies, so they push those companies' products. Others are just lazy or ignorant of wider possibilities for you.

☐ *How many insurance companies do you represent that offer the type of insurance I want?*
An "independent" agent who says he represents one company, even if he's independent, isn't likely to do you much good. The number of firms offering certain types of insurance varies. For example, there are more insurance companies offering automobile insurance than disability insurance. You want an agent who represents at least two or three companies with disability. Most types of insurance are offered by enough companies that the agent should represent a minimum of four to five companies.

☐ *What are the industry ratings of the companies you represent?*
If the agent doesn't give you a direct answer to this question, claims he doesn't know, or tries to convince you it's not important, then likely he represents poorly rated companies. Keep away.

Stockbrokers

The public thinks brokers are investment advisors or financial planners. Some are and have earned their certification. However, most are not. Their investment recommendations usually come from the brokerage firm's research department. All the firm's brokers (which can number in the hundreds or thousands) get the same recommendations. My recommendation: Generally avoid brokerage firm recommendations.

The one and only correct way to use a stockbroker is to execute transactions. (For investment information, rely on objective third parties, such as Standard & Poor's and Morningstar.) To buy stocks, bonds, mutual funds, annuities, REITs, RELPs, commodities, futures, and other financial instruments, you need to use a broker or a financial planner who is a broker or who works with a broker. If you choose your own investments, you don't need investment-planning advice. All you need is an inexpensive order taker. I've recommended in the next chapter complete portfolios with specific investment recommendations. If you follow these sample portfolios, you don't need much, if any, help.

Those who buy mutual funds and annuities, which are the primary investments I recommend in this book, can use a financial planner, discount stockbroker, or full-service broker for virtually the same cost. You pay the same commissions for these investments no matter who you buy them through.

15

SAMPLE PORTFOLIOS:
How Many Baskets, How Many Eggs?

Earlier, I discussed the power of the asset allocation model to maximize returns while minimizing risk. Creating a true asset allocation model is quite complex because of the difficulty of balancing all the elements and providing the desired degree of diversity.

Following are sample portfolios for those who are willing to assume low, medium, or high risk based on data I developed. The percentage of each portfolio devoted to the eight types of investments listed came from a sophisticated computer program used by Edward Carr Franks, an economist in Pasadena, California. Franks has a masters degree from the Massachusetts Institute of Technology and a Ph.D. from the Rand Graduate School at the Rand Corporation in Santa Monica, California, and has written about asset allocation and applied it as an executive at various money management firms. I thank him for his help with these sample portfolios.

Important note: The percentages for the sample portfolios listed below remain constant, no matter how much money you have to invest. If, for example, you are a medium-risk investor with $20,000 to invest, you would put 10 percent ($2,000) in domestic stocks. Likewise, if you have $300,000 and were a medium-risk investor, you would put 10 percent ($30,000) in domestic stock.

First let's look at an overview showing how the percentage of your assets in different investments, from Treasury bills through gold to real estate, changes according to the risk level (Table 10). Then we'll look at some special considerations before developing each risk portfolio separately, fleshing out the initial percentages by looking at the particular investments you might choose in each category.

▶ **TABLE 10**

Sample Portfolios—An Overview

	Portfolio (%)		
	Low Risk	Medium Risk	High Risk
Treasury bills/cash	35	4	0
U.S. small-company stocks	0	7	26
Treasury bonds	17	10	7
Domestic stocks	0	10	15
International stocks	0	24	32
International bonds	18	20	0
Gold	10	12	0
Real estate	20	13	20
Expected annual rate of return (%)	9.5	13.0	16.0

Treasury bills/cash. Treasury bills are short-term instruments (three months, six months, or one year) sold by the U.S. Treasury. Cash, of course, is cash. Treasury bills and cash are used for depression bulletproofing. During a depression, we expect prices to decline, making cash and cash equivalents more valuable. The more prices fall, the greater the purchasing power of cash. Treasury bills and cash have important characteristics:

1. They are highly liquid. Cash is the most liquid of all assets, with Treasuries being a close second because they can quickly and easily be converted to cash. This makes cash and Treasury bills (often called *cash equiva-*

lents since individuals and businesses use them as a place to hold cash and earn interest until the cash is needed) ideal for emergencies and for when you want to buy other assets.

2. Their values fluctuate less than long-term investments, thus making them low risk. That's why the low-risk portfolio has 35 percent of its assets in cash while the high-risk one has none.

U.S. small-company stocks. U.S. small-company stocks are domestic companies whose market capitalization is less than $750 million. A firm with 2 million shares outstanding and a share price of $10 is said to have a market capitalization of $20 million ($10 × 2 million). Two reasons account for emphasizing small-company stocks:

1. They tend to outperform the market. Being smaller than large corporations, such as General Electric and IBM, they have more growth and profit potential, so their stocks tend to increase more than large companies over time.

2. They are riskier than large-company stocks. That's because small firms are, as a group, younger and less established than large corporations. That's why 26 percent of the high-risk portfolio is comprised of small-company stocks, whereas they are not in the low-risk portfolio at all.

Treasury bonds. Treasury bonds are 30-year notes issued by the U.S. Treasury. The longer a bond is from maturity, the more its price fluctuates. That's why you buy Treasuries when issued. A 30-year Treasury with only one year to maturity is a short-term bond. You want long-term ones. Because Treasuries are government securities, they are liquid and the investor runs virtually no risk that they won't be repaid. The low-risk portfolio has more of these bonds than the high-risk one to maintain overall balance.

Domestic stocks. Domestic stocks are the stocks of U.S. companies with a market capitalization of more than $750 million. We talked at length throughout the book about stocks, such as their 50-year track record of 12 percent compound annual growth. Their tendency to fluctuate makes them a moderate risk.

International stocks. Stocks of foreign companies traded overseas are international stocks. These are riskier than domestic ones. They are also more difficult to understand, and the information about them is usually not as complete as with U.S. companies. Over the past decade or more, international stocks have outperformed domestic ones.

International bonds. The short-, medium-, and long-term bonds of foreign governments make up this category of investments. They are not as risky as international stocks but more risky than domestic bonds.

Gold. Gold is an excellent inflation hedge, making it an important component of our inflation bulletproofing. Gold was discussed in Chapter 10. Gold can be bought in a variety of ways. Bullion (pure gold) is not recommended because it is expensive to keep and difficult to trade. Gold futures and options are far too risky. I recommend two forms of gold ownership: Gold bullion coins are the least risky way to purchase gold because almost all their value is in the gold itself, which is why I recommend them for the low-risk portfolio. Gold mutual funds, which invest in gold stocks, are relatively volatile while being the most convenient form of gold ownership. This makes gold mutual funds suitable for all types of portfolios.

Real Estate. Like gold, real estate was discussed at length in Chapter 10. You can own it directly or indirectly through mutual funds, REITs, and RELPs. The more leverage involved, the riskier the investment.

The above portfolios deserve a couple of additional comments:

No corporate bonds. While researching asset allocation, the optimizer program I used concluded that corporate bonds did not fit into our model. Their prices fluctuated similarly to other investments that had better risk/reward relationships. That's why you won't find corporate bonds in any of the portfolios. However, corporate bond funds are useful for those wary of buying stocks. Many of my clients new to the stock market place their money in a bond fund, which gives them a feeling of security and then, using dollar-cost averaging, take the money from this fund and invest it over time in stocks until they are out of the bond fund entirely.

Rates of return. Each portfolio has expected rates of return listed at the bottom of Table 10. Of course, there are no guarantees. The standard deviation for the low-, medium-, and high-risk portfolios is 6.2, 10.0, and 15.0 percent, respectively. This means that 67 percent of the time (that's the *confidence level* obtained from one standard deviation), the rate of return of each portfolio will fall between the expected rate of return plus or minus the standard deviation. Spelled out in numbers, as below, you'll quickly see the differences between risk levels.

Low-risk portfolio. 9.5 percent + 6.2 percent = 15.7 to 3.3 percent. We expect that 67 percent of the time, the return on the low-risk portfolio will fall between 15.7 and 3.3 percent. In fact, we can move to the second standard deviation, which gives us a 95 percent confidence level (we're 95 percent sure this will happen) by doubling the 6.2 percent factor:

9.5 percent + 12.4 percent = 21.9 to −2.9 percent.

This second calculation says that 95 percent of the time the rate of return of the low-risk portfolio will fall between 21.9 and −2.9 percent (a loss). This portfolio has little chance for loss, but its opportunity for big gains is low, too. This is what we would expect from a low-risk portfolio since risk and reward are directly related.

Medium-risk portfolio. The standard deviation for the medium-risk portfolio is 10.0. Using the same calculations as above, we find

67 percent confidence level: 23 to 3 percent.
95 percent confidence level: 33 to −7 percent.

Here the potential gains are greater than those of the low-risk portfolio (33 percent versus 21.9 percent), the risk of loss is greater, and the expected rate of return (13 percent), is more, too.

High-risk portfolio. The standard deviation here is 15.0. Using the same calculations as above, we find

67 percent confidence level: 31 to 1 percent.
95 percent confidence level: 46 to −14 percent.

As expected, the portfolio with the highest risk has the

greatest potential for profits and losses, and its expected rate of return is the highest of all the portfolios.

These results are what you would expect. The riskier the portfolio, the greater the price fluctuations and the more chance you will make money—and lose money. That's why the expected rate of return goes up with the increasing risk level and why the range of each confidence level is wider (due to greater price fluctuations).

Portfolio Investments

Here are recommended investments for each portfolio. For specifics about each mutual fund, see Chapter 8; Chapter 9 covers the annuities; Chapter 10 discusses gold and real estate. I've made two portfolios for each risk level—tax deferred and taxable. You usually want to put your money first into the tax-deferred investment when possible and then the taxable one. Sometimes there is no tax-deferred choice, so you must use the taxable one.

Low-Risk Portfolio

Treasury bills/cash (35 percent of portfolio)

Tax deferred: Treasury bills, cash, and American Funds' U.S. Treasury Money Market Fund.

Taxable: Treasury bills, cash, and American Funds' U.S. Treasury Money Market Fund. There are no tax-deferred equivalents.

U.S. small-company stocks

Not used with this portfolio.

Treasury bonds

Tax deferred: Franklin Valuemark II and/or zero coupon bonds that come due in 2010 (17 percent of portfolio).

Taxable: 30-year Treasury bonds (17 percent of portfolio).

Domestic stocks

Not used with this portfolio.

► FIGURE 4

► FIGURE 4

Low-Risk Portfolio.

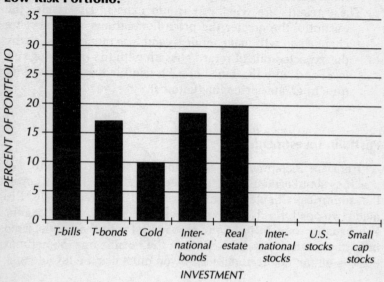

International Stocks
    Not used with this portfolio.

International bonds
    Tax deferred: Templeton Investment Plus Income Fund (18
                  percent of portfolio).
    Taxable: MFS Worldwide Government Trust (18 per-
                  cent of portfolio).

Gold
    Tax deferred: Franklin Valuemark II Gold Fund (10 percent
                  of portfolio).
    Taxable: Gold bullion coins (10 percent of portfolio).

Real estate
    Tax deferred: Franklin Valuemark II Real Estate Securities
                  Fund (20 percent of portfolio).
    Taxable: Templeton Real Estate Securities Fund (20
                  percent of portfolio).

Medium-Risk Portfolio

Treasury bills/cash

Tax deferred: Treasury bills (4 percent of portfolio), and American Funds' U.S. Treasury Money Market Fund.

Taxable: Treasury bills (4 percent of portfolio), and American Funds' U.S. Treasury Money Market Fund.

U.S. small-company stocks

Tax deferred: Pioneer Three Fund (7 percent of portfolio). There is no tax-deferred alternative here.

Taxable: Pioneer Three Fund (7 percent of portfolio).

Treasury bonds

Tax deferred: Franklin Valuemark II Zero Coupon Funds maturing in 2010 (10 percent of portfolio).

Taxable: 30-year Treasury bonds (10 percent of portfolio).

▶ **FIGURE 5**
Medium-Risk Portfolio.

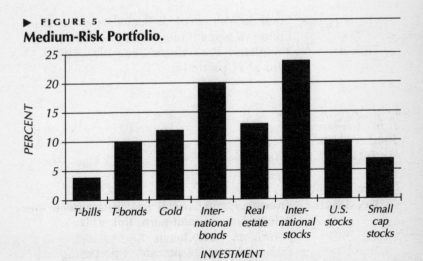

Domestic stocks

    Tax deferred: American Legacy II Growth Fund (10 percent of portfolio).

    Taxable: American Funds Washington Mutual Investors Fund (10 percent of portfolio).

International stocks

    Tax deferred: American Legacy II International Fund (24 percent of portfolio).

    Taxable: Templeton Foreign Fund (24 percent of portfolio) plus American Funds' Washington Mutual Investors (10 percent).

International bonds

    Tax deferred: Templeton Investment Plus Income Fund (20 percent of portfolio).

    Taxable: MFS Worldwide Government Trust (20 percent of portfolio).

Gold

    Tax deferred: Franklin Valuemark II Precious Metals Fund (12 percent of portfolio).

    Taxable: Franklin Gold Fund (12 percent).

Real estate

    Tax deferred: Franklin Valuemark II Real Estate Securities Fund (13 percent of portfolio).

    Taxable: Templeton Real Estate Securities Fund (13 percent of portfolio).

High-Risk Portfolio

Treasury bills/cash

    Not used with this portfolio.

U.S. small-company stocks

    Tax deferred: Pioneer Three. There are no desirable tax-deferred investments in this category. (26 percent of portfolio).

    Taxable: Pioneer Three (26 percent of portfolio).

► FIGURE 6
High-Risk Portfolio.

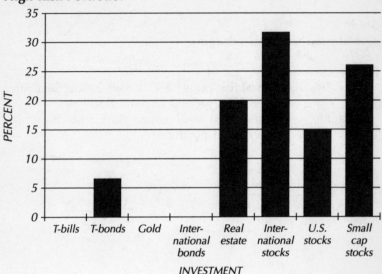

Treasury bonds
 Tax deferred: 30-year strips (7 percent of portfolio). There
 are no desirable tax-deferred investments in
 this category.
 Taxable: 30-year strips (7 percent of portfolio).

Domestic stocks
 Tax deferred: American Funds' American Legacy II Growth
 Fund (15 percent of portfolio).
 Taxable: American Funds' Washington Mutual Inves-
 tors Fund (15 percent of portfolio).

International stocks
 Tax deferred: American Funds' American Legacy II International Fund (32 percent of portfolio).
 Taxable: Templeton Foreign Fund (32 percent of portfolio).

International bonds
   Not used with this portfolio.

Gold
   Not used with this portfolio.

Real estate

Tax deferred:	Franklin Valuemark II Real Estate Securities Fund (20 percent of portfolio).
Taxable:	Templeton Real Estate Securities Fund (20 percent of portfolio).

Appendix

Appendix

INSURANCE COMPANY AND BOND RATINGS

The following are the ratings for insurance companies and bonds made by the major rating services. Typically, a ratings service that rates both insurance companies and bonds (Standard & Poor's and Moody's) will use the same or very similar ratings for each. The following is based on material provided by the rating services.

Standard & Poor's

AAA	The highest rating, where the ability to repay is considered "extremely strong."
AA	Differs from the highest rating "only in small degree."
A	"A strong capacity" to repay.
BBB	"An adequate capacity" to repay.

Debt rated BB, B, CCC, CC, and C has "predominantly speculative characteristics with respect to capacity" to repay.

BB | "Has less near-term vulnerability to default. . . . However, it faces major ongoing uncertainties or exposure to adverse business . . . conditions."

B | "Has greater vulnerability to default" but has the capacity to repay at this time.

CCC | Vulnerable to default and dependent on favorable economic conditions to repay.

CC | "Typically applied to debt subordinated to senior debt which is assigned an actual or implied CCC rating."

C | May indicate imminent default.

D | When payments are in default or company in bankruptcy.

+ or − Used for ratings AA to CCC and shows relative standing within the major rating categories.

Duff & Phelps

AAA | Highest rating. "Risk factors are negligible."

AA+/AA/AA− | "Very high claims paying ability . . . risk modest."

A+/A/A− | "High claims paying ability. Protection factors are average."

BBB+/BBB/BBB− | "Below average protection factors but still considered sufficient for prudent investor."

BB+/BB/BB− | "Uncertain claims paying ability and less than investment grade quality. However, the company is deemed likely to meet these obligations when due."

B+/B/B− | "Possessing risk that policyholder and contractholder obligations will not be paid when due."

CCC | "There is substantial risk that policyholder and contractholder obligations will not be paid when due."

DD | Company is under an order of liquidation.

Weiss Research

A | Excellent. "We believe that this company has the resources necessary to deal with severe economic conditions."

B | Good. "This company offers good financial security and has the resources to deal with a variety of adverse economic conditions."

Companies with a rating of B+ or higher are included on Weiss's recommended list.

C | Fair. "This company offers fair financial security and is currently stable. But during an economic downturn ... may encounter difficulties."

D | Weak. "This company currently demonstrates ... significant weaknesses which could negatively impact policyholders. In an unfavorable economic environment, these weaknesses could be magnified."

E | Very weak. "This company currently demonstrates ... significant weaknesses and has also failed some of the basic tests that we use to identify fiscal stability. Therefore, even in a favorable economic environment ... policyholders could incur significant risks."

F | Failed. "Company is under the supervision of state insurance commissioners."

+ | "With new data, there is a modest possibility that this company could be upgraded."

—   "With new data, there is a modest possibility that this company could be downgraded."

A.M. Best

AA+/A+   Superior. Companies that "have a very strong ability to meet their . . . contractual obligations over a long period of time."

A/A−   Excellent. Companies that "have a strong ability to meet their . . . contractual obligations over a long period of time."

B++/B+   Very good. Companies that "have a strong ability to meet their . . . contractual obligations, but their financial strength may be susceptible to unfavorable changes in underwriting or economic conditions."

B/B−   Good. Companies that have a "generally adequate ability to meet their . . . contractual obligations, but their financial strength is susceptible to unfavorable changes in underwriting or economic conditions."

C++/C+   Fair. Companies that "generally have a reasonable ability to meet their . . . contractual obligations, but their financial strength is vulnerable to unfavorable changes in underwriting or economic conditions."

C/C−   Marginal. Companies that "have a current ability to meet their . . . contractual obligations, but their financial strength is very vulnerable to unfavorable changes in underwriting or economic conditions."

D   Below minimum standards.

E   Under state supervision. Does not include liquidation.

F   In liquidation.

Moody's Investors Service

Aaa   These bonds are of the "best quality."

Aa   Judged to be of "high quality."

A   "Possess many favorable investment attributes and are . . . upper-medium grade obligations.

Baa   "Medium grade obligations."

Ba   "Speculative elements, their future cannot be considered as well-assured."

B   "Generally lack characteristics of the desirable investment. Assurance of interest and principal payments . . . over any long period of time may be small."

Caa   Are of "poor standing. . . . May be in default."

Ca   "Speculative in a high degree. Such issues are often in default."

C   "The lowest rate class of bonds."

GLOSSARY

401(k)   A Pension plan used by private-sector businesses; provides either tax deductions, tax deferrals, or both.

403(b)   A Pension plan used in the public sector; provides either tax deductions, tax deferrals, or both.

Actuaries   Insurance company mathematicians who use statistics to calculate the probability of certain events, such as the probability of a person getting sick. Insurance premiums are based on such probabilities.

Appreciation   When an asset increases in value.

Asset   Something that has monetary value. Usually thought of as something able to provide benefits to its owner, such as bonds that pay interest.

Asset allocation   A strategy of investing based on diversifying one's investments to minimize risk and maximize returns based on theories and practices that won three economists the Nobel Prize in economics in 1990.

Back-end charges   Mutual fund and annuity fees and commissions charged when money is withdrawn. *See* Front-end charges.

Beta   A statistical technique used to measure a stock's or mutual fund's volatility compared with the stock market as a whole.

Bond   A long-term debt instrument.

Bondholder   The owner of a bond.

Bond mutual fund　A mutual fund that invests in bonds. *See* Mutual fund.

Bulletproof protection　A strategy using a carefully calculated mix of investments designed to respond in predictable ways to various economic situations; for example, some investments go up with inflation whereas others decline, so the investor using this strategy balances the predictable losers with winners. A hedging strategy that provides protection against every serious economic catastrophe that can occur; eliminates the need to predict what the economy will do.

Bullion　Gold itself (rather than jewelry or gold company stocks) in the form of bars, ingots, or coins.

Buy-and-hold strategy　When an investor invests for the long term, namely, many years, rather than buying and selling frequently.

Call feature　The right of a bond issuer to redeem (call in) the bond during a certain time period under specified conditions; usually invoked when interest rates have fallen and the issuer wants to turnover the old bonds so as to issue new ones at the lower prevailing interest rate.

Capital gains　Profit made from the sale of a security or property due to an increase in price.

Certificate of deposit (CD)　A form of savings account that pays a specified interest rate for a certain period of time.

Charitable remainder unitrust (CRUT)　A trust that when dissolved has its assets go to charity but whose income goes to an appointed beneficiary that frequently is the donor. *See* Trusts.

Closed-end mutual fund　A mutual fund that, at its founding, issues a set number of shares that does not change; the shares are bought and sold just like shares in corporations. See Open-end mutual and sold just like shares in corporations. See Open-end mutual fund.

Co-op education　A college plan where work and education are combined in a formal program.

Collectibles　Tangible assets that are collected with the expectation that they will rise in value, such as art, coins, stamps, and antiques. *See* Tangible assets.

Compound interest　When interest is paid not only on the principal of a loan but on interest previously earned.

Corporate bond　A bond issued by a corporation.

Deflation　A decrease in the general price level.

Depreciation　When an asset decreases in value.

Depression　A prolonged period when economic activity significantly declines.

Depression protection   Part of the bulletproof protection strategy using U.S. government securities as a hedge against the decline in value of other assets. When implemented properly, it assures that the investor's total portfolio retains its assets at a time of depression or severe recession. See Bulletproof protection and Inflation protection.

Devastation dividend   The additional earnings one can earn by investing in assets that are out of favor, such as real estate when the real estate market is distressed.

Diversification   When a portfolio is invested in many types of investments; used to reduce risk.

Dividend   Money paid to shareholders; usually used by companies as a way to distribute their earnings to their shareholders.

Dollar-cost averaging   An investment strategy based on periodic investments where the same amount of money is invested according to a set timetable.

Downside potential   The potential for loss. See Upside potential.

Elimination period   The time between when one is disabled and when insurance begins to pay; used with disability insurance.

Face value   The value shown on the front of a security, such as a bond.

Fixed annuity   A loan to an insurance company. The insurance company guarantees the return of principal but generally does not guarantee the rate of interest that will be paid See Variable annuity.

Fixed-income investments   Investments that pay a fixed (unchanging) interest rate or dividend, such as a bond.

Front-end charges   Mutual fund and annuity fees and commissions charged at the time money is invested. See Back-end charges.

Goal   An objective; used to give shape and direction to one's financial plan.

Gold coins   Coins with a very high content of gold, such as American Eagles and Canadian Mapleleafs.

Growth mutual fund   A mutual fund whose goal is to increase in value by investing in assets that will increase in value.

Hard assets   Usually used synonymously with tangible assets. See Tangible assets.

Illiquidity   A situation where it is difficult to turn an asset into cash. See Liquidity.

Income   Money earned through labor, investments, and business.

Income mutual fund   A mutual fund whose goal is to generate a stream of income for fund owners. *See* Growth mutual fund.

Individual retirement account (IRA)   A tax-sheltered retirement plan for the individual.

Inflation   A general rise in prices and wages.

Inflation protection   Part of the bulletproof protection strategy, using such hard assets as real estate and gold as a hedge against the decline in value of other assets. When implemented properly, it assures that the investor's total portfolio retains its purchasing power at a time of severe inflation. *See* Bulletproof protection and Depression protection.

Inflation-adjusted dollars   The value of money after taking into account the decline in value caused by inflation.

Interest   To someone who lends, interest is the money paid for the use of the money; to someone who borrows, interest is the cost of money.

Interest rates   The percentage charged for the use of money.

Junk bond   An unrated bond or one issued by a company that has fallen on hard times; typically pays a high rate of interest.

Keogh-type plan   A pension plan where contributions are based on salary and/or profit sharing.

Leverage   The magnifying effects of borrowing. If you purchase real estate with 20 percent down, you can buy five times as much real estate than if you didn't borrow anything; by borrowing, you've gained a leverage factor of 5.

Liability   A debt owed.

Liquidity   The ease by which an asset can be converted into cash; the easier it is, the more liquid the asset. *See* Illiquidity.

Load mutual fund   A mutual fund that sells shares to the public with a sales charge of up to 8½ percent.

Long term   A period of time whose length varies depending on the investment or a person's preference. It is used in this book to refer to a recommended time period for holding investments of five years or more. *See* Short term and Medium term.

Margin   When used in reference to investments, it refers to buying stocks or bonds on credit.

Maturity date   The date a loan or bond is due.

Medium term   A period of time to hold an investment; used in this book to refer to a time period of between one and five years. *See* Short term and Long term.

Mortgage   When property is pledged as collateral for a loan.

Municipal bond   A bond issued by a state, city, or county; not subject to federal income taxes and frequently not to state taxes, either.

Mutual fund   A company that pools investors' money and invests in a variety of investments.

Net worth   Assets minus liabilities.

No-load mutual fund   A mutual fund that sells shares to the public without a sales charge.

Numismatic coins   Coins whose value, because of rarity or beauty, is above the value of the material in the coin itself or its face value.

Open-end mutual fund   A mutual fund that issues new shares when investors buy and buys back shares when investors sell. See Closed-end mutual fund.

Portfolio   An individual's investments.

Precious metals   Metals with great value, such as gold, silver, and platinum; frequently used as investments.

Present value   The value today of a future payment or stream of payments that has been discounted by a discount rate. It relates to the fact that money has a time value; generally, money today is worth more than the same amount in the future.

Price level   An average of prices for a wide number of goods and services.

Principal   The original amount of money invested or lent, such as the amount invested in a stock or the amount borrowed on a loan.

Real estate investment trust (REIT)   Similar in concept to a mutual fund that invests only in real estate. Investors are shareholders in the REIT, which is a corporation.

Real estate limited partnership (RELP)   A partnership that invests only in real estate and is run by one or more general partners. Investors are limited partners.

Recession   A period of economic slowdown. It is defined by the government as a period of two successive quarters when the gross national product declines.

Risk   The chance that a choice someone makes may result in a loss of value of an asset.

Risk management   Using insurance to limit the effects of loss, i.e., medical insurance helps manage the financial risks associated with poor health.

Risk–reward ratio   The relationship between the risk of loss and the potential for profit of a given investment.

Rolling recession   Where economic doldrums strike various regions of the country rather than the entire country at one time. See Recession.

S&P 500   An index of the stocks of 500 major corporations compiled by the publishing firm Standard & Poor's; used to measure stock market movements.

Simplified employee pension plan/individual retirement account (SEP/IRA)   A pension plan where both the employer (the SEP part) and the employee (the IRA part) can contribute. Frequently used by small businesses and professionals.

Sequence of investing   An order of investment priority based on the tax exposure of various investments; (1) invest in those investments that provide both tax deductions and tax deferrals, (2) invest where one receives tax deferrals, and (3) invest in fully taxable investments.

Short term   When one invests for less than one year. See Medium term and Long term.

Stock   A share in the ownership of a corporation.

Stockholder   Someone who owns stock.

Stock mutual fund   A mutual fund that invests in stocks. See Mutual fund.

Strip   A bond whose interest portion has been removed (stripped) and, as a result, sells at a large discount from its face value.

Tangible asset   A physical property—such as real estate, coins, and art—that has value.

Tax deductible   An investment where the money paid into the investment is deductible from the investor's taxable income. See Tax deferred.

Tax deferred   An investment whose income and capital appreciation is not taxable until it is withdrawn from the investment. See Tax deductible.

Term life insurance   Strictly life insurance where a specified sum is paid to beneficiaries upon the death of the insured. See Whole life insurance.

Timing   An investor's attempt to time investments so purchases and sales are done at the "best" time (buy when prices are lowest and sell when prices are highest).

Treasury bill   A short-term (not more than one year) U.S. government security.

Treasury bond   A 30-year U.S. government security.

Treasury note   A 2- to 10-year government security.

Trusts   A legal entity that is a depository for assets.

Turnover rate   The number of times a mutual fund's or annuity's investment portfolio is bought and sold annually.

Unearned income   Income earned not directly from one's efforts, such as interest.

Upside potential   The potential to make money. *See* Downside risk.

Variable annuity   Like a tax-deferred mutual fund; bought from an insurance company that makes no guarantees on return of principal or rate of interest paid. *See* Fixed annuity.

Volatility   The up and down movement of prices. The more volatile an investment, the more rapid and more pronounced are the price movements.

Whole life insurance   Insurance where a portion of one's premium pays for life insurance and a portion is an investment managed by the life insurance company. *See* Term life insurance.

Zero coupon bond   A bond whose interest portion has been removed and, as a result, sells at a large discount from its face value. *See* Strip.

NOTES

1. Ravi Batra, *The Great Depression of 1990* (New York: Dell, 1988).
2. George W. Wilson, *Inflation: Causes, Consequences and Cures* (Bloomington, IN: Indiana Univ. Press, 1982).
3. Peter S. Spiro, *Real Interest Rates and Investment and Borrowing Strategies* (New York: Quorum Books, 1989), p. 191.
4. Jonathan Clements, "Why It's Risky Not to Invest More in Stocks," *Wall Street Journal*, February 11, 1992, p. C1.
5. Gary P. Brownstone, L. Randolph Hood, and Gilbert L. Beebower, "Determinants of Portfolio Performance," *Financial Analysts Journal*, July–August 1986, pp. 39–44.
6. Roger C. Gibson, *Asset Allocation* (Homewood, IL: Dow Jones–Irwin, 1989), p. 12.
7. Barbara Donnelly, "Stock Investors Pay High Price for Liquidity," *Wall Street Journal*, April 28, 1987, p. 41.
8. Barbara Donnelly, "Stock Investors Pay High Price for Liquidity."
9. Charles Mackay, *Extraordinary Popular Delusions and the Madness of Crowds* (New York: Farrar Straus & Giroux, 1932). (Original work published 1841.)
10. A Merrill Lynch study quoted in Jerome B. Cohen, Edward D. Zinbarg, and Arthur Zeikel, *Investment Analysis and Portfolio Management*, 4th ed. (Homewood, IL: Irwin, 1982), p. 155.
11. *American Demographics*, June 1987, p. 10. The Federal Reserve Bulletin was March 1986.
12. Gibson, *Asset Allocation*, p. 69.
13. Ibid.
14. Ibid.
15. Ibid., p. 72.
16. Quoted by Gibson, *Asset Allocation*, p. 75, from Charles D. Ellis, *Investment Policy* (Homewood, IL: Dow Jones–Irwin), p. 13.

17. Warren Bronson, "Betting on Dark Horses," *Sylvia Porter's Personal Finance*, September 1988, p. 39.

18. Eric N. Berg, "Financial Plight of a Top Insurer May Shake Faith in the Industry," *New York Times*, July 15, 1991, p. A1.

19. Ibid., p. C8.

20. Bernard Baumohl, "A Lack of Assurance," *Time*, August 5, 1991, p. 46.

21. Susan Pulliam, "Prudential Insurance Loses Top Rating as Moody's Lowers Firm to Double A-1," *Wall Street Journal*, January 27, 1992, p. A4.

22. Barry Vinocur, "Checking Out Insurance Ratings," *Stanger's Investment Advisor*, July 1991, p. 35.

23. Susan Pulliam, "Prudential Insurance Loses Top Rating as Moody's Lowers Firm to Double-A-1."

24. "Term Insurance: Why Plain Vanilla Is Best," *Consumer Reports*, June 1986, p. 379.

25. "Both Fidelity Investors and Firm Are at Sea as Magellan Boss Goes," *Wall Street Journal*, March 29, 1990, p. A1.

26. Ibid.

27. Jonathan Clements, "Behind Every Fund Stands a Manager—For How Long," *Wall Street Journal*, April 4, 1990, p. C1.

28. The figures in this and the above paragraph came from Jonathan Clements, "Mutual Funds with Low Turnover Find Penny Saved Is Penny Earned," *Wall Street Journal*, May 17, 1990.

29. This number comes from *Consumer Reports*, September 1991, p. 630.

30. Richard Donahue, "Baby Boomers Will Have a Rough Time Retiring," *National Underwriter*, November 27, 1989.

31. Ibid.

32. Karen Slater, "Social Security Records Deserve a Check in Planning Retirement," *Wall Street Journal*, July 13, 1990, p. C1.

33. Ibid.

34. Social Security Administration, "Medicare" (pamphlet).

35. Barbara Donnelly, "IRAs Still Offer Some Tax Advantages, But Pitting Pluses vs. Minuses Is Tougher," *Wall Street Journal*, March 12, 1991, p. C1.

36. "Retirement Plans: Part 1: 401(k) and 403(b) Programs," *Consumer Reports*, January 1990, p. 16.

INDEX